Human Language
and Knowledge
in the Light of Chalcedon

American University Studies

Series VII
Theology and Religion

Vol. 187

PETER LANG
New York • Washington, D.C./Baltimore
Bern • Frankfurt am Main • Berlin • Vienna • Paris

Stephen W. Need

Human Language
and Knowledge
in the Light of Chalcedon

PETER LANG
New York • Washington, D.C./Baltimore
Bern • Frankfurt am Main • Berlin • Vienna • Paris

Library of Congress Cataloging-in-Publication Data

Need, Stephen William.
Human language and knowledge in the light
of Chalcedon/ Stephen William Need.
p. cm. — (American university studies. Series VII, Theology
and religion; vol. 187)
Includes bibliographical references and index.
1. Language and languages—Religious aspects—Christianity. 2. Knowledge,
Theory of (Religion). 3. Jesus Christ—Person and offices. 4. Man (Christian
theology). 5. Council of Chalcedon (451). I. Title. II. Series.
BR115.L25N44   230'.014—dc20   95-1301
ISBN 0-8204-2728-4

Die Deutsche Bibliothek-CIP-Einheitsaufnahme

Need, Stephen William:
Human language and knowledge in the light of Chalcedon/
Stephen William Need. –New York; Washington, D.C./Baltimore; Bern;
Frankfurt am Main; Berlin; Vienna; Paris: Lang.
(American university studies: Ser. 7, Theology and religion; Vol. 187)
ISBN 0-8204-2728-4
NE: American university studies/ 07

Cover design by James F. Brisson.

The paper in this book meets the guidelines for permanence and durability
of the Committee on Production Guidelines for Book Longevity
of the Council of Library Resources.

© 1996 Peter Lang Publishing, Inc., New York

Printed in the United States of America.

For my Mother

'. . .the greatest thing by far is to be a master of metaphor.'
Aristotle, *Poetics* (1459a).

ACKNOWLEDGEMENTS

The following material is reprinted with permission:

Excerpt from "The Dry Salvages" in FOUR QUARTETS, copyright 1943 by T.S. Eliot and renewed 1971 by Esme Valerie Eliot, reprinted by permission of Harcourt Brace & Company. Excerpts from "Choruses from 'The Rock'" and "The Love Song of J. Alfred Prufrock" in COLLECTED POEMS 1909-1962 by T.S. Eliot, copyright 1936 by Harcourt Brace & Company, copyright ©1964, 1963 by T.S. Eliot, reprinted by permission of the publisher. All excerpts from the poetry of T.S. Eliot are reprinted from THE COMPLETE POEMS AND PLAYS by T.S. Eliot, copyright 1969, by permission of the Eliot Estate and of Faber and Faber Ltd. Excerpt from "Chimneys" in COMPLETE POEMS 1904-1962 by e.e. cummings, copyright 1994, reprinted by permission of the Liveright Publishing Corporation. Excerpts from SYSTEMATIC THEOLOGY by Paul Tillich, copyright 1951, 1957, reprinted by permission of the University of Chicago Press.

I would also like to thank all those who have assisted in any way with the publication of this book, especially L.S.U. College, Southampton for financial support; my colleagues in the Theology Department at L.S.U. for their help and encouragement; Mr. Tim Cain for help with page layout; Professor Leslie Houlden for proof-reading the final manuscript; Mrs Ann Hudson for creating the Index; and Mr. Chris Hardman and the Art and Design Department at L.S.U. for their help and hospitality.

A note on the system of references:

Actual quotations within the text are followed by details in parentheses, also within the text. In the first quotation from a work the author's name, the date of publication (referring to the Bibliography) and the page number are included. In subsequent quotations from the same work, only the page number is given. When a new work is quoted, full details occur again. Other references and points requiring clarification are followed by numbers in square brackets which refer to a system of Endnotes included at the end of the main text, before the Bibliography.

CONTENTS

Part Two: The Inner Logic of Language

Part Three: The Inner Logic of Knowledge

Introduction

INTRODUCTION

What is 'Bankruptcy'?

During his time as Headmaster of Repton School in Derbyshire, William Temple contributed to a subsequently controversial collection of essays entitled *Foundations*. The subtitle of this volume was 'A Statement of Christian Belief in Terms of Modern Thought' and Temple's essay carried the heading 'The Divinity of Christ'. Temple's line of thought certainly bore the stamp of modernity in that he rejected the Chalcedonian Definition of the person of Christ as 'bankrupt'. For Temple, at this stage in his life, the terms and concepts used by that document represented a 'breakdown of theology'. Temple claimed that:

> The formula of Chalcedon is, in fact, a confession of the bankruptcy of Greek Patristic Theology. The Fathers had done the best that could be done with the intellectual apparatus at their disposal. Their formula had the right devotional value; it excluded what was known to be fatal to the faith; but it explained nothing. To the Latin mind there was little or nothing to be explained; the same man may be both consul and augur, the same Christ may be both God and Man. This is true if one is thinking of functions, but is irrelevant if one is thinking of substances. The formula merely stated the fact which constituted the problem; it did not attempt solution. It was therefore unscientific; and as theology is the science of religion, it represented the breakdown of theology (Temple 1912 p.230).

Temple reveals his modernity in this essay in a number of ways in addition to the actual rejection of the formula. He separates the language of devotion from that of scientific 'explanation' and is dissatisfied with notions of 'substance'. The sense that Christology on the one hand and human language and knowledge on the other, operate separately leads him later in the article to declare the Chalcedonian formula to be 'philosophically valueless' (p.232).

Although this negative judgement upon the Chalcedonian Definition is the one for which Temple has been remembered, it is not his final word concerning it. At a later stage in his life, having borne something of the brunt of the debates arising out of his article in *Foundations* and having become Bishop of Manchester, he retraced his steps somewhat in his book *Christus Veritas*, whilst still maintaining reservations concerning the formula. In the later work he says:

> The truth is that this great formula derives part of its value from the clearness with which it refuses to explain. It does in one sense represent 'the bankruptcy of Greek patristic theology'; it marks the definite failure of all attempts to explain the Incarnation in terms of Essence, Substance, Nature, and the like. It is content to reaffirm the fact. But that is all that an authoritative formula ought to do (Temple 1924 p.134).

By this stage Temple has changed his position significantly whilst trying not to reject his original words. In a footnote he broadens the accusation of bankruptcy to the 'history of the whole controversy' (p.134). He now thinks, however, that 'it would be disastrous if there were an official Church explanation of the Incarnation' (p.134). With this claim he has come to see something of the real strength of the Chalcedonian Definition, that is, its avoidance of clear explanation along the lines of modern science and its power to sustain an insight which would be lost entirely if all were somehow 'clearly explained'.

Overall, Temple is confused about how his central metaphor of 'bankruptcy' should be understood. In the earlier work he clearly sees Chalcedon to be completely without value and the 'bankruptcy' is a wholly negative matter. In the later work, however, the bankruptcy is a positive thing reflecting something of the real insight into the Incarnation which the document has. Temple's general confusion over Chalcedon is typical of the Enlightenment critique of classical christology. Indeed, a major feature of so-called modern christology has been precisely this misunderstanding of Chalcedon and a gulf has opened up between those who are basically in sympathy with it and those who are not. In a very important sense, then, Temple's legacy has remained with us down to the present day.

The main concern in this book is with the nature of theological language. The aim is to rehabilitate the Chalcedonian Definition specifically with a view to enabling a more fruitful notion of human language about God. It seems that wherever Chalcedon is rejected, notions of how human language and knowledge operate in relation to God go astray. The separation of christology from language and knowledge has been responsible for the modern sense of the meaninglessness of a great deal of theological language. The argument in this book is that to view human language about God in the light of the Chalcedonian Definition would contribute significantly to the revitalization of notions of theological language. We shall follow Temple's second sense of the bankruptcy metaphor, maintaining that the bankruptcy encountered in the Chalcedonian Definition is a positive matter. However, as we shall see, this needs pressing much further than Temple realized, even in his later writing, if its full importance for our understanding of theological language is to emerge. First of all, however, let us address the problem of human language about God more specifically.

A Master of Metaphor

Talking about God in the modern world can be a difficult matter. Enlightenment presuppositions relating to human language and knowledge bring about situations in which talk about God and his revelation in the world often sounds hollow and meaningless. The language of 'devotion' has been separated from the language of scientific 'explanation'. Notions of truth have become narrowly positivistic and scientistic and the meaning of talk about God often becomes eclipsed [1]. However, many of the problems which arise in human speech about God, although they are exacerbated by modern presuppositions, have deeper roots in the more widespread human difficulty of speaking of a God who is known to us but is also beyond us. From the earliest times, human experience of God has brought with it a sense of limitation in speaking about him. We believe in a God who makes himself known to us in revelation and yet we are aware that he comes to us as one unknown. From within this context, however, we feel that we must speak of him and we do so in a number of different ways. It is here that the actual nature of human language about God becomes all-important.

In Exodus 3:14 the God of Israel is revealed as one still unknown, but named in a riddle: I am who I am. Human naming of God takes place in riddles, that is, in language which does not operate in its primary sense. We use analogy, metaphor and symbol in order to articulate the one who is known to us as unknown. In using such language, we are attempting to speak of the divine in human terms. We are bringing the human and the divine together in our speech. In the present climate there is frequently a lack of understanding on the part of believers and non-believers alike concerning just how this language achieves its meaning. Too frequently it is taken solely at face value. There is a severe need today, therefore, to renew the sense of the riddle in human speech about God and its rootedness in the revelation of God in Jesus Christ.

In the work of two recent writers on theological language, George Lindbeck and Sallie McFague, some important problems have arisen. Their views of language leave human talk about God ultimately drifting in the direction of subjectivism. The rootedness of human language about God in the reality of God itself is not taken nearly seriously enough. Also, these authors' views of such language are accompanied either by a 'regulative' view of classical christology, as in the case of Lindbeck, or by an outright rejection of such christology, as in the case of McFague. It is clear from these writings that there is an inner, unacknowledged connection between language and christology. Notions of language are closely related to notions of christology. Looking at the patristic and other debates about Christ, we can see that there are inherent connections between language and christology and that an imbalance in one area is often associated with an imbalance in the other.

Furthermore, it has frequently been specifically in relation to the christology of Chalcedon that difficulties with language have arisen. For example, Schleiermacher's rejection of Chalcedon gave rise to a view of language as essentially expressive. We have already seen that Temple's rejection of Chalcedon was associated with a separation of the language of devotion and that of scientific 'explanation'. In the fifth century, the christology of Chalcedon achieved a balanced view of the relation between the human and the divine within the person of Christ. It acknowledged the distinction between the two elements as emphasised by the Antiochenes, but also their simultaneous unity, as emphasised by the Alexandrians. These two emphases together, as found in the christology of Chalcedon, constitute what we shall call the 'inner logic of christology'. In this book it will be argued that because of the inner connections between christology and language, Chalcedon can also achieve a balanced view of the relation between human and divine in human language about God.

Human language about God is permeated by analogy, metaphor and symbol. These are all inherently related, and our basic insights in relation to one area apply easily to the others. However, even those who have affirmed the importance of such language for Christian theology have not always seen the connection with christology. Thomas Aquinas, in responding to the problem of the relation between the positive and the negative ways in theology, provides us with some useful notions of analogy. However, he does not bring his notions together into a synthesis which really accounts for the fact that human language applies to God and yet is also limited. He has not emphasised the connection between language about God, and christology. A similar thing happens in relation to Paul Tillich's notion of symbol. Although he is aware of the 'distinction in unity' which lies at the heart of the way in which symbols work, he does not really balance the human and the divine elements. Furthermore, he is unhappy with Chalcedonian christology.

Aristotle claimed that 'the greatest thing by far is to be a master of metaphor' (*Poetics* 1459a) [2]. In this book it will be maintained that analogy and symbol are very closely related to metaphor and that metaphor is the basic and controlling phenomenon of the human speaking and knowing processes. At the heart of the three areas, analogy, metaphor and symbol, lies a particular view of metaphor which sees it as both united with what it speaks of and yet also really limited. There are, of course, many views of metaphor. Most people would be agreed, however, that the heart of metaphor lies in the fact that it 'speaks about one thing in terms of another'. How, more particularly, is this to be understood? Some have seen the two elements in metaphor as existing side by side, providing us with no more than a basic simile or ambiguity. Some have insisted that metaphors must be taken in a single straightforward sense and be dismissed as meaningless, serving only to attract our attention to something left unsaid. Others have spoken of 'interaction' and 'controversion' and even of contradiction between the two elements in metaphor.

It is acknowledged increasingly, however, that the significance of a really good metaphor lies in the simultaneous affirmation and denial which lies at its heart. In metaphor we find a primary or literal level and a secondary or metaphorical level. There is falsity at the primary level, but truth and immediacy at the metaphorical level. Thus, in the metaphor 'God is a rock', there is falsity at the primary level, but truth at the metaphorical level. God is clearly not literally 'a rock', but this does not leave the utterance meaningless or false. The metaphor communicates a truth concerning the nature of God through its two elements operating together. It is the two dimensions *together* which form the inner power of the metaphor. The metaphor achieves its meaning through the collision of these two elements *together*. The two levels unite, but retain their distinction. Thus, some have spoken of 'stereoscopic vision', or of 'split reference' in relation to the way in which metaphors achieve their meaning. This 'distinction in unity' which lies at the heart of metaphor constitutes what we shall call the 'inner logic of language'.

All language, and especially human language about God, presupposes or implies a view of knowledge. If human language is fundamentally metaphorical in its 'inner logic', then the structures of epistemology will be continuous with this. Indeed, metaphor turns out to be the guiding principle not only of human language, but also of human knowledge. As in language, so in knowledge, the concern is once again with the relation between the human and the divine. The epistemology worked through in this book will not separate the knowing mind from the known object, as did the philosophers of the Enlightenment, but see them 'fused' in a unity, as did Coleridge. The primary human faculty of perception is the imagination which is essentially a 'combining' faculty, the producer of analogy, metaphor and symbol. With an 'imaginative rationality' we carry out a 'heuristic conversation' in which, searching for truth, we are united with the known object whilst retaining our distinction from it in the process. This 'distinction in unity' which lies at the heart of the processes of human knowing constitutes what we shall call the 'inner logic of knowledge'.

Christology, language and knowledge are inherently united in the revelation of the God who is known to us as unknown and named in a riddle. There are many views of language and of metaphor. The question is, in the words of Humpty Dumpty, 'which is to be master?'[3]. Metaphor is certainly the master of language and, therefore, of knowledge. It is christology, however, especially that articulated in the Chalcedonian Definition of the Faith, which is the master of metaphor. The 'inner logic' of the three areas is continuous. The Chalcedonian Definition enables a notion of language about God which maintains both the limitedness of that language and its rootedness in God himself. It is in this context, therefore, that human language about God begins to make sense.

It is important to note that most of the work done on metaphor, the basic element in the processes of human speaking and knowing, has been done outside theology and certainly without any reference to christology. However, the concern in this book is with human language about God and we shall find that as all human language about God is permeated by metaphor, general discussions of the nature of metaphor are very important. It is clearly not the case that the view of metaphor which is supported here can only be found through christology. It is possible to arrive at this view of metaphor, and at the Chalcedonian 'inner logic', in purely literary or linguistic terms. However, in Christian theology, language and christology are inherently related in revelation and the connection between language and Chalcedon is crucial in finding a Christian notion of how human language about God really operates. Colin Gunton has remarked that:

> If orthodox or even Chalcedonian doctrines can be reached by methods more in harmony with modern assumptions and epistemology it would indeed be a great gain, achieving maximum communication with minimum loss of distinctive Christian content (Gunton 1983 p.10).

Certainly some of the contemporary views of metaphor take us into the heart of the 'inner logic of language'. It is a short step then to the 'inner logic of christology' and thus to Chalcedon itself. The traffic between language and christology runs in both directions. If we turn first to Chalcedon, we shall come to a more fruitful understanding of human language about God.

Theological language and christology are inherently related because they are both essentially about God. The human and the divine are related in a particular way within the context of revelation. A consideration of the way human language about God works leads directly to christology. The specific contribution of this book, therefore, is that problems of human language about God should be addressed in the light of the Incarnation or the 'enfleshment of the Word', especially as this is understood in the Chalcedonian Definition of the Faith. William Temple saw this central connection, even in his earlier essay, when he remarked that 'the wise question is not, "Is Christ divine?" but, "What is God like?" And the answer to that is "Christ"' (Temple 1912 p.259). In this book also, the main question, 'What is language about God like?' leads very quickly into christology and thus to the heart of the argument. With this question in mind, we shall turn first to the problem of theological language itself and then pass on to consider the Chalcedonian Definition in detail. In Parts Two and Three, we shall consider how human language and knowledge might look in the light of this christology.

Part One:
The Inner Logic
of Christology

'The hint half guessed, the gift half understood, is Incarnation.'
T.S. Eliot, *Four Quartets*.

I

LANGUAGE AND CHRISTOLOGY

The Problem of Theological Language

In the first chapter of his treatise *The Divine Names*, Dionysius the Areopagite speaks of the incomprehensibility of God and of the difficulty of speaking of him adequately in human language. If the divine nature is beyond us, he asks, how then is it to be named?

> But if It is greater than all Reason and all knowledge, and hath Its firm abode altogether beyond Mind and Being, and circumscribes, compacts, embraces and anticipates all things while itself is altogether beyond the grasp of them all, and cannot be reached by any perception, imagination, conjecture, name, discourse, apprehension or understanding, how then is our Discourse concerning the Divine Names to be accomplished, since we see that the Super-Essential Godhead is unutterable and nameless(Rolt 1940 p.59)?

Later in the same work, however, Dionysius notes that the process of naming the divine nature does, nevertheless, take place. His main concern is with how this can occur:

> Now is not the secret Name precisely that which is above all names and nameless, and is fixed beyond every name that is named, not only in this world but also in that which is to come? On the other hand, they attribute names to It when, for instance, they speak of It as declaring: 'I am that I am'... (p.61).

We shall consider this two-dimensional problem of knowing and speaking about God in order to discover, in so far as this is possible, the inner workings of each. God is different from us and yet we do speak of him. He is both known and unknown. It is clear from the outset that there is a 'tension' in the way human knowledge and language operate in relation to God. Because we are human and God is divine, our language about him operates in a particular way. We are concerned with both the human and the divine elements in our speech about God. The aim here, therefore, is to find a notion of our language about God which respects both of these aspects. Because human language is the wider and more immediate of the two phenomena, we shall begin with language and then pass on to knowledge. Hans-Georg Gadamer has made the point that 'language is the universal medium in which understanding itself is realised' (Gadamer 1979 p.350). We approach the problem, therefore, through the medium of language and pass on to the question of knowledge afterwards.

The problem of speaking of God and of naming God has been a continuous and widespread feature of human experience of God in many religions. The sense of God's 'otherness' has raised the question of how merely human language can be adequate to name him. Theologians and philosophers of religion, in reflecting upon the nature of human language about God, have drawn attention to the difficulties which arise in speaking about the one who is known as unknown. The philosopher Brian Davies has stated this dilemma in the following words:

> Here, then, is the problem. If one says that God is very different from anything else, can one really talk significantly about him at all? How can one say that God is good or wise but not in the sense that ordinary good and wise things are? Is there not a real dilemma here for those who believe in God? Are they not caught between the stools of meaninglessness and misrepresentation? (Davies 1982 p.9).

Both Davies and Dionysius articulate the problem with which we are concerned and which lies at the centre of all theology and all theological discourse: how are we both to acknowledge our experience that God is beyond all human naming of him and yet also simultaneously make the claim that we really do speak of him?

This fundamental problem cuts across the entire canvas of all theological utterance and demands an investigation into the nature of the very language we use of God and how this language might be understood to operate. There have, of course, been many attempts in the past to characterize this basic problem and to contribute to some sort of solution. Davies responds in terms of analogy, whilst Dionysius sees symbolic theology as the way forward. At the present time, the situation regarding the meaningfulness of theological language has become so complex that theologians and philosophers of religion are attempting to deal with this basic issue with a renewed sense of urgency. One such theologian is the American George Lindbeck who has characterized the various possible ways of viewing theological language in a particularly useful way. We therefore turn to his contribution to the debate first.

The Nature of Doctrine

In *The Nature of Doctrine,* George Lindbeck works with three possible paradigms for understanding theological language. His work is influenced by scholars from a mixture of disciplines but his basic contribution is indebted to the legacy of the later Wittgenstein. Lindbeck's work has received a variety of reactions, but his attempt to characterize the ways in which theological language can be seen to function polarizes the options conveniently. These characterizations are of tendencies in notions of theological language rather than exclusive views held by individuals, but they provide an appropriate way of moving forward. We shall look at these three views in order to clarify some of the ways in which human language about God may be thought to function.

The first possible way of understanding the language of religion is, according to Lindbeck, the 'cognitive-propositionalist' view. For such a view, the propositions found in religious discourse are permanently true. On this scheme, the cognitive dimension of such propositions is emphasized and statements are seen to be informative and descriptive. The stress is on the objectivity and permanence of the truth-claims. Lindbeck says that 'for a propositionalist, if a doctrine is once true, it is always true, and if it is once false, it is always false' (Lindbeck 1984 p.16). He points out that although classical theology grew up under a realist epistemology, nevertheless the epistemology which lies behind modern 'cognitive-propositionalist' views stems not only from Plato, but more specifically from Descartes and Newton. Here, the view can be seen to be characterized by a one-to-one isomorphic correspondence between the knower and the known.

Lindbeck cites the view of theological language against which Hans Küng is writing in his work *Infallible?* as an example of this type of view. Küng is arguing broadly against the Roman Catholic doctrine of Papal infallibility, but has much to say on the nature of propositions in theology. Clearly, in rejecting Papal infallibility, Küng is rejecting any view which would see theological propositions as static and unchangeable. An even better example of the view which Lindbeck has in mind here is the view of language found in the early writing of Ludwig Wittgenstein, especially the *Tractatus Logico-Philosophicus*. For the early Wittgenstein, human language 'pictures', once and for all, a state of affairs which exists apart from the language. We might say that there is a 'one-to-one' correspondence between the language and the situation pictured by the language [1]. Although it is fairly clear what Lindbeck wishes to reject under this first heading, his characterization of it is in fact rather crude. It is, indeed, very hard to find anything resembling this concept of theological language in even the most orthodox theologians in the Christian tradition, although Alister McGrath cites a few examples [2]. This, however, does not directly affect Lindbeck's argument and he is, in any case, arguing against such an understanding.

The second possible way of understanding religious language characterized by Lindbeck is that which he calls the 'experiential-expressive' type. For this view, religious doctrines are 'non-informative and non-discursive symbols of inner feelings, attitudes, or existential orientations' (Lindbeck 1984 p.16). Here Lindbeck sees a polyvalence in the way doctrines function and they can have different meanings at different times and in different circumstances. The crucial dimension here is not whether doctrines are permanently true, but rather how effective they are at articulating or expressing what is essentially an experience of the subject or community. The measure now is a doctrine's symbolic efficacy in its actual use.

This tradition of 'experiential-expressivism' can, according to Lindbeck, be traced back to Schleiermacher. The basic religious experience is prior to the language about it. The language then expresses that experience and can do so in a number of different forms relative to time and context. There are some difficulties here with Lindbeck's characterization, as Schleiermacher's concept of the function of doctrines within the Christian tradition was one which saw them rooted in christology and the Christian community, not in the isolated solipsism of an individual who experiences 'absolute dependence' on his own. Nevertheless, it is once again fairly clear what Lindbeck is rejecting when he rejects 'experiential-expressivism'. An understanding of religious experience and theological language as rooted in personal faith and then needing expression, is what lies at the heart of this view. Rooted as it is in a form of subjectivism, this epistemological type leads easily to views of theological language which see it as instrumentalist or voluntarist. The views of R.B. Braithwaite and Don Cupitt come most readily to mind here [3].

Before discussing his main view, Lindbeck mentions a third and intermediary view which attempts to combine the first two, but which he sees as collapsing into one of the earlier views. He calls this intermediary view the 'two-dimensional' view. This is obviously an attempt to combine the view of doctrine as cognitive and permanently true with that of doctrine as merely expressive. Lindbeck alludes to the work of Rahner and Lonergan as examples of this view, but he does not pursue it as a serious option. This is unfortunate, for this 'two-dimensional' view combines the two interests which Lindbeck is trying to bring into harmony.

Lindbeck's third and most important option for understanding religious doctrines is the view which he himself is writing to support. He calls this view the 'cultural-linguistic' view. Here, the emphasis is on an analogy with the learning of 'acquired skills'. When learning a language or growing up in a culture there are no initial questions as to whether the rules or procedures are permanently true or adequately expressive. Rather, the concern is with learning rules or with inhabiting a world of codes. Here the skills are acquired and the result is a binding together of those who take part. Religious doctrines are exactly like this. They function as rules in a language or in a community-based activity in which the language makes sense in its use. Lindbeck also calls this theory a 'rule' theory. He says:

...a religion can be viewed as a kind of cultural and/or linguistic framework or medium that shapes the entirety of life and thought....It is not primarily an array of beliefs about the true and the good (though it may involve these), or a symbolism expressive of basic attitudes, feelings or sentiments (though these will be generated) (p.33).

Here in this view, we can see the obvious influence of the writings of the later Wittgenstein, especially the *Philosophical Investigations,* in which the claim is that the meaning of language lies in its use within a particular 'language game' or 'form of life' [4]. Again, the community-based and contextual emphases are important.

Lindbeck's attempt has been to avoid the pitfalls of both objectivism and subjectivism. In order to do this he has sketched a 'cultural-linguistic' concept of language following the later Wittgenstein in stressing meaning as use. The problem with this concept for theological language, of course, concerns the truth status of the language. In what sense, if there are no 'cognitive-propositional' truths in any sense, can there be said to be any truths at all? This is the very problem which arises with the later Wittgenstein himself. Lindbeck inherits both the view and the problem.

In order to deal with this essentially Kantian dilemma of trying to establish some form of objective truth whilst putting a great deal of weight on the subjective element, Lindbeck makes the distinction between 'intrasystematic' and 'ontological' truth (p.64). Intrasystematic truth exists when there is a coherence between truths *within* the system and total context concerned. Things are, therefore, false when they do not cohere in this fashion. Truth is thus a phenomenon internal to a particular system and is related to the communal existence and life of a community of believers skilled in a particular set of 'rules'. Concerning 'ontological' truth, Lindbeck does admit that it can exist, but maintains that it would not be a 'one-to-one', 'permanently true' sort of truth. Such truth would arise in the context of 'intrasystematic' truth, which can nevertheless exist without it.

It is in this area of the relation between 'intrasystematic' and 'ontological' truth that Lindbeck is at his weakest. He does not pursue questions concerning the ontological status of theological language and this leaves open the question of whether such language has any significance apart from its speakers. McGrath says of Lindbeck:

Indeed, at points he seems to suggest that conceiving theology as the grammar of the christian language entails the abandonment of any talk about God as an independent reality and any suggestion that it is possible to make truth claims (in an ontological rather than intrasystematic sense) concerning him. 'Truth' is firmly equated with - virtually to the point of being reduced to - internal consistency (McGrath 1990 p.29).

Arguing along similar lines against this weakness in Lindbeck's scheme, David Fergusson says that 'the learning of a religious language will certainly involve practical skill, our concepts will in large measure be inadequate; yet what truth we do confess is established ultimately by the way things are independently of our performance' (Fergusson 1990 p.198). The overwhelming problem with Lindbeck can be seen to lie with the weak ontological roots of the 'cultural-linguistic' view he encourages. There is a fundamental cleavage here between language and ontology, between human language and reality itself.

One aspect of Lindbeck's discussion is introduced as a passing historical example, but in fact can be seen to be of paramount importance. This concerns his treatment of the christological statements of Nicaea and Chalcedon. Lindbeck states early on in his work that 'the Nicaenum in its role as a communal doctrine does not make first-order truth claims' (Lindbeck 1984 p.19). By this, he means that the creed of Nicaea and its statement concerning 'consubstantiality' involves neither ontological truth, nor 'cognitive-propositionalist truth', but regulative truth. Speaking of Athanasius' key role at Nicaea and of the concept of consubstantiality, Lindbeck claims that 'the theologian most responsible for the final triumph of Nicaea thought of it, not as a first-order proposition with ontological reference, but as a second-order rule of speech. For him, to accept the doctrine meant to agree to speak in a certain way' (p.94). For Lindbeck the same is true of Chalcedon. He claims that the ontological or 'first-order' concern developed in the Middle Ages [5].

This concept of 'regulative christology' brings us to the heart of our observations concerning Lindbeck's understanding of the function of theological language. Our hypothesis is that language and christology are inherently connected. Where the one is viewed inadequately, the other will be impoverished. Whichever we take first, the other will be affected by our view of it. Thus, with a view of language as purely regulative, or at least where the ontological dimension of that language is underestimated, the resulting christology will also emerge as regulative. The basic insight that christology is regulative for language is, of course, fundamental and we uphold this. Lindbeck himself is clear that in their regulative function, Nicaea and Chalcedon are not simply to be repeated, but are to guide the formation of new doctrines even when their own specific language has fallen out of use [6]. The problem is that in Lindbeck's scheme the language is not nearly regulative enough because it is stripped of its content. That is to say, it has no ontological roots [7].

A great deal of the response to Lindbeck's view of doctrine and theological language as regulative, has seen it as ontologically inadequate. McGrath says that 'Lindbeck's concept of doctrine is strongly reductionist, facilitating theoretical analysis at the cost of failing to interact fully with the phenomenon in question' (McGrath 1990 p.34). This weakness has shown up in Lindbeck's passing reference to christology as regulative. If this were corrected, our view of the nature of doctrine and of the nature of theological language generally would be more adequate to the phenomenon it seeks to articulate. If we approached our understanding of language through our christology, the functions of our theological language would look very different.

Thus, Lindbeck has articulated three possible ways of understanding theological language: the 'cognitive-propositional' view; the 'experiential-expressive' view; and the 'cultural-linguistic' view. In this book we follow his own chosen view, the 'cultural-linguistic', but affirm the need to take the content of the language much more seriously. We suggest that this can best be facilitated by a reassessment of the christological roots of theological language.

The renewed sense of urgency with which theologians and philosophers of religion have approached the question of the meaningfulness of human language about God has often meant that the appropriate links with other features of the 'theological terrain' have not been made. Also, in the present 'post-Enlightenment' climate, the aim is often to overlook or reject the interrelatedness of theological questions, stripping things down to single issues. Lindbeck is not alone in neglecting the importance of christology where the nature of theological language is concerned. Sallie McFague moves in similarly shallow waters. For, although she does associate her notion of Jesus as 'parable of God' with her understanding of theological language, she misses the deeper links between the two areas. However, since she does provide some key concepts in relation to how human language about God works, we turn to her now in order to clarify matters further.

Metaphorical Theology

A possible way of understanding human language about God which, surprisingly, is not mentioned by Lindbeck, is in terms of metaphor(cf. above pp.7-9). We shall approach this phenomenon through the work of Sallie McFague. McFague has written a number of works in this field of which *Metaphorical Theology* is the most important [8]. In this work she makes an attempt to steer a path between the two pitfalls which she sees threatening an adequate understanding of the function of theological language. She calls these two threats 'idolatry' and 'irrelevance' (McFague 1983 p.4). If language about God is taken literally, she maintains, the result is idolatry, that is, identifying the language with the divine. If, as she maintains is increasingly the case at the present time, language about God becomes irrelevant, then it is rendered meaningless. Her aim is to find 'a way of speaking of religious language as referring to God without identifying it with the divine' (p.4). Once again the problem lies between a 'cognitive-propositionalist' view and an 'experiential-expressive' view.

McFague maintains that the way to understand theological language is to acknowledge its metaphorical structure. We shall consider the nature of metaphor in more detail in Part Two. Here we are concerned only with the salient features and the strengths and shortcomings of McFague's argument. Her overriding point is that metaphor consists of a simultaneous 'is and is not'. She says that 'metaphorical theology, most basically, insists on the dialectic of the positive and the negative, on the "is and is not", and that tension permeates every aspect of it...' (p.65). Her stress is on the tensive quality of metaphor which avoids both the identification of theological language with God and its being made completely meaningless. The double aspect of assertion and denial renders this language perfectly suitable for speaking about God in a manner which is consistent with human experience of God.

McFague's discussion of metaphor also involves discussion of models. Models, both in theology and in the sciences, operate in essentially the same way. A model, for McFague, is 'a sustained and systematic metaphor' (p.67) and it therefore functions as a metaphor. The quality which enables models to function adequately is, once again, the 'is and is not' which constitutes the essential tension required and which avoids the pitfalls to which we have referred. McFague says that 'the principal danger in the use of models is...the loss of tension between model and modeled. When that distance is collapsed, we become imprisoned by dogmatic, absolutistic, literalistic patterns of thought' (p.74). In our use of models, as in the less 'sustained' metaphors, the way forward in our articulation of our subject matter lies in maintaining the tensive element in our language. Thus, to speak about God adequately, we must avoid 'idolatrous' and 'meaningless' notions of theological language and preserve the essential tension which enables that language to remain adequate.

The second major concern here in looking at McFague's metaphorical theology lies in the link she makes with christology. Her aim is to construct a picture of Christianity in which Jesus is seen as the 'parable of God' and in which Jesus' parables are of the type of language which sustains the tension she maintains is so central. Our interest lies not so much in this suggestion, however, as in her rejection of 'incarnational christology'. Very early on in the main work she claims that she cannot support such a christology [9]. The reasons are the standard ones amongst those who share this view. She claims that 'an incarnational christology is inevitably static and nature-oriented, rather than dynamic and human-oriented' (p.196). The interesting feature here is that McFague rejects incarnational christology and yet bases her entire system on an 'is and is not' ontology. Although she never discusses her reasons for understanding nature and substance in an incarnational christology as 'static', it is here that the heart of the matter lies. In fact, with a different, and, we shall maintain, more satisfactory reading of the word 'nature' in such christology, the very 'tensive' ontology for which McFague is searching is readily provided.

A final area of concern here is the underlying epistemology in McFague's discussion of metaphorical theology. It is especially interesting to note that an undiscussed Kantian element in her overall view of metaphor seems to be linked with her rejection of incarnational christology. As was the case with Lindbeck, this problem could be eliminated by a different reading of this christology. McFague emphasizes the need for a fundamentally relational view of language and that metaphors are 'images of a relationship' (p.166). However, in spite of the insistence on the 'is and is not' as the basic structure of this relation, McFague is never really clear how strong the 'is' is intended to be. McFague frequently claims that metaphors are not merely ornaments (p.50), but that they are 'cognitively oriented for the purpose of understanding the world' (p.92), that models involve both 'discovery' and 'creation' (p.101) and that they 'give intelligibility to the unintelligible' (p.73). Nevertheless, her view that metaphors must be developed without limit tends in one of the directions she is trying to avoid, that of meaninglessness [10]. She says that '...a metaphorical theology will insist that *many* metaphors and models are necessary, that a piling up of images is essential, both to avoid idolatry and to attempt to express the richness and variety of the divine-human relationship' (p.20). With such a plethora of metaphors could it not be the case that the 'is not' in the attempted tension will prevail over the 'is'?

The central hypothesis here is now beginning to emerge. It is this: that if a satisfactory reading of incarnational christology is found, then the 'is' and the 'is not', which McFague has rightly articulated as the heart of metaphor and theological language generally, will be more clearly secured. The Chalcedonian Definition of the Faith, which, for McFague, is static, limiting and too 'neat', can actually be seen to stress a fluid relation between the human and the divine natures [11]. On such a reading, the divine reality is conceptually more stable than McFague allows in her overall picture. McGrath pointed out that Lindbeck, in producing his theory of theological language, has drained it of all content. McFague is in danger of doing the same. As both of them largely fail to attend to christology, the suggestion here is that a christological approach to theological language might be of considerable benefit in securing the essential feature of that language, that is, the 'is and is not' feature.

We must now turn to examine a further dimension of our basic problem. With both Lindbeck and McFague we have found an attempt to come to a view of language which carries the essential double aspect. If God is different from us how do we speak of him successfully? The original question is still with us as we attempt to take into account both the human and the divine elements in human talk about God. Lindbeck and McFague both lose sight of the ontological pole of meaning: in this case, God himself. McGrath says that Lindbeck's view seems to involve 'the abandonment of any talk about God as an independent reality' (McGrath 1990 p.29). It is important to note that neither Lindbeck nor McFague speaks of the revelation of God in relation to their understanding of language about him. Certainly, if we are to understand human language about God, we must take into account the nature of him of whom we speak. We turn now, therefore, to a consideration of the relation between language and revelation.

Language and Revelation

The language which human beings use of God is rooted in the relationship in which we come to know him, that is, in the dynamic relationship in which God makes himself known to us. This concept of God's 'making known' his own nature to his people lies at the heart of the Judeo-Christian and other concepts of God. In the Christian experience this is rooted particularly in the experience of Christ as the one who makes God known to his people. Here we see the three elements of language, revelation and christology firmly meshed together. Once again, through a consideration of these elements, we can observe the fundamental tension of 'is and is not' at the heart of them all.

In Exodus 3:14, Yahweh reveals himself to Moses in the theophany of the Burning Bush. Moses' question concerns the naming of the one who has made himself known. His desire is to comprehend fully and to name adequately. The response is only *eheyeh asher eheyeh*, commonly translated 'I am who I am'. This Exodus narrative articulates the revelation of Yahweh which lies at the heart of Israel's religious experience. It is not, however, a revelation which makes the God of Israel known perfectly clearly. Rather, it is the revelation of one whose knowability is in question and whose name lies in a riddle. Even though he is known and named, this naming is not a final naming, for the identity of the one revealed and named is still in question. This basic naming in a riddle lies at the heart of the Exodus narrative and of the Jewish experience of God. It is the basic insight in relation to knowing and naming God which was noted by Dionysius.

Exactly this concept of the revelation of God lies at the heart of the theology of Karl Barth. It is now, however, specifically in Christ that this hidden revelation occurs. Barth's theology is, of course, rooted in the notion of Incarnation as found in John 1:14. The 'making flesh' of the Word is the central event in God's revealing himself to humanity. It is here in 'the way of the Son of God into the far country' that the hidden one is revealed. Barth says that 'He is the same God who was truly gracious to Israel in the hiddenness of His love in the form of His righteous wrath' (Barth 1956 p.176). In the revelation of God in his Son Jesus Christ, there is for Barth, however, both a making known and a hiding. For Barth, it is God in his revelation in Jesus Christ who makes possible the naming of God. But there is a hiddenness which affects this naming. Thus, Barth claims frequently that 'between God and us there stands the hiddenness of God' (Barth 1957 p.182) and that 'the true God is the hidden God' (p.193). He is still a God, however, who must and can be named.

The situation concerning the naming of God for Barth is characterized, as it is in Exodus 3, by the essentially tentative nature of human language about God. Barth says that 'the pictures in which we view God, the thoughts in which we think Him, the words with which we can define Him, are in themselves unfitted to this object and thus inappropriate to express and affirm the knowledge of Him' (p.188). This hiddenness requires that there be constant revision of words concerning God. It is also clear, however, that for Barth God must be named. There is a fundamental necessity that we make this attempt and there is also a known content to that naming. The situation of naming is one of tentativeness. Thus, in his discussion of the application of the term 'Son of God' to Jesus Christ, Barth speaks of it as 'a true but inadequate and an inadequate but true insight and statement' (Barth 1956 p.210).

It is crucial to Barth's theology, and to the argument here, that the revelation of God in Jesus Christ does not directly involve the revelation of propositions. God reveals his own nature, not propositions about it. Nevertheless, the naming of God is crucial, even if this must be in a riddle.

Herbert Hartwell, in speaking of Barth's view of the Church's doctrinal propositions, summarizes this point as follows:

> As the work of man they are only a human attempt to formulate the content of the divine revelation and thus are always only on the way to the truth of revelation. In revelation God reveals and communicates neither general truths nor doctrines but Himself, His work and His will for the world and for man (Hartwell 1964 p.71).

The language of naming God is not thus a matter of unchanging propositions revealed once for all and permanently true. Barth is fully aware of the idolatry which lies in such a view. It is rather a case of 'is and is not', a riddle at the heart of the naming.

The rootedness of human language about God in the revelation of God in Jesus Christ in Barth's thinking means that we must take seriously both the language and the content if we are to understand Barth's claims concerning the naming of God. The content is the divine life itself, graciously given. Ingolf Dalferth has recently stressed this rootedness of human language about God in the divine life itself, as follows:

> Revelation is not the divine promulgation of propositions about things which we do not (yet) know through means beyond the ordinary course of nature. It is an act of direct, yet mediated, communication between God and us which opens our eyes to the ultimate reality of our existence *coram deo* - not through propositional information from (or about) God but through personal confrontation with God (Dalferth 1988 p.158).

It is, therefore, not information about God, but God himself with which we are concerned in finding the locus of theological language. The primacy of the object spoken of is crucial. Dalferth again says that 'the object is determinative of the knowledge, not vice versa' (Dalferth 1989 p.18). Both language and knowledge of God find their roots in that experience of the divine life made known in Jesus Christ.

Again, however, we must stress that for Barth this personal knowledge of God in which human language about him has its roots, retains a crucial hiddenness. He says that the Word of God does not come to us directly, but comes clothed 'in the garments of creaturely reality' (Barth 1936 p.189). This naming of God, for Barth, has to do, not with a direct communication, but with a heavily veiled communication. Barth says that 'the veil is thick. We do not possess the Word of God otherwise than in the mystery of its worldliness' (p.188). Thus, it is the relation of the human and the divine as established in the revelation of God in Jesus Christ which Barth sees as the foundation of human speaking about God. Once again, the 'enfleshment of the Word' lies at the heart both of revelation and of language.

The speaking and naming can now be seen to be neither descriptive nor expressive, but as arising out of the heart of the relation between humanity and the revealed yet hidden God. The language and the content together arise in the relation established in the revelation of God in Jesus Christ. Hartwell again summarizes well when he says that 'the worldly form and the divine content have to be grasped in their togetherness in order to be comprehended and known as the Word of God' (Hartwell 1964 p.64). This togetherness of the language and its content, the content of revelation, is crucial to understanding how human language about God operates. There lies in the veiling and unveiling of the divine nature in Christ, a tension which governs the way in which human language about God operates. Here, the 'inner logic of language' is rooted in the 'inner logic of christology'.

Barth's identifying feature as a theologian of the twentieth century is his reversal of the epistemological project of the Enlightenment. Whereas the philosophers of the Enlightenment, to whose epistemology we shall turn in Part Three, sought to 'understand so that they might believe', Barth follows Anselm in 'believing so that he may understand'. More particularly, Barth's epistemological programme is grounded, as we have seen, in the revelation of Jesus Christ. Barth says that 'the truth of Jesus Christ is not one truth among others; it is the truth' (Barth 1949 pp.26+70). This shows that for Barth this revelation of God in Jesus Christ is the basic truth. All others flow from it. His epistemology is fundamentally christological:

...Christology, is the touchstone of all knowledge of God in the Christian sense, the touchstone of all theology. 'Tell me how it stands with your christology and I shall tell you who you are'. This is the point at which ways diverge, and the point at which is fixed the relation between theology and philosophy, and the relation between knowledge of God and knowledge of men, the relation between revelation and reason, the relation between Gospel and Law, the relation between God's truth and man's truth, the relation between outer and inner, the relation between theology and politics. At this point everything becomes clear or unclear, bright or dark. For here we are standing at the centre. And however high and mysterious and difficult everything we want to know might seem to us, yet we may also say that this is just where everything becomes quite simple, quite straightforward, quite childlike (p.66).

Christology for Barth is where human knowledge and speaking of God find their roots. Here things may become 'bright or dark'. It is here in christology, in the revelation of God in Christ, that human language about God begins to make sense. Roger White underlines this feature of Barth's contribution when he says that 'it is a central leitmotif of the *Dogmatics* and perhaps one of the deepest lessons we may learn from it, how much more radically we must be prepared to look to divine revelation - and above all to Jesus Christ - to learn about the very words we use in theology' (White 1982 p.224). With this in mind, we shall turn shortly to examine christology in some detail.

Language and Chalcedon

We have seen that there is a basic problem in human speech and knowledge about God. This was articulated by Dionysius and by Brian Davies. The problem is that if God is not human, but is beyond us, how can we speak adequately of him and know him? The experience of the inadequacy of human speech for God is widespread. In spite of this, we do still speak of him and name him. We have seen that there are several ways of understanding how human language about God works. It could operate in Lindbeck's 'cognitive-propositional' sense, but this might open the door to identifying the language we use with God himself and lead us into idolatry. Alternatively, it could be understood as an expressive phenomenon, only loosely, if at all, linked with the reality it seeks to articulate. The problem here is that this could lead us into a form of subjectivism which left our language about God meaningless and lacking in any real content. Lindbeck and McFague have offered alternative ways of understanding human language about God, but whilst they make some positive contributions, there are, nevertheless, some drawbacks.

It seems that both Lindbeck and McFague have produced notions of theological language which are less than adequate because they have not attended properly to christology. Lindbeck specifically rejects Nicaea and Chalcedon as anything more than 'regulative'. McFague rejects 'incarnational christology', which is clearly typified by Chalcedon. We have seen from Barth that this inner connection between language and christology is rooted in revelation itself, another feature neglected by these two writers. Furthermore, our comments on revelation and christology can already be seen to have the potential for providing the very understanding of language for which these two are searching. When we look at language in relation to christology, do we not find that a great deal of light is shed upon some of the the problems we have noted? The central tension of 'is and is not', which McFague especially is concerned to emphasize, appears in all its significance.

It is, therefore, to the heart of christology that we need to turn in order to make sense of human speech about and knowledge of God. At the heart of the Christian understanding of the revelation of God in Christ there has lain, theologically and historically, the Chalcedonian Definition of the Faith (451 A.D.). There are a number of reasons why we should turn to this christology in order to shed light upon human language about God. First, Lindbeck specifically reduces this christology to a 'regulative' status and McFague, by implication, rejects it. This reduction at the christological level alerts us to a connection between christology and language in these two writers, especially as their views of language turn out to be inadequate. It seems that the connection runs much deeper than appears at first sight and that it is in this realm of christology that a solution might be found to some of the problems which arise in their views.

Secondly, it is interesting to note that where Chalcedon has been rejected in the past, there has also been a disturbance at the level of language. We began to see this in the writings of William Temple, but Protestant theologians of the nineteenth century, for example Schleiermacher and Ritschl, had already established an Enlightenment critique of classical christology [12]. In Schleiermacher, of course, we find christology, language and revelation all fundamentally associated. However, the questions which hang over his christology also hang over his notion of God and then over his notion of language. His specific rejection of Chalcedon forms the background to McFague's. They both think that the Definition understands 'nature' to be 'static' and that its claim that there are two natures in one 'hupostasis' is therefore illogical [13]. Again, language and christology can be seen to be closely connected. Colin Gunton notes that 'Schleiermacher's first criticism of the tradition...is a linguistic one' (Gunton 1983 p.89). Schleiermacher's christology is closely associated with this criticism of the tradition. It drifts in an anthropological direction. We then find an element in his notion of theological language which suggests 'expressivism'. He says that 'Christian doctrines are accounts of the Christian religious affections set forth in speech' (Schleiermacher 1928 p.76). Language and christology go hand-in-hand in Schleiermacher and the tradition with which he is associated is characterized by an 'expressivism' in both areas [14].

We can begin to see that a rejection of Chalcedon brings with it a view of language which often turns out to be inadequate to the God about whom we are trying to speak. Paul Tillich is another example of one who wishes at least to revise Chalcedonian christology [15]. The inner connection between language and christology, however, leaves Tillich's notion of language tending in the direction of idealism. We can see that there are family likenesses here between Tillich and McFague. This inner connection between christology and language operates in a similar way wherever one looks. Aquinas' notions of analogical predication, valuable as they are in coming to understand our language about God, fail to strike a balance between divine and human components. Aquinas does not explicitly relate his notions of analogy to christology. Barth, of course, uses patristic categories and, as we have seen, relates his notion of language to his christology. As a result, he is fully aware of the 'inner tension' in our language about God. We shall also see that Coleridge maintains a fine balance between the human and the divine in his understanding of human language about God, speaking of the 'translucence of the eternal in and through the temporal'. In our final chapter, however, we shall see that Ian

Ramsey's attempt to provide us with 'an empirical placing of theological phrases' founders for reasons similar to those in Lindbeck and McFague.

Thirdly, and most importantly, we turn to the Chalcedonian Definition of the Faith because of its 'inner logic'. We shall see that the christological tension which lies at the heart of this Definition and which is interpreted in terms of the unity of 'hupostaseis' and the distinction of 'phuseis', is thoroughly continuous with the 'inner logic' of our language about God. This is especially true of our metaphorical language. The 'is and is not' which McFague has identified as central to theological language, is found at the heart of Chalcedon. It is for these three reasons, the rejection by Lindbeck and McFague and their subsequent problems with language, the presence of this feature elsewhere in the history of theology, and the 'inner logic' of the christology of Chalcedon itself, that we turn to this document.

It must be emphasized, finally, that the point is not that the Chalcedonian Definition itself provides the only adequate view of language. Rather, the point is that this Definition articulates the relation between the human and the divine in such a way that, as in the debates about christology itself, in constructing a notion of human language about God we shall do well to keep this relation in view. We have seen something of the importance of the enfleshment of the Word of God, both for revelation and for language. We now propose to pursue the problem of human language about God in the light of the relation between the human and the divine articulated by the Fathers of Chalcedon. We can now see that such a venture will shed a great deal of light upon the nature of human language about God. In particular, we shall look for similarities and parallels between the 'inner logic of christology' and the 'inner logic of metaphor'. In order to expose the 'inner logic of christology', however, we must turn first to an examination of the Chalcedonian Definition and especially to the 'tensive christology' to be found there.

II

THE CHALCEDONIAN DEFINITION

Divine-Human Relations

We have observed that the rejection of Chalcedonian christology gives rise to views of human language about God which turn out to be less than adequate. Notions of christology have a bearing upon notions of language. We noted that Schleiermacher's rejection of Chalcedonian christology was accompanied by a view of theological language in which there are some weaknesses. Both Lindbeck and McFague operate on 'revised' concepts of the person of Christ which have all sorts of implicit features which are left undiscussed. Two things are clear, however: that their concepts of theological language are flawed and that this is related to their christologies. The matter is wider than at first appears. The fundamental link between language and christology is rooted in the revelation of God in Christ. The 'inner logic of language' arises out of the 'inner logic of christology'.

The most important feature linking the two here is the relation between the divine and the human. In each case we are dealing with the way in which these two primary elements are related. The problem of how we speak about the God who is incomprehensible and yet known to us is continuous with that of how the two natures are related in Christ. Both deal with human nature, divine nature and the relation between the two. Thus, christology shows itself to be central not only because a shift here brings about a shift in the way theological language is thought to operate. It is central also in that it is concerned with articulating the same relation as is a theory of theological language, that is the relation between the divine and the human.

When we turn specifically to christology we maintain that the model which has articulated the relation between the divine and the human most adequately has been the Chalcedonian Definition of the Faith. We have also seen that it has been the rejection of Chalcedon which has brought about weaknesses in related notions of language. It could be, therefore, that a consideration of how theological language is to be understood should be carried out in the light of an understanding of the Chalcedonian Definition.

In this study of Chalcedon we shall turn first to a consideration of the two traditions which fed this Definition and of the relation between language and christology in these. We shall observe two basic 'models' in christology, the Antiochene and the Alexandrian. Charles Waldrop summarizes the respective emphases of these two schools conveniently when he says that 'the Antiochenes and the Alexandrians conceive the unity of the person of Christ differently. The latter emphasize the oneness, while the former stress the duality. Each side attempts to deal adequately with the opposite emphasis' (Waldrop 1984 p.25). Wolfhart Pannenberg calls these two types 'disjunction christology' and 'unification christology' respectively (Pannenberg 1968 p.287). We shall call them the 'model of distinction' and the 'model of unity'. Having observed the characteristics of these types and the place of language within these christologies, we shall turn specifically to the Chalcedonian Definition in order to observe how these two models come together and how the divine and the human are seen to relate. In this way we shall show how we may best understand human language about God.

The Antiochene Model

Two basic issues will occupy us in this section. These are, once again, language and christology. We shall observe first how, in the Antiochene tradition, a concern with language used in christology turns out to be the touchstone of the christology itself and indeed of the concept of God which is at work there. We shall consider two elements of this concern with language which arise in the two extreme proponents of the christology of this school, namely Theodore of Mopsuestia and Nestorius. These two elements are the rejection of the terms θεοτόκος (theotokos: God-bearing) and *communicatio idiomatum* (interchange of properties), at least as the Alexandrians understood them. Secondly, concerning christology, we shall note the emphasis on the duality within the unity of the person of Christ and its tendency to drift into a separation of the two elements. This will be done, as before, through a consideration of the relation between the language and the christology. We shall see that specific words are all-important.

First, the rejection of the two terms. Both Theodore of Mopsuestia and Nestorius rejected the term θεοτόκος or 'God-bearing' for the Virgin Mary. It is Nestorius who has come to be specifically associated with this, but the issues are exactly the same in each case. The word θεοτόκος was already in circulation by the time its weaknesses were drawn out by the Antiochenes. Nestorius' main objection to the word as used of Mary was that it gave the impression that the divine had undergone a human birth. It failed to articulate the fact that it was the man Jesus, recognized as divine, who was, strictly speaking, 'born of Mary', not God himself. Nestorius' preference was to preface θεοτόκος by ἀνθρωποτόκος (anthropotokos: 'man-bearing') or to use the word Χριστοτόκος (Christotokos: 'Christ-bearing') which he felt articulated the distinction in unity most adequately. Even the word θεοδόχος (theodochos: 'God-receiving') would be preferable to a word which suggested that God had undergone a human birth.

The main concern here lies in the relation between language and christology. Nestorius' rejection of a word used in christology exposes the fundamental link between the concepts of christology and of language. To speak of Mary as the bearer of God might imply both that the Son is divine but not human and that God has had a birth. To reject its unqualified use, however, was to imply a rejection of the divinity of the Son, that is, that Mary had given birth to a mere man. This latter was seen as precipitating a drift into 'psilanthropism', the teaching that Jesus was a 'mere man'. This teaching was associated with Paul of Samosata and had been rejected. The dispute over θεοτόκος provided a catalyst which sparked off the need to focus the language and the christology together. It also obviously had a bearing on the way in which God was understood to be involved with the world.

We turn secondly to the expression *communicatio idiomatum* or 'interchange of properties'. Here we find exactly the same underlying issue at work. How is the language concerning Christ to be understood? Both the 'inner logic of language' and that of christology are apparent here, for we have the problem of how the language about Christ relates to him alongside that of how the two natures within Christ relate to each other. In the Alexandrian tradition the *communicatio idiomatum* referred to the belief that propositions and terminology appropriate to the human nature of Christ could equally well be used of the divine nature and *vice versa*. They maintained that this was the result of the unity of the natures. Thus, references in the gospels to 'human' actions could be predicated of the divinity of Christ and references to the 'divinity' could be predicated of the humanity. There was an 'interchange of properties' and the terms could, therefore, be used interchangeably.

For Nestorius and the Antiochenes, however, the language of the gospels which speaks of the 'human' events of Christ's life was to be taken as referring to the human nature, whilst the language referring to the 'divine' events was to be taken as referring to the divine nature. This distinction is developed especially in the christology of Theodore. R.A. Norris observes that 'this habit of his is well known and can be abundantly and tiresomely illustrated from his works' (Norris 1963 p.197). Thus, reference to the growth and development of Jesus, his hunger or tiredness, would obviously be taken as reference to his human nature. Language referring to miracles, foreknowledge or other 'superhuman' events in the life of Christ, would be taken as reference to his divine nature. The language referred to either one or the other element. Rowan Greer in his work on Theodore says that 'predication had to be either to the human nature or to the divine nature' (Greer 1961 p.61).

We can see here that once again the Antiochenes deal with language and christology together. To maintain the Alexandrian usage would, for Theodore and Nestorius, result in a confusion of the two elements. For the Alexandrians, the language is interchangeable and so, therefore, are the natures within the person of Christ. The Antiochenes thus prefer to separate the language in order to guard a distinction between the elements in Christ. In this case, as in that of θεοτόκος, a variation in the view of language is controlling the christology. Interestingly, Nestorius is prepared to allow a limited use of the *communicatio idiomatum* if it is used in relation to 'Christ' or another appropriate unitive term. The important feature here is that the language controls the christology and *vice versa*. A variation in one effects a variation in the other.

We must now turn specifically to the christology at work here in the Antiochene tradition. We have called the Antiochene christology the 'model of distinction'. In this tradition, as can be seen clearly from the observations we have made concerning the language used in relation to the person of Christ, a central concern was to affirm a distinction between the two elements in Christ. The reaction was against the Alexandrian tendency to merge and confuse them. The concern over θεοτόκος and *communicatio idiomatum* was precisely to do with the way in which the two elements, the divine and the human, were to be thought of as being related. The christology of Theodore and Nestorius was a reaction against the tendency to undermine the humanity of Christ producing thereby some sort of *tertium quid*, something which was neither human nor divine. The way forward here is to look briefly at some of the words used in this tradition. Once again, the christology and the language are integrally related, but also these words are words which form the heart of Chalcedonian christology and we shall return to them in more detail later.

Central to understanding both the Antiochene and Alexandrian positions is an appreciation of four key words: οὐσία (ousia), φύσις (physis), ὑπόστασις (hypostasis) and πρόσωπον (prosopon). For the present we can work with brief definitions of these, but it should be observed that their meanings are broad and complex and sometimes overlap to the extent of synonymity. Basically, οὐσία (by this period) indicates the identity or genus of a thing, what makes that thing specifically what it is. It is sometimes translated into English as 'being'. Secondly, φύσις is the 'nature' of a thing, obviously overlapping with οὐσία. Thirdly, ὑπόστασις is 'that which stands under' a thing, or its concrete reality. Finally, πρόσωπον is the 'mask', 'face' or 'outward appearance' of a thing, that which presents itself to the senses. However, πρόσωπον can also mean 'defining properties' and may thus not be limited to external appearances. We shall be concerned here especially with two of these words, πρόσωπον and ὑπόστασις.

In the Antiochene tradition and especially in the christology of Theodore and Nestorius, there is a concern, within the context of affirming unity, to articulate as clearly as possible the distinction between the divinity and the humanity of Christ. This is achieved through the use of particular words. Nestorius rejects any idea of unity at the levels of οὐσία, φύσις or ὑπόστασις. Indeed, at these levels of 'nature' and of the actual identity and concrete reality of the elements, there could be said to be two realities, the divinity and the humanity. It was at the level of the πρόσωπον that the unity existed. The 'external appearance', which, we must remember, may imply 'the defining properties', and not mere appearance, was the level at which the unity was held to exist. Nestorius thus speaks of a 'prosopon of unity'. There are not two 'prosopa' which are unified, but one 'union of prosopon'. This union is constituted by a mutual reciprocity or dynamic interchange of humanity and divinity at this 'prosopic' level.

The second key word at this point is ὑπόστασις. There has been a great deal of misunderstanding here because of the ambiguity of the word and because its use in the Antiochene tradition is different from that at Chalcedon. However, both Theodore and Nestorius are clear that they reject the idea that there is unity at the level of the ὑπόστασις. They view this element in a more static way than the Alexandrians and link it specifically to πρόσωπον. Theodore observes that 'it cannot be said that a hypostasis is without its prosopon' (Sellers 1940 p.187). For this reason both Theodore and Nestorius assert two ὑπόστασεις (hupostaseis), that is two real underlying realities within the union. The suggestion that there might only be one immediately smacks of confusion. Although the underlying realities are fundamentally linked with the 'prosopic unity', we must be clear at which levels unity is asserted and at which levels distinction is asserted. A. Grillmeier summarizes as follows:

> ...Theodore always puts physis and hypostasis side by side. *Prosopon* is distinguished clearly from them. A being has a *prosopon* in so far as it is a physis and a hypostasis. The duality in Christ is to be sought on the side of the physis and the hypostasis, and the unity is on the side of the *prosopon* (Grillmeier 1975 p.439).

We can see from this that the distinction between the divinity and the humanity is thought to exist at the deepest levels, those of ὑπόστασις and φύσις [16]. The unity exists in the πρόσωπον. It is because of this assertion in the Antiochene tradition of a distinction at the most fundamental levels in the person of Christ, that the distinction slips into a duality. Where we have such a duality, we have what is spoken of today as 'Nestorianism', that is the complete separation of the natures with only a semblance of unity.

It is interesting to note here that in order to avoid the confusion which the Alexandrians fell into when speaking of the relation between the two elements in Christ, the Antiochenes avoided such words as κρᾶσις (krasis: mixture), μίξις (mixis: commingling or blending), σύγκυτος (sugkutos: confusion) and ἕνωσις (henosis: oneness). Rather, the word συνάφεια (sunapheia: close connection or conjunction) is preferred. We can see here also the tendency to overemphasize the distinction. More importantly, however, we can see that the concern with language is very closely associated with the type of christology which emerges.

We must now summarize the basic observations here. In the Antiochene tradition language and christology are fundamentally related. The concern to understand the language properly is related to the need to articulate the relation between the two elements in the person of Christ adequately. If the language is used incorrectly, an imbalanced christology emerges and this has implications for the fundamental question of God's relation with the world. In spite of attempts to the contrary, Theodore and Nestorius work with a model of christology which slips from emphasizing a distinction into operating with a duality. This is the 'model of distinction' which tends towards duality. The key point here is that in their attempts to guard against the confusion of the two elements and to avoid such language as implied this, the Antiochenes overemphasized the distinctions in both areas. It would take Chalcedon to balance the christology and we can begin to see now that Chalcedon might also enable us to produce a balanced understanding of theological language. Before turning specifically to Chalcedon, however, we must turn to the second model in christology, the Alexandrian 'model of unity'.

The Alexandrian Model

When we turn to the 'model of unity', the Alexandrian christological tradition in which the main emphasis was the union of the two elements in the person of Christ, we find that once again there is a fundamental link between language and christology. The theologians who typify this tradition at its extreme are Apollinarius of Laodicea and Eutyches. Clearly the Alexandrian school found no problem in using the concepts of θεοτόκος and *communicatio idiomatum* in relation to their christology. It had been against the Alexandrian use that Theodore and Nestorius had reacted so strongly. The Alexandrians were equally aware of the inner connection between christology and language, however, and had been quick to appreciate the implications of denying, for example, that Mary was θεοτόκος. To avoid the term completely was to undermine the unity and to slip into erroneous dualisms. Once again we note that there is a close connection between the way the language is understood and the type of christology which emerges. The main concern here is with a series of words which occur regularly in Alexandrian christology and which assist in a 'model of unity' slipping into a 'model of confusion'. First, however, we must outline Apollinarius' christology.

Apollinarius was the first to attempt to articulate fully the relation between the human and the divine elements in Christ. He was, of course, reacting against such Antiochene dualisms as we have considered. His overriding concern was, therefore, to assert the unity of the two elements. Frances Young says that 'whatever the problems or implications, the union is Apollinarius' chief concern' (Young 1983 p.188). In order to secure this union Apollinarius set out to enable a full understanding of the humanity in Christ by considering human psychology. In spite of various changes and developments in Apollinarius' thinking in this area, certain key features persist and are essential to understanding his attempt to articulate the union of the two elements in Christ.

It is normally acknowledged that for Apollinarius the human person is made up of three elements: the σῶμα (soma: body), the ψυχή (psyche: vital principle), and the νοῦς (nous: rational principle). These elements form a hierarchy with the νοῦς, the rational or intellectual principle at the top. This νοῦς is the feature which separates man from the animals. The νοῦς is the seat of human freedom, of free will and thus of guilt and of innocence or sinlessness. Next, we have the ψυχή, which is the animating principle which human beings share with the animals. This is the non-material part of the personality of a human being. Finally, at the bottom of the ladder, we have the material aspect, the σῶμα. The latter is also sometimes called σάρξ (sarx: flesh), but this usage links it up to the lower soul or ψυχή. It is with this scheme of understanding the human person that we are involved when we raise the question of Apollinarius' christology.

The central question for Apollinarius is, as Maurice Relton puts it, 'How could two perfect natures be united in one person, since two natures involve two personalities?' (Relton 1917 p.19). Apollinarius' reply is that in the unity of the two elements in Christ, the divine Λόγος (Logos: Word) has taken the place of the human νοῦς, the rational principle, the seat of human free will, of guilt, sin and innocence. As a result of this, we have a unity in which the divine Λόγος forms the seat of intelligence and freedom and is thus the primary element within the union.

If the divine Λόγος has taken the place of the human νοῦς in Christ, however, then the humanity within the union has been undermined and the v˙ ₂w that the flesh of Christ was divine and even pre-existent begins to emerge. If the divine Λόγος is the sole life-giving principle in the union, then the drift into docetism, into undermining the humanity, has begun and a scheme which was attempting to articulate a union has slipped over into a scheme maintaining a 'confusion'. This drift into a mixing of the elements and even an elimination of one of them is shown in Apollinarius' use of the expression μία φύσις (mia phusis: one nature). At the very best it is the Λόγος which controls or rules (ἡγεμονικός, hegemonikos) the humanity. Indeed, H.A. Wolfson in his work on the philosophy of the church Fathers maintains the view that we have in Apollinarius' christology a 'union of predominance' in which the active divine Λόγος predominates over the passive, human flesh (Wolfson 1970 p.441).

How, more specifically, does Apollinarius understand this unity? Is it fair to maintain that the 'union' in his scheme has become a 'confusion'? In order to try to clarify the union between human and divine, Apollinarius uses the model of the human body-soul relation. The nature of the unity between these two elements had occupied Aristotle and its use as a model in christology is widespread amongst the early Christian Fathers. Norris summarizes the position in relation to Apollinarius when he says that 'as the soul is mixed with its body without thereby being altered in its nature, so the Logos is mixed with a body, the while remaining transcendent over it and unchanged by it' (Norris 1963 p.107). The analogy is clear enough.

The question is whether or not the natures in the union in Christ do remain unchanged in Apollinarius' christology. It is significant that it is the language which Apollinarius uses which seems to pull him in the direction of a confusion of the elements. The words which appear most frequently in Apollinarius' writings, in relation to the unity of the two elements in the person of Christ, suggest that we are indeed dealing here with a confusion of the elements.

We turn now, therefore, to a closer consideration of the nature of the union of the two elements in the person of Christ in Apollinarius' christology through an investigation of the language he uses. This demands a look at the concept of 'mixture' and its background, evident in the christology. Apollinarius frequently uses language associated with the idea of mixing. Such words as μίξις, κρᾶσις, σύγκρασις and σύνθεσις (mixis, krasis, sugkrasis and sunthesis) occur regularly in his articulation of the union. These are words which had been avoided by the Antiochenes. They have specific backgrounds, but remain meaningless until defined, especially in this context. We must, therefore, look at their possible meanings in turn.

Three main types of 'mixture' concern us here. Two of them can be found in a distinction made by Aristotle and the third can be found in Stoicism [17]. These three possibilities are straightforward, but there are 'sub-distinctions' within them. Aristotle makes the distinction between σύνθεσις (sunthesis) and κρᾶσις (krasis) or μίξις (mixis). By σύνθεσις he means a juxtaposition in which the different parts retain their distinctive elements without any loss. His example is grains of barley or wheat. He also calls this type 'continuous', in the sense that pieces of wood bound together or held together by glue are 'continuous'. In this type there is no reaction of the elements upon each other.

By κρᾶσις (normally used for liquids) and μίξις (normally used for solids) Aristotle means a mixture in which the two elements react upon each other, changing and being changed and forming a *tertium quid*. The elements involved turn away from themselves to the other. Here a compromise between the elements occurs. These elements could, in principle, return to their original states. In some cases, one element in the mixture may be dominated by the other, forming an imbalance between stronger and weaker elements. In certain cases, as with a drop of wine thrown into ten thousand gallons of water, one of the elements can be eliminated in the mixture and the 'unity' is then comprised of only one of the original elements. Comparing the two main types which he distinguishes, Aristotle maintains that no level of σύνθεσις can become κρᾶσις or μίξις.

In Stoicism, these distinctions are taken up in the context of the debate concerning the relation between body and soul in human beings. Because of the inadequacy of the distinctions made by Aristotle for the purpose required (the human soul and body are for the Stoics neither separate nor a *tertium quid*), the Stoics sought further clarification and distinction. They spoke of σύγκυσις (sugkusis) and κρᾶσις δι' ὅλων (krasis di' holon). By σύγκυσις they meant a mixture in which both elements undergo change and which in principle might not return to their prior states. Interestingly, the Stoics held that a drop of wine in the ocean would retain its presence as wine [18]. By κρᾶσις δι' ὅλων they meant, according to Norris, '...a mutual and total interpenetration of two material substances, in which each contained all of its characteristic properties unaltered, so that even in their intimate union the two substances remain distinct' (Norris 1963 p.69). This clearly strikes the balance of unity and distinction and it is significant that Apollinarius uses the Stoic κρᾶσις δι' ὅλων in his christology. Apollinarius observes that 'the qualities of things which are mixed are mixed and not destroyed, so that certain [portions] stand apart from the ingredients which have been mingled - as, for example, wine from water' (p.106). However, in spite of using this expression, Apollinarius frequently uses other words (μίξις, κρᾶσις and σύγκρασις) for the relation between the elements and his overall success in securing an adequate distinction is still greatly in question.

There have been a number of interpretations of Apollinarius' christology, but the basic outline and the potential for slipping into 'confusion' is clear enough. Certainly, after Apollinarius' time, the extreme Alexandrian view which he typifies developed in the direction of 'Monophysitism', that is, a view of the person of Christ which completely undermines the human nature. This was to be the contribution of Eutyches whom J.N.D. Kelly notes as 'the founder of an extreme and virtually Docetic form of monophysitism, teaching that the Lord's humanity was totally absorbed by His divinity' (Kelly 1977 p.331). Even though Eutyches' real identity may be lost to us, he stands as one who turned the 'model of union' into a 'model of confusion'. It was to be the role of Chalcedon to stem the tide in these developments.

The particular interest here is in the connection between the christology and the language. We have observed that the willingness to call Mary θεοτόκος was a symptom of a certain christology: it overemphasized the divine element by calling her the bearer of God. So also with the *communicatio idiomatum*. Here the view was that language could be used interchangeably of both human and divine elements. The same thing can be seen with the issues arising from a study of particular words. Charles Raven draws attention to the connection between Apollinarius' language and his christology when he says that 'his insistence upon the need for a real union, and his use of words like "mixture" and "combination" to express it, laid him open to the charge, later deservedly brought against the Monophysites, of confusing together human and divine' (Raven 1978 p.208). The language, because it is so fundamentally linked to the christology, had a serious bearing on the christology which emerged. Confusion in one produced confusion in the other. As in the Antiochene tradition, fundamental questions are raised here concerning the nature of God's relation with the world. It would take Chalcedon to balance the christology and we can begin to see, once again, that Chalcedon might well also enable a more adequate understanding of human language about God.

From this consideration of the two traditions which fed the christology which was to emerge at Chalcedon, we have discovered a number of crucial points. As we suspected, language and christology are very closely related to each other. A deficiency in one of these is closely associated with a deficiency in the other. Where we have found a 'distinction' or a 'mixing' in one of these areas, we have also found it in the other. The two models of 'unity' and 'distinction' have shown us what happens where certain emphases prevail and are taken to their extremes: we so easily find ourselves slipping into confusion or separation. If Chalcedon was to achieve a unique insight at the level of christology, could it not also be the case that it might achieve this at the level of language, particularly given the close connections between the two?

We must now turn to a consideration of the Chalcedonian Definition

in order to see how the two models of christology which we have discussed
are brought together and how the divine and the human relate there. This
will expose the 'inner logic of christology' whose characteristic feature
will be shown to be an 'is and is not' structure. We shall then be in a position
to turn much more specifically to the question of how this christology can
shed light on our understanding of the language we use about the God
who is known to us as unknown, in the revelation of God in Jesus Christ.

THE CHALCEDONIAN DEFINITION OF THE FAITH

THE CENTRAL SECTION

Ἑπόμενοι τοίνυν τοῖς ἁγίοις πατράσιν, ἕνα καὶ τὸν αὐτὸν ὁμολογοῦμεν Υἱὸν τὸν Κύριον ἡμῶν Ἰησοῦν Χριστόν, καὶ συμφώνως ἅπαντες ἐκδιδάσκομεν, τέλειον τὸν αὐτὸν ἐν θεότητι, τέλειον τὸν αὐτὸν ἐν ἀνθρωπότητι, Θεὸν ἀληθῶς, καὶ ἄνθρωπον ἀληθῶς, τὸν αὐτὸν ἐκ ψυχῆς λογικῆς καὶ σώματος, ὁμοούσιον τῷ Πατρὶ κατὰ τὴν θεότητα, καὶ ὁμοούσιον τὸν αὐτὸν ἡμῖν κατὰ τὴν ἀνθρωπότητα, κατὰ πάντα ὅμοιον ἡμῖν χωρὶς ἁμαρτίας· πρὸ αἰώνων μὲν ἐκ τοῦ Πατρὸς γεννηθέντα κατὰ τὴν θεότητα, ἐπ᾽ ἐσχάτων δὲ τῶν ἡμερῶν τὸν αὐτὸν δι᾽ ἡμᾶς καὶ διὰ τὴν ἡμετέραν σωτηρίαν ἐκ Μαρίας τῆς παρθένου τῆς θεοτόκου κατὰ τὴν ἀνθρωπότητα, ἕνα καὶ τὸν αὐτὸν Χριστόν, Υἱόν, Κύριον, μονογενῆ, ἐν δύο φύσεσιν ἀσυγχύτως, ἀτρέπτως, ἀδιαιρέτως, ἀχωρίστως γνωριζόμενον· οὐδαμοῦ τῆς τῶν φύσεων διαφορᾶς ἀνῃρημένης διὰ τὴν ἕνωσιν, σῳζομένης δὲ μᾶλλον τῆς ἰδιότητος ἑκατέρας φύσεως, καὶ εἰς ἓν πρόσωπον καὶ μίαν ὑπόστασιν συντρεχούσης, οὐκ εἰς δύο πρόσωπα μεριζόμενον ἢ διαιρούμενον, ἀλλ᾽ ἕνα καὶ τὸν αὐτὸν Υἱὸν καὶ μονογενῆ Θεόν, Λόγον, Κύριον Ἰησοῦν Χριστόν· καθάπερ ἄνωθεν οἱ προφῆται περὶ αὐτοῦ, καὶ αὐτὸς ἡμᾶς ὁ Κύριος Ἰησοῦς Χριστὸς ἐξεπαίδευσε, καὶ τὸ τῶν πατέρων ἡμῖν παραδέδωκε σύμβολον. (Bindley/Green 1950 p.193)

Therefore, following the holy Fathers, we confess and all unanimously teach our Lord Jesus Christ, one and the same Son, the same perfect in Godhead, the same perfect in Manhood; truly God and truly Man; the same (consisting) of a rational soul and body; of one substance with the Father concerning the Godhead and the same of one substance with us concerning the Manhood, like us in all things apart from sin; begotten of the Father before all ages concerning the Godhead; the same in the last days for us and for our salvation, born of the Virgin Mary, Theotokos, concerning the Manhood;

one and the same Christ, Son, Lord, Only begotten, made known (recognized) in two natures, unconfusedly, unchangeably, indivisibly, inseparably; the distinction of the natures being in no way denied because of the unity, but rather the characteristic property of each nature being preserved, running together into one 'Prosopon' and one 'Hupostasis', not divided or parted into two 'Prosopa', but one and the same Son and only-begotten God, Word, Lord Jesus Christ; just as from the beginning the prophets taught concerning him, and our Lord Jesus Christ himself taught, and the Symbol of the Fathers has handed down to us. (My own translation using Sellers' division.)

The Chalcedonian Definition

Karl Barth drew attention to the centrality of christology for all human knowledge of God and speech about God. It is here in christology, he maintained, that everything else becomes 'bright or dark' (Barth 1949 p.66). We have observed especially the relation between christology and language and have noted the close association between the two. The Enlightenment critique of classical christology, as typified in Ritschl and Schleiermacher, brought with it a disturbance at the level of language. We have already observed that it was Schleiermacher, with whose theology Barth struggled to the end of his life, who helped to establish a notion of theological language which, to some extent at any rate, lies behind the 'experiential-expressivism' noted by Lindbeck. It can be seen, once again, that christology and language are related at the most fundamental level in the modern period.

Schleiermacher articulated the problems of christology clearly in his major work *The Christian Faith* when he said that:

> ...all the results of the endeavour to achieve a living presentation of the unity of the divine and the human in Christ, ever since it was tied down to this expression, have always vacillated between the opposite errors of mixing the two natures to form a third which would be neither of them, neither divine nor human, or of keeping the two natures separate, but either neglecting the unity of the person in order to separate the two natures more distinctly, or, in order to keep firm hold of the unity of the person, disturbing the necessary balance, and making one nature less important than the other and limited by it (Schleiermacher 1928 p.394).

He maintained, however, that the solution was to begin christology elsewhere. Although he rejected the language and structure of Chalcedon because of a misunderstanding over the meaning of 'nature', he has outlined correctly here the pitfalls which that Council was attempting to avoid. The problems of 'mixing the two natures' and of 'keeping the two natures separate' constitute the backdrop to any consideration of Chalcedon. We have seen these problems already in the previous sections.

In turning now to the document which Schleiermacher rejected, we are mindful once again that christology is related to language. Schleiermacher turned away from Chalcedon and helped instigate an 'expressivist' drift in notions of human language about God. We are turning towards Chalcedon in order to avoid the pitfalls which face us in understanding human language about God.

McFague, it will be recalled, although rejecting 'incarnational christology', emphasized the importance of 'metaphor' in theology and saw the key element in metaphor to be its 'is and is not' structure. We observed that McFague rejected incarnational christology on the grounds of the static character of 'nature'. Schleiermacher had done the same. The interesting thing here is that both Schleiermacher and McFague end up with concepts of language which turn out to be lacking. If McFague had made the appropriate links between the 'is and is not' of metaphor and the 'is and is not' of Chalcedon, a more balanced view of theological language could have emerged. Clearly a reconsideration of Chalcedonian christology is what is required in order to begin to solve at least some of the problems.

Barth's crucial insight that it is with christology that things become 'bright or dark' draws our attention to the importance of an appreciation of ontology and metaphysics. Frequently, where religious language has been seen to be either meaningless or idolatrous, it has been divorced from a balanced christology. In these cases the content of religious language has become eclipsed and reduced either to a confusion or to a separation of the elements. All human language, about even the most commonplace things, presupposes some understanding of knowledge and therefore operates within an ontology. The wider issue of language always presupposes and implies an ontological system in which this is set. This is not peculiar to language about God. We have stressed the link between language and christology. This is an inherent link between the subject and the way it is spoken of. Through an understanding of Chalcedonian christology we can move towards a fuller appreciation of how human language about God works. This will presuppose and imply ontological elements which in fact emerge as we look at the central words in the Chalcedonian Definition.

When we turn to the Chalcedonian Definition itself, we find that a series of words and expressions dominate its christology. These words, emerging as they did from Greek metaphysical thinking, were crucial to the entire patristic christological enterprise and, therefore, to the emergence of christology as such. Some of these words have arisen already in the discussion of the two basic 'models' from Antioch and Alexandria. Some will now emerge for the first time. The basic observation here will be that the two 'models', that of unity and that of distinction, now come together to form a christology which is based on an 'is and is not' structure. This dynamic metaphysical structure exposes the 'inner logic of christology' and also provides the crucial link with the way human language about God works.

We shall now consider the following words and phrases separately before turning to a more general overview of the Chalcedonian Definition. In this way we shall expose the main dynamics of the 'inner logic of christology'. The words and phrases to be considered here are: (1) οὐσία and ὁμοούσιος (ousia and homoousios); (2) πρόσωπον (prosopon); (3) ὑπόστασις (hupostasis); (4) ἐνυπόστατος (enupostatos); and (5) φύσις (phusis).

οὐσία and ὁμοούσιος

Possibly the most important word in patristic christology and certainly one of the most important here in the Chalcedonian Definition is the word ὁμοούσιος. The background to this word lies in the word οὐσία of which ὁμοούσιος is a compound. These words are normally translated into English as 'substance' and 'of the same substance', respectively. In addition to its centrality at Chalcedon, ὁμοούσιος also has an important background in the creed of the Council of Nicaea where it is more important than it is here in the Chalcedonian Definition. It is, however, used here in this document twice, in relation to both humanity and divinity. The background to οὐσία and ὁμοούσιος is extremely complex, ambiguous and vague, but the central thrust of meaning in the context of early christology can be stated clearly enough for the purpose here: it affirms unity. We shall now briefly examine the background to these two words in order to shed light on this basic meaning.

οὐσία: The immediate problem in relation to this word is that, outside specific contexts, there is no single meaning associated with it. J.N.D. Kelly observes that:

> There were few words in Greek susceptible of so many and so confusing shades of meaning as ousia. Its fundamental significance can be at once defined as 'being', 'essence', 'reality', but these synonyms only bring out the cause of the ambiguity. The precise meaning attached to ousia varied with the philosophical context in which it occurred and the philosophical allegiance of the writer (Kelly 1972 p.243).

The basic philosophical background lies in Aristotle's two works the *Categories* and the *Metaphysics*. In these works the breadth of meaning is striking. In the *Categories* we find the classic distinction between 'primary' and 'secondary' substances. The main concern here is with things and categories of things which exist. In the *Metaphysics*, the concern is far wider and there is a whole host of concepts of substance. The complexity and incoherence in the arguments and terms in this work means that little light is shed upon the meaning of the word substance. We shall, therefore, concern ourselves primarily with Aristotle's ideas as they emerge in the *Categories*.

In the *Categories*, Aristotle lays out his distinction between primary and secondary substances as follows:

> Substance, in the truest and primary and most definite sense of the word, is that which is neither predicable of a subject nor present in a subject; for instance, the individual man or horse. But in a secondary sense those things are called substances within which, as species, the primary substances are included; also those which, as genera, include the species. For instance the individual man is included in the species 'man', and the genus to which the species belongs is 'animal'; these, therefore - that is to say, the species 'man' and the genus 'animal' - are termed secondary substances (5:1f).

Here we can see that the 'primary substance', the πρώτη οὐσία (prote ousia) as Aristotle calls it, is the 'individual thing'. The primary substance is essentially something which is 'neither said of a subject nor in a subject', that is, it cannot be predicated of something, but is a thing in itself. Thus, for example, a particular man or a particular horse are substances in the primary sense. The 'secondary substance' or δευτέρα οὐσία (deutera ousia), on the other hand, refers to the genera and species to which such particulars belong. Thus, the particular man belongs to the species 'man' and the particular horse belongs to the species 'horse', whilst both belong to the genus 'animal'. The basic distinction between primary and secondary substances is essentially a distinction between the particular and the universal.

Later in the same chapter, Aristotle affirms that if there were no primary substances 'it would be impossible for anything else to exist' (5.2b). This gives the impression that whilst he uses the word οὐσία in a wide variety of senses, the base meaning has to do with the individuality of something, that distinctive element which makes it what it is. For both senses of substance, in fact, it seems that the emphasis is on the 'defining characteristics' of something.

It is important to note that there has been a great deal of debate concerning whether the *Categories* has to do primarily with words or with things referred to by words. This, of course, raises the fundamental philosophical issue of how words relate to what they mean, in addition to Aristotle's view of the matter. The issues are wide and complex and we cannot examine them in detail here [19]. Ideas concerning Aristotle's real interest in relation to this matter have varied, but Porphyry, whose view has on the whole predominated, maintained that Aristotle's concern is with both. Stead summarises Porphyry as follows:

> ...the *Categories* is concerned primarily with words, though not in the same way as a grammar or literary criticism; rather, it considers the natural divisions of our language as reflecting a corresponding division in the order of nature; indirectly, therefore, it contributes to our theory of the universe (Stead 1977 p.56).

According to this view, the distinctions articulated in language are also distinctions within reality. The real point of interest here is the fundamental link, however this is conceived, between human language and that which the language is about.

We may thus conclude two points: first, that οὐσία has to do with the defining characteristics of a particular or universal; and, secondly, as in our observations of the relation between language and christology, that there is an inherent relation between words and the realities which words depict.

ὁμοούσιος: When we turn to the word ὁμοούσιος, a word of special significance in the creed of Nicaea and used here in the Chalcedonian Definition twice, we encounter even more complexity. As with οὐσία, the word ὁμοούσιος proves to be more complex the more it is investigated. Obviously as a compound adjective coming from οὐσία, ὁμοούσιος brings with it all the complexities of the basic word. The Greek word is made up of ὁμός (homos: same) and οὐσία (substance, being) and the straightforward meaning of ὁμοούσιος is obviously 'having the same substance'. Stead translates it as 'made of the same element' or 'belonging to the same order of beings' (Stead 1977 p.193). The Latin equivalent *unius substantiae* is found in Irenaeus (Stead p.191), whilst the word 'consubstantial' is widely used in English. G.L. Prestige defines ὁμοούσιος as follows: 'The original signification of homoousios, apart from all theological technicality, is simply "made of the same stuff". "Stuff" here bears a generic sense, necessarily, since no objects of physical experience are composed of identical portions of matter; it really means "kind of stuff"' (Prestige 1952 p.197). Prestige adds to his discussion that, down to the Council of Nicaea, ὁμοούσιος was always understood to refer to material substance and that 'it conveyed a metaphor drawn from material objects' (p.209). Indeed, one of the reasons the word was so widely misunderstood, as Bernard Lonergan points out, was because it was interpreted in materialist terms [20]. The importance of understanding this language as metaphorical is fundamental here to a proper appreciation of the claims being made.

It may seem that examining the etymology of ὁμοούσιος goes little way towards illuminating actual meaning. The breadth of usage encountered in relation to this word still renders it almost meaningless until specific contexts are looked at. Fortunately, we do have a wealth of usage from the patristic period upon which we can draw. Some of this will provide us with a picture adequate enough for the purpose here. The term ὁμοούσιος first emerged in the second century in Gnostic circles and it can be found in the descriptions and criticisms of Gnostic teaching which comes down to us from Irenaeus. Its use was not exclusively Gnostic, but the Gnostics especially seem to have taken up the word and used it with regard to God's relation to the world. Stead has discovered forty-seven occurrences of the word in pre-Nicene literature and the predominant meaning has to do with common derivation or having the same source [21]. This is to be understood in the widest possible way, however, and it is important to note Stead's observation that 'the word allows, but does not entail, organic connection. And it allows, but does not entail, equality of status' (Stead 1977 p.201). This leaves some rather large holes in our understanding of what the word might mean. It is clear, however, following Stead and Prestige, that the broad concept of unity of source and derivation is intended. The context in each case fills out the further clarification needed.

In the third century, the key writers to use this term were Clement and Origen. As with Irenaeus, the context in Clement is one in which he is reacting to Gnostic thinking. The main use occurs when he attacks the view of the Valentinians that a superior race of human beings is responsible for bringing life to a dead world. Clement argues that such a race would be taking the place of Christ, unless it be said that he is ὁμοούσιος with them. Stead thinks that the word may be equivalent to ὁμογενής (homogenes: of the same race or family) here, or that it 'implies some closer identity' (p.207). Clement also uses the word in relation to creation and especially Genesis 1:26. The creator takes dust from the earth and creates a material soul which is ὁμοούσιος with the beasts. There is, in addition, a psychic element which is ὁμοούσιος with the creator. The two ὁμοούσιοι (homoousioi: those who are of the same being) are the image and the likeness [22]. Concerning Clement's use of the word, Stead concludes that 'in general, Clement's use of the term homoousios agrees with that of Irenaeus. It means "belonging to the same order of being"...' (p.208). It can be seen that, even before we consider the uses of the word ὁμοούσιος in connection with the relations of the persons of the Trinity, its general use has to do with common derivation or unity, even if not exclusively so.

It is with Origen that the word is first used in relation to the persons of the Trinity, although he does use it in a more general way as well and it is not yet a 'technical term'. It is also with Origen that some of the richest metaphors for the relation of the Λόγος to the Father appear [23]. This is especially important as it is such metaphors as the sun and its light, the source and its stream and the father and his son which clinch the very consubstantiality which the word ὁμοούσιος is also attempting to clinch. As far as Trinitarian relations are concerned, Origen is concerned to speak of the derivation of the Son from the Father. Within the very rich and complex understanding of the cosmos in which Origen's christology is set, he is out to assert the superiority of the Λόγος over the other beings. In short, the concern in using this word is with the continuation and unity which exists between the Father and the Son.

When we approach the Council of Nicaea and the christology of Athanasius, the complexity in finding the meaning of ὁμοούσιος thickens. Obviously, taken in the sense of 'common derivation', the word could be seen to merge the Son with the Father and tend in the direction of Modalism or Sabellianism because it gave the impression of meaning 'one thing'. It was rejected by the Arians and even many of those on the 'orthodox' side were wary of the term. It is clear, however, that the main concern of Nicaea was to challenge those who were claiming that the Λόγος was not one with God. The context, therefore, shows us that the main understanding and intention of this word as it was asserted at Nicaea concerned the assertion of unity. Stead says that 'the phrase simply denies that the Son had an origin outside, or independent of, the Father' (p.241). Stead also notes that, in order to maintain the hint of a distinction between Father and Son, the Fathers of Nicaea left their terms deliberately ambiguous: 'This formula of theirs was essentially a formula of compromise' (p.242).

The diversity of meanings associated with the word ὁμοούσιος means that it is impossible to say in narrow and precise terms what the word did and did not mean. Furthermore, we can never be absolutely sure that when either οὐσία or ὁμοούσιος occur, the writer has Aristotle's meanings firmly in mind. The meanings of ὁμοούσιος seem to range from 'the same' to 'different'! However, the term, as we find it in its historical context of denying the teaching of Arius, is used at Nicaea and also at Chalcedon to assert unity and common derivation. In relation to the complexity of the word ὁμοούσιος, Stead says that:

Homoousios guarantees very little; it can be used of things which
resemble one another merely in belonging to the created order, or
to the category of substance; it can relate collaterals to each other,
or derivatives with their source; it does not exclude inequality of
status or power. Secondly, however, the term is often used to indicate
a relationship which is in fact closer than mere membership of the
same species or similar material constitution, for instance that of a
stream to the actual fountain from which it flows, or that of an
offspring to his own parent. To call a son *Homoousios* with his father
implies more than merely their common membership of the human
race; and the further implication need not be merely that of their
physical linkage; the term can evoke their whole biological and social
relationship (p.247).

We have seen that, although the meaning of this word can be extremely
broad, it is the second sense above, the sense of close relationship, which
is central to ὁμοούσιος at Nicaea and Chalcedon. According to Kelly, the
use of this word at Nicaea was more likely to have had a generic sense.
Logically, however, in relation to the Godhead it requires more the sense
of identity [24].

    We can conclude, therefore, that the words οὐσία and ὁμοούσιος as used
in the Chalcedonian Definition are concerned with affirming the unity
between the defining characteristics of two things, that is a common
derivation, continuity or unity between the Λόγος and the Father, on the
one hand and between Jesus' humanity and common humanity, on the
other.

πρόσωπον

    We have already discussed the meaning and place of πρόσωπον in the
christology of Nestorius. We must now identify its role in the Chalcedonian
Definition. Originally πρόσωπον meant 'face', 'mask' or the 'external
appearance' of a thing. The emphasis is on the concrete or empirical
dimension. It is basically that which is presented to the senses. Prestige
defines it as 'the external being or individual self as presented to an

onlooker' (Prestige 1952 p.157). It could, therefore, mean the 'individuality' of a thing. It has a semitic origin and was, therefore, popular with the Antiochenes. The Latin equivalent is *persona*.

We saw that Nestorius' concept of 'prosopon of union' constituted the level at which he saw the unity between the elements in Christ. For him, there was still a fundamental distinction at the level of ὑπόστασεις. Here in the Chalcedonian Definition we have the claim that there is ἓν πρόσωπον καὶ μίαν ὑπόστασιν (one prosopon and one hypostasis). We are thus dealing here with a concern to assert unity at every level. The Alexandrian concern to secure unity prevails in the assertion of one πρόσωπον and one ὑπόστασις. Theodore and Nestorius had claimed that each πρόσωπον had its ὑπόστασις and that whilst there was a 'prosopic union', the ὑπόστασεις remained distinct. In Chalcedon we find only one ὑπόστασις concurring with one πρόσωπον. In terms of the πρόσωπον, the view is the same in Chalcedon as in the Antiochene tradition, but its fundamental link with ὑπόστασις brings about a crucial difference. At this point, union has been expressed at the expense of distinction, but this is to come in the second half of the main section of the Definition.

ὑπόστασις

The word ὑπόστασις is extremely difficult to translate into a single English word. Basically the meaning originally had to do with the sediment of liquid and meant simply 'what settles'. It came later to refer to the particular underlying concrete reality of a thing. It meant 'reality and genuineness' and had very physical overtones (Sellers 1953 p.139). Cyril uses the word, especially in his expressions μία ὑπόστασις ἡ του λόγου σεσαρκωμένη (mia hupostasis he tou logou sesarkomene: one person of the Word incarnate) and ἕνωσις καθ' ὑπόστασιν (henosis kath hupostasin: hypostatic union). This was the word used especially in the Alexandrian tradition to assert the fundamental and underlying unity of the two elements in Christ [25]. Whilst the Alexandrian understanding of ὑπόστασις was one of a dynamic unity, the Antiochene view, preserving the impassibility of the divinity and the distinction between the elements involved, saw it as a static phenomenon. There was no movement between the two ὑπόστασεις.

In the Chalcedonian Definition we find that there is only one ὑπόστασις. The Alexandrian use of the word, to assert the unity, has prevailed. It must be said, however, that the lack of a human ὑπόστασις in the Chalcedonian Christ is a point of weakness in this Definition and it is not until an adequate concept of ἐνυπόστασια (enhypostasia) has been articulated that this problem can be said to have been overcome. Until this weakness has been overcome, there remains an undermining of the humanity of Christ and the balance between union and distinction is not secured. John McIntyre suggests that the concept of 'enhypostasia' found in the theology of Ephraim of Antioch offers the best solution to this problem. We turn now, therefore, to a closer look at this.

ἐνυπόστατος

This word is not actually found in the Chalcedonian Definition, but first emerged in a significant way in Leontius of Byzantium. It emerged by way of an attempt to secure a real humanity in the incarnate Christ, whilst adhering to Cyril's concept of 'hypostatic union' and the Chalcedonian μίαν ὑπόστασιν and at the same time overcoming their difficulties. Leontius' view was that the human ὑπόστασις was 'enpersoned' ('enhupostatized') in the divine ὑπόστασις. The problem with this was that whilst it helped eliminate the problematical ἀνυπόστασια (anhupostasia: the belief that in the Incarnation only 'general humanity' came into union with the Λόγος and not a particular individual man), it left the humanity of Jesus still at least potentially undermined and thus left open a door leading to further docetism. If a particular humanity were to be articulated as part of the union, then the logic of ἐνυπόστατος needed pressing further.

Ephraim's concept of ἐνυπόστατος comes the closest, according to McIntyre, to articulating adequately the union between the two elements in the person of Christ. Ephraim speaks of a σύνθετος ἡ ὑπόστασις (sunthetos he hupostasis: composite hypostasis). The humanity of Jesus is at its most personal when it comes into composite union with the divine ὑπόστασις. Here, the problem of the impersonal human nature of the Christ of Chalcedon receives its most adequate treatment. The humanity is at its fullest and most personal when it is in composite union with the divine ὑπόστασις, thus forming a 'composite hypostasis' [26]. Having thus articulated the union, the distinction remains at the level of the natures as in the Definition of Chalcedon. Thus, a personal union securing full hypostases and distinction of natures is articulated.

φύσις

In turning to the word φύσις or 'nature', we are turning to the word which in Chalcedon articulates the distinction between the two elements. We must remember that it is here also that there has been considerable misunderstanding leading to the rejection of the whole Definition. Our understanding of the type of christology with which we are dealing here depends upon how we interpret the word φύσις. Geoffrey Lampe defines it as follows: 'nature; essence of a person or thing with the attributes proper to it; essence considered from the point of view of activity or function' (Lampe 1961 p.1496). There are overlaps with οὐσία and ὑπόστασις here, but the sense of the 'function' of the 'thing in itself' or of the 'individual person', predominates. It could also be seen in generic or collective terms as a species. It was used widely in theology and philosophy, in relation to the divine nature, the Trinity, christology and the natural world.

In the Antiochene tradition φύσις was used to articulate the 'distinction' within the unity of the person of Christ. Theodore and Nestorius spoke of 'two natures' in order to maintain the two realities within the Incarnation and to avoid any confusion at the most fundamental levels. The Alexandrian tradition, especially Cyril and Eutyches, saw φύσις more as individual than generic and, therefore, saw a threat to the unity of Christ in the Antiochene claim to two natures. Thus, the Alexandrians affirmed the unity in terms of nature: two natures before the union, but one after [27]. In the Chalcedonian Definition, the Antiochene practice is maintained and the distinction is articulated as ἐν δύο φύσεσιν (en duo phusesin: in two natures). The unity is spoken of in terms of μίαν ὑπόστασιν (mian hupostasin: one hypostasis). Although there is overlap in the meaning of the terms, they are used in the Definition in this way in order to articulate both the unity and the distinction.

It should be noted here that there has been considerable debate concerning the original text of the Chalcedonian Definition at this point. The uncertainty lies in whether the original text had ἐν δύο φύσεσιν (en duo phusesin: in two natures) or ἐκ δύο φύσεων (ek duo phuseon: out of two natures). Clearly if it was 'out of' two natures, it could imply 'into one nature', that is, two natures before the union and one after the union. This was precisely what was at issue between Cyril and Nestorius and the Alexandrian and Antiochene christologies. 'Out of two natures' and 'into one nature' was the Alexandrian view, unifying the natures. 'Out of two natures' and 'in two natures', was the Antiochene view, preserving the distinction at the level of natures. By far the majority of manuscripts of the Chalcedonian Definition have ἐν δύο φύσεσιν and Sellers is clear that 'there can be no doubt...that the correct text is "in two natures"' (Sellers 1953 p.121). This is also the view taken here.

What, more specifically, does the word φύσις mean, however? The underlying divide is between those who interpret the word in a static sense, on the one side, and those who interpret it in a fluid and dynamic sense, on the other. In his *Metaphysics*, Aristotle gives seven meanings of the word φύσις. The predominant meaning given is that it has to do with 'movement'. Aristotle says that it is 'the source from which the primary movement in each natural object is present in it in virtue of its own essence' (1014b). R.G. Collingwood comments that it is this sense which 'Aristotle regards as the true and fundamental meaning, and this, therefore, is how he uses the word himself. It certainly does accurately correspond with the ordinary Greek usage' (Collingwood 1945 p.81). This element of the 'movement' or 'behaviour' peculiar to a thing making it what it is, lies at the heart of the Greek notion of φύσις.

In the modern period, it has been the misinterpretation of this word that has led to the misunderstanding of Chalcedonian christology. Schleiermacher interpreted φύσις in a static sense, concluding that two 'natures' could not be spoken of as one. He understood it as a 'limited existence, standing in opposition to something else' (Schleiermacher 1928 p.393). An interpretation of this sort reduces the content of the document to a meaningless riddle similar to that of trying to square the circle [28]. Those who reject Chalcedon in the present day, McFague amongst them, normally do so along these lines. However, those who interpret φύσις in a fluid or dynamic sense, perhaps in relation to 'being', save the content of the Definition by acknowledging that the phrase ἐν δύο φύσεσιν encapsulates the insight that two phenomena can exist in a totally unified relation, whilst still retaining their individual identity. We noted that Lampe defined the word as 'essence considered from the point of view of activity or function' and that 'movement' and 'behaviour' typify this notion.

John Macquarrie brings this point out very well when he stresses how important it is to understand this word in its dynamic sense, if we are to grasp what the Chalcedonian Definition is really about:

> If we take *phusis* to mean 'essence', understood as a fixed stock of characteristics, then it would be very hard to make sense of two natures concurring in one subsistence. But here we may remember that the Greek word *phusis* was originally a very dynamic term, with some such meaning as 'emerging'. Even in Aristotle, according to Christopher Stead, *phusis* could mean 'an immanent formative principle that controls the development of living things'. The Latin equivalent *natura* had originally a similar dynamic meaning. It is formed from the future participle of the verb *nasci*, to be born, so that *natura* meant everything that might arise or be born out of something....So the idea of the two natures concurring in the one person of Jesus Christ makes very good sense, if we conceive the language in a dynamic way (Macquarrie 1979 p.70).

Thus, we can see that a dynamic sense of φύσις and indeed of ὑπόστασις in the sense of Ephraim's ἐνυπόστατος, leaves us with a thoroughly fluid ontology, in relation to both the unity and the distinction articulated at Chalcedon [29].

The Inner Logic of Chalcedon

We can see from this discussion of the main words used in the Chalcedonian Definition that the two elements which we found in the

Antiochene and Alexandrian traditions come together in Chalcedon to form a single dynamic christology. Two basic features are articulated together to form the single insight which is found here in this document for the first time. The two features are: first, the affirmation of unity, achieved essentially through the words ὁμοούσιος, πρόσωπον, ὑπόστασις (and ἐνυπόστατος). It should be noted that the word ὁμοούσιος affirms unity of the divinity of the Λόγος with the Godhead on the one hand, and of the humanity of Jesus with general humanity on the other. The two other words affirming unity are affirming unity between the humanity and the divinity within Christ. Secondly, the affirmation of distinction, articulated with the word φύσις interpreted in a dynamic sense. The single insight is that of the simultaneous 'distinction in unity'. This 'is and is not' is the fundamentally unique contribution of this document to the christological debate concerning how humanity and divinity relate. In Chalcedonian christology the two elements of humanity and divinity are united and yet distinct.

When we turn to some more general observations concerning the christology of the Chalcedonian Definition, we find the same features underlined. The overall intention of the document is positive both in tone and content. The first concern is to reassert the christology which had been laid down at the Councils of Nicaea and Constantinople in an attempt to re-assert continuity with what had gone before. The main insights of these councils had, of course, been concerned with affirming positively the union of the Son with the Father. The purpose of Chalcedon was not initially to negate developments which had taken place since those councils, although this did in fact form part of the articulation of a balanced christology. Other parts of the document of Chalcedon continue this extremely positive dimension, in alluding to the past, '...even as the prophets of old have spoken concerning him...', in 'confessing' the christology to which they now bear witness, and in affirming frequently throughout the document the phrase which stems ultimately from Irenaeus' *Adversus Haereses*, εἷς καὶ ὁ αὐτός (heis kai ho autos: one and the same) [30].

Other aspects of the Definition confirm this emphasis. Of particular importance is the use of the word θεοτόκος for Mary, the meaning of which, and the problems relating to which, we have discussed in relation to

Nestorius. Here in the Definition, the term prevails despite Nestorius' warnings. The distinction which he was concerned to maintain by qualifying this word is not honoured here. The unity of the two elements is firmly in mind at this point and the emphasis on distinction comes only later.

At the heart of the Definition lie the four negative terms which have led so many to see the whole document as negative: ἀσυγχύτως, ἀτρέπτως, ἀδιαιρέτως, ἀχωρίστως (asugkutos, atreptos, adiairetos, achoristos: unconfusedly, unchangeably, indivisibly, inseparably). Harnack in his *History of Dogma* despised the formula of Chalcedon, speaking of its 'four bald negative terms' as 'profoundly irreligious' and 'wanting in warm, concrete substance' (Harnack 1958 p.222f). Indeed, he considered the document an overall failure largely because of these negative terms: '...a theology which, in what is for it the most important of all questions, has recourse to mere negatives, is self condemned' (p.223).

Harnack's disdain in relation to Chalcedon stems from his reading of these terms as merely negative and thus missing the heart of what the document is concerned to safeguard. For, although we are at the most negative point here in terms of grammar, the terms used safeguard the crucial insight in a very positive way [31]. The positive intention here is to stave off the two errors of merging the union into a confusion and of turning the distinction into a duality. There are two words for each (Apollinarianism and Nestorianism), negating the errors, yet affirming the truths of their respective insights. Again the two natures are affirmed: 'the distinction of the natures being in no way denied because of the unity'. Here we are not to understand a 'mixing' or a total separation of the elements, but a harmonization of the two natures, a 'running together into one' (συντρεχούσης: suntrechouses), a distinction within a unity.

In addition to the various words and phrases which we have considered and which underline both positive and negative elements in this christology, there is also an issue relating to the general structure of the central section of this Definition which is worthy of attention. Sellers notes that the passage falls into two halves. The first half emphasizes the positive aspects of the christology, that is the dimension of unity. The second half emphasizes the negative aspects of the christology or the dimension of distinction. After this, we return quickly to the union. Sellers says that:

...the formal confession can be divided into two parts on doctrinal grounds; for whereas central to the first is the doctrine of the unity of the Person of Jesus Christ, central to the second is that of the reality of His two natures. Or, to put it another way, once the confession is divided in this way, its foundations are more clearly revealed... (Sellers 1953 p.211).

Sellers notes also that the two traditions of christology, the Antiochene and the Alexandrian, are brought together here at the heart of this document. Grillmeier makes a similar point when he says that 'the position of the Chalcedonian Definition in the history of theology is determined not merely by the concepts which it contains but also by its basic christological framework, i.e. by the particular way in which it gives a theological interpretation of the person of Jesus Christ' (Grillmeier 1975 p.552). The very structure of the Definition bears witness to the christology and once again the language and the christology, the form and the content, are united.

A final word will conclude these basic observations concerning the 'inner logic' of Chalcedonian christology. We have seen that a fundamental unity and distinction, an 'is and is not' element, lies at the heart of Chalcedon. It is a simultaneous distinction-within-unity. The Definition has frequently been thought a failure because of its incoherence. It has been thought by some, from the beginning, to be a compromise. Relton, in his work on patristic christology, illuminates the real value of Chalcedon when he says that:

It may be conceded at once that the Definition is not an explanation of the mystery of the Incarnation. The very failure of the Definition to solve the insoluble is its best recommendation to our careful consideration. The framers of the Definition were not concerned so much to formulate a theory as to safeguard the truth from two attempted solutions of an erroneous character, and to preserve for us the truth hidden in both these errors (Relton 1917 p.36).

He later adds that:

the Chalcedonian formula admirably fulfilled the purpose for which it was drawn up, namely, to exclude two possible explanations of the mystery, and to provide a convenient summary of essential facts which must be borne in mind by all those who attempted to penetrate still further into the mystery. The four characteristic words, *asugkutos, atreptos, adiairetos, akoristos,* were four convenient sign-posts, each with a warning to the traveller that he might know what to avoid in his journey as a seeker after the truth (p.37).

Relton's observations draw attention to the fact that the basic contribution of Chalcedon is one of providing a 'safeguard' which can be used for guidance as we move ever more deeply into the truth of the revelation of God in Christ. To return to Temple's metaphor, it is 'bankrupt' only in the sense that it fails to 'solve the insoluble'. This, however, as we have seen, is its great richness and strength.

Conclusion

We turn now to summarize the basic insights of this chapter. First of all, we have seen that there is in fact a close relation between christology and language. In both the Antiochene and Alexandrian traditions we have observed that issues of language lie at the heart of christological debates. Specific words and phrases, accepted or rejected, are crucial in the emergence of an adequate christology. Thus, θεοτόκος and *communicatio idiomatum* turned out to be very important issues both in terms of christology and in terms of language. We saw also that specific words used in the christology of Apollinarius were closely related to the direction his christology eventually took. It has now become clearer that a shift in one of these areas can cause a shift in the other. We may compare once again the way in which in the tradition begun by Schleiermacher we have a significant shift both in christology and in language.

This link between christology and language pointed to our overall observation that with these two traditions we are dealing with two 'models' in christology. One emphasizes the union between the two elements in the person of Christ and could drift in the direction of 'confusion'. The other emphasizes the distinction between the two elements and could drift in the direction of 'duality' or complete separation of the elements. These two traditions combine in the Chalcedonian Definition to form an insight which clinches a crucial 'is and is not' relation between the elements. That is, an affirmation both of unity and of distinction within the unity. We found from a study of specific words that the Chalcedonian Definition, interpreted in the light of Ephraim of Antioch's understanding of the relation between the two elements in Christ, affirms this distinction within unity. Specific words and phrases, namely ὑπόστασις and πρόσωπον, affirmed the unity, whilst the distinction was largely articulated by the word φύσις or 'nature', which we stressed was to be understood in a dynamic rather than a static way.

The link between christology and language and the 'is and is not' feature of the Chalcedonian Definition helps us to see that if we are to come to a more adequate understanding of the way human language about God operates, we shall do well to turn to the central insight articulated in this document. The coming together of the human and the divine, the enfleshment of the Word, is of crucial importance here. Both Lindbeck and McFague operated on a revised christology and their understandings of language proved to be inadequate. Because of the inherent link between the two, we can see that a reconsideration of christology will enable a more adequate and coherent concept of human language about God. We can see that the threats to a concept of theological language, as laid down by Lindbeck, are exactly paralleled in the traditions which fed Chalcedon. Over-identifying the two elements leads to a confusion. Too much stress on the distinction leads to a total separation. In terms of language, these weaknesses are Lindbeck's 'cognitive-propositionalism' and 'experiential-expressivism'. The language might either become identified with that which it depicts or become totally separated from it. McFague's emphasis on the 'is and is not' aspect of metaphor went a long way towards producing an adequate understanding of language, but her christology left that notion of language weak at important points.

The Chalcedonian Definition provides an insight into christology which perfectly suits the 'is and is not' structure which McFague is so keen to maintain and avoids the pitfalls into which both she and Lindbeck have fallen. With the Chalcedonian Definition, therefore, we have a christological structure, which, used 'heuristically' in the search for knowledge of God and adequate speech about him, can go a long way towards enabling us to find an adequate notion of what we are doing when we talk about the God who is known to us as unknown and named in a riddle. Dionysius and Davies both knew the problem. Lindbeck and McFague also discussed it, but did not deal adequately with the difficulties which arose. It is clearer now that, because of the inherent relation between language and christology, the Chalcedonian Definition can lead us forward. Davies, McFague and Dionysius respond to the problem of speaking about God in terms of analogy, metaphor and symbol respectively. In the light of this discussion of Chalcedonian christology, therefore, we now turn to a consideration of these three important dimensions of theological language. In Part Two we shall see how the 'inner logic of christology', as found in the Chalcedonian Definition of the Faith, can help focus a concept of the 'inner logic of theological language'.

Part Two:
The Inner Logic
of Language

'...Knowledge of words, and ignorance of the Word.'
T.S. Eliot, *Choruses from 'The Rock'*.

III

ANALOGY

The Speakability of God

Stressing the revelation of God in Jesus Christ as the only possible context for legitimate speaking about God, Eberhard Jüngel emphasizes the need to avoid misuse and abuse of the word God. The whole purpose of theology in this respect, he says, is to maintain the proper use of this word:

> Theology, in distinction from all possible other uses of the word 'God', is talk about God which in its positive usage is obligated to prevent the misuse of this word. As such, it constantly must attend to the kind of speech which corresponds to God, in that it allows him to speak himself (Jüngel 1983 p.227).

Jüngel is concerned that the word God and, stemming from this, all language about God be acknowledged in its proper context and not be reduced so that the divinity itself be lost. The problem of talking about God lies at the very heart of all theology. Jüngel says that 'the problem of theology, which ultimately decides the issue of the thinkability of God, is the question as to how one can talk about God humanly and not miss his divinity in so doing. We call this the problem of the speakability of God' (p.230).

The problem of the 'speakability of God' is concerned not only with the fact that finite human beings find speech about the infinite God problematical. It stems also from the desire to acknowledge the fact that if the language we use of the revealed God is identified with him, we might reduce him to the language and drift into idolatry. If we deny that we really do speak of God, however, we shall drift into scepticism and meaninglessness. The concern is, thus, to speak of God responsibly and adequately. The difficulties drawn out by Lindbeck and McFague are once again evident. Dionysius had articulated the problem that whilst God is beyond us, yet we really do speak about him and name him. We have seen that this naming of God is fundamentally linked with christology. Having established this link, we now turn to an examination of the 'inner logic of language' taking our main insights from the christology of Chalcedon with us.

Three fundamental areas lie before us. These were associated in the opening chapter with Davies, McFague and Dionysius. They are analogy, metaphor and symbol and are all very closely related. In the context of language about God, of course, they all have to do with the fundamental relation between humanity and divinity. We turn to analogy first for a number of reasons. Jüngel is clear that 'there can be no responsible talk about God without analogy' (p.281). Certainly, notions of analogy have played a particularly important role in the ways in which theologians have responded to the problem of human talk about God. It is reasonable, therefore, to begin here with the question of what is involved in analogy and analogical predication.

Analogies consist fundamentally of 'stretching' our language in order to make a comparison between two things. In some respects we have with analogy an intermediate stage between language used in its straightforward sense and language used metaphorically. In this sense, analogy and simile are closely related. With analogy the language comes to have wider application as it is 'stretched' and a comparison is created. Seeing similarities in the dissimilar and combining the diverse is crucial here. A great deal of human discourse is made up of analogies and these form a large part of the way in which we make sense of the world. Analogy, therefore, inevitably also functions as one of the most basic features of human language about God. Concerning the nature of analogy, Thomas Fawcett says:

...an analogy is primarily constituted by the use of an image which corresponds in one or more respects with the reality of which it speaks. We can define this more closely if we observe that an analogy possesses both *positive and negative characteristics*. The positive content of an analogy consists of that which it has in common with that for which it stands. The negative content consists of those features which are not shared. The extent to which there is a correspondence determines the strength and usefulness of an analogy (Fawcett 1970 p.55).

The 'stretching' of language in analogy and the resulting positive and negative sides to the way in which analogy works remind us immediately of the link which we have seen between human language about God and christology. In turning to analogy, there is an immediate sense that the positive and negative elements, the 'is and is not' structure, are related to Chalcedonian christology.

In addition to the notion of the stretching of language and the general use of 'analogues' in order to speak more clearly about something for which we have no adequate language, there are also Aquinas' notions of all language about God as 'analogical'. These areas are, of course, related and Aquinas, broadly speaking, is struggling to come to terms with how human language about God operates when it is so stretched. These notions of analogical predication are our particular concern here. It is interesting to note that the close relation between christology and analogical predication has been neglected in recent years. Patrick Sherry says: 'I am surprised...at how rarely discussions about divine attributes and about analogical predication introduce the question of the Incarnation, which is very important both for deciding what attributes are to be ascribed to God and for considering the relationship between human and divine perfections' (Sherry 1976 p.437). A reassessment of this close relation will, therefore, yield some important insights. It is of special interest, however, particularly in relation to Sherry's comment, that Aquinas' notions of analogy turn out to be somewhat confusing and that his discussions of human language about God are not carried out specifically in relation to christology. Once again the separation of language and christology looks significant. For these reasons, we turn to analogy first and then to metaphor and symbol.

Before turning specifically to analogy, however, we need to address two elements in the Christian tradition which provoked Aquinas' response to the problem of human language about God in terms of analogy. These are the 'apophatic' and the 'cataphatic', the negative and the positive ways.

Apophatic and Cataphatic Theology

The problem of the 'speakability of God' lies at the heart of Christian theology and of the Christian tradition. Two major elements in the response to this problem will occupy us before we turn specifically to analogical predication. These two elements are the negative and the positive and to some extent they parallel the two traditions in christology which we have considered, the Antiochene and the Alexandrian. Let us take these two dimensions of language in turn.

The tradition of the 'negative way' or *via negativa* has its roots in the Greek philosophical tradition. Socrates' insistence that the heart of his knowledge lay in knowing that he knew nothing, stands at the beginning of this tradition in western philosophy and theology. Plato is clearly of this opinion when he maintains in the *Republic* that 'the good...far exceeeds essence in dignity and power' (509). This notion also lies at the heart of the Jewish tradition forming the central insight of the Burning Bush theophany of Exodus 3:14 and of Moses' encounter with God on Sinai in Exodus 33. It is continued in the writings of Philo, in many of the early Christian Fathers and is found in such differing quarters as the philosophy of David Hume, the early Wittgenstein and the theology of Karl Rahner [1]. The central feature here is the notion that there is something about which we have difficulty in speaking.

The response to the problem of the 'speakability of God' in this tradition has been to maintain, first of all, that God must be spoken of by way of negation. Dionysius and Aquinas, who follows him closely, agree that a crucial part of the business of knowing and speaking about God lies in acknowledging that we cannot know and speak of him. Aquinas says that 'we cannot know what God is, but only what he is not; we must therefore consider the ways in which God does not exist, rather than the ways in which he does' (Aquinas 1964b p.19). Speaking about God thus proceeds by way of negation, or along the 'apophatic way'.

In this dimension of speaking about God it is maintained that we cannot make straightforwardly positive statements about him because of our essential difference from him. We make statements, therefore, about what he is not. God is unknowable, ineffable, immutable or infinite. Grammatically positive statements are understood in a negative way, as when we say that God is good or wise, but not as human beings are good or wise. The *via negativa* may also operate in a more obviously negative manner, 'God is not thus or thus'. This negative path enables the differences between human and divine to be maintained and the business of idolatry to be avoided. The problem here is that if we proceed only by negatives, we are in danger of landing in a *cul-de-sac*. To say only what God is not, cannot ultimately lead us to a knowledge of what God is. More particularly, we would soon slip into scepticism and meaninglessness, in the style of Heraclitus and Cratylus [2]. Human language would be rendered totally inadequate in relation to God and he would thereby be rendered 'unspeakable'.

We do, however, speak of God and name him. Along with the tradition of negative or 'apophatic' theology, therefore, we have also the insistence that the way of negation is to be balanced by the positive, affirmative or 'cataphatic' way. In this dimension of the tradition it is maintained that positive statements about God are, indeed, both possible and necessary. To proceed only by negation would leave us with no real speech or knowledge of God. Thus, positive statements, such as that God is good or wise, omnipotent or omniscient, are also part of speaking of God. Here we are back with Dionysius' observation that in spite of the difficulty of speaking of the God whom we experience as beyond us, we nevertheless do speak of him and name him. Dionysius was aware that we name God in a riddle, however, and that we are therefore involved in a circular process of 'is and is not' as we try to understand the way in which our language about God operates. For Dionysius, both the negative and the positive ways together are crucial.

The observations which we have made so far have drawn attention to the centrality in the Christian tradition of two strands of speaking about God, the 'apophatic' or negative and the 'cataphatic' or positive. Together these form a concern for the 'is and is not' element which is essential to human speech about God. They also alert us once again to the Chalcedonian christological structure in which models of unity and distinction come together. The central connection between language and christology is once again becoming evident. Let us turn now more specifically to Aquinas' notions of analogical predication with this connection between language and christology in mind.

Analogy in Aquinas

Notions of analogy have formed an important part of the theological activity of many of the greatest theologians as they have sought to clarify our understanding of the relation between the human and the divine [3]. The word itself (from ἀνα and λóγoς: 'ana' and 'logos') has to do with 'reckoning up' in the sense of 'similarity' or 'proportion'. Its origins lie in Greek mathematics, although it came to have a wide variety of applications. It is the uses of this word found in the theology of Thomas Aquinas to which we now turn because he uses the word particularly in relation to human language and its role in knowing and naming God.

The scholarly output in recent years on Aquinas' views of analogy is both comprehensive and complex. There are two elements which we must note before turning to Aquinas himself. First, Aquinas' discussion of language about God can only be understood within the context of his understanding of the cosmos. His comments upon analogical predication take their place within his wider philosophical and theological system. Rooted as it is in Platonist and especially Aristotelian presuppositions, Aquinas' understanding of the cosmos consists essentially in an understanding of reality as a hierarchy of beings descending from God to creatures. The creatures are dependent upon the creator and participate in his attributes. The creator is not dependent upon the creatures. The doctrine of relation here, that of cause and effect, is fundamental. Within this system, Aquinas argues from the world of the finite and the sensible to the infinite. He then attempts to show that it is possible to ascribe certain attributes to God because we already know creatures.

Secondly, there are severe problems within Aquinas' writings concerning the various uses of the word 'analogy'. It was in the work of Cardinal Cajetan in his *De Nominum Analogia* of 1498 that one particular strand in Aquinas' thinking was elevated above the others, obscuring the variety of uses in Aquinas himself [4]. If we return to the Aquinas texts themselves, rather than interpretations of him, we find that matters are very blurred indeed. David Burrell has recently drawn attention to the fact that there is no single 'doctrine of analogy' in Aquinas' theology [5]. Rather, we have to do with an ongoing struggle with the relation between the creaturely language about God and God himself. William J. Hill commenting upon

Burrell's work on Aquinas says that:

> Theological reflection is seen here not as science, nor as
> transcendental reflection, nor even as hermeneutics, but as skill in
> the discriminating use of language about God. Thus Burrell finds
> no neat theory of analogy in Thomas but a sensitivity to the flexibility
> and even the ambiguity of language when it is deployed in thought
> about the transcendent, with meaning emerging from the usage to
> which language is put. Perfective terms undergo an alteration of
> meaning as they are placed in differing contexts. It follows from this
> that analogy always retains a dimension of metaphor (Hill 1987
> p.703).

Certainly Aquinas uses the word 'analogy' in a wide variety of senses and
there appears to be no straightforward picture of what he thought overall.

Although Aquinas is struggling to articulate the way in which human
language about God operates in relation to God and although it can now
be seen that he is more sensitive to the inherent flexibility of language when
used of God, there remain some fundamental gaps in the way this comes
over. It is of considerable importance to the case here to note that Aquinas'
discussions of language about God and of analogical predication are not
set specifically within the context of christology [6]. It seems that once again
the fundamental relation between these two dimensions has been
overlooked and that this may well explain some of the difficulties which
remain in Aquinas' views. Once again we shall see that viewing our
language about God in the light of the Chalcedonian Definition would
begin to provide a more consistent picture of the way human language
about God operates. First, however, what does Aquinas actually say about
analogy?

Aquinas is well aware of the problem that the language we use about
God is human language and therefore arises out of human experience. He
says that

> ...God is known from the perfections that flow from him and are to
> be found in creatures yet which exist in him in a transcendent way.
> We understand such perfections, however, as we find them in

creatures, and as we understand them so we use words to speak of them. We have to consider two things, therefore, in the words we use to attribute perfections to God, firstly the perfections themselves that are signified - goodness, life and the like - and secondly the way in which they are signified. So far as the perfections signified are concerned the words are used literally of God, and in fact more appropriately than they are used of creatures, for these perfections belong primarily to God and only secondarily to others. But so far as the way of signifying these perfections is concerned the words are used inappropriately, for they have a way of signifying that is appropriate to creatures (Aquinas 1964c p.57).

Thus, within the hierarchical cosmology and within the cause-effect relation of God to the creatures, there are two elements to be noted: that which is signified and the words used to signify that which is signified. The 'mode of signification' is human language and as it arises within human experience it cannot simply be applied to God without further note.

Aquinas speaks of two possible ways of understanding human language about God and rejects them both. Either language is to be understood univocally or equivocally. In the first case, the univocal use of language is essentially the same as Lindbeck's 'cognitive-propositionalism'. In this view, human language simply refers directly to God in the same sense and with the same meaning as it refers to human beings. In ordinary language a word is used univocally if it means the same thing in two contexts. Two human beings may be said to be good or wise. On the univocal view of language about God, if we say that God is good or wise, or loving or omnipotent, the language refers in exactly the same way as it would if the words were used of a human being. Aquinas rejects this view as inadequate. We have seen that it can drift into idolatry. It identifies God with the language and ends up losing the element of divinity about which it is attempting to speak in the first place.

The second way of understanding language about God which is rejected by Aquinas is the equivocal way. This view is similar to Lindbeck's 'experiential-expressivism'. In that it maintains that the language used of God is to be understood in an entirely different way from its ordinary usage, it separates the language from God. In ordinary language the word 'bat' may be used of an implement used in cricket or of an animal. The word means something different in the two cases. Thus, if God is called good or wise, loving or omnipotent, and these words are understood as having completely different meanings from their application to human beings, then they are separated from human experience and rendered useless. A gap opens up between the language and God. In fact, logically the language can have no meaning because, on this view, creatures would not have access to such meaning.

In the two ways rejected by Aquinas, the familiar pitfalls are clear: identifying the language with God, or separating the language from God. Copleston says that 'Aquinas' answer to the problem is that when terms like "wise" or "good" are predicated of God they are predicated neither univocally nor equivocally but in an analogical sense' (Copleston 1955 p.134). Thus, Aquinas opts for a third way when he speaks in his various ways of 'analogical predication'. It is here in these concepts of analogy that we find Aquinas struggling with the essential tension which exists when human beings speak of God. Neither of the two ways referred to already is sufficient. In Jüngel's terms, neither is a responsible way of understanding human language about God. Both lead to misuse and abuse. Analogical predication, however, begins to acknowledge the 'is and is not' element which is so crucial. We must follow Aquinas closely here.

In a number of places Aquinas refers to two modes of analogical predication [7]. The first mode involves three entities and occurs when one thing is predicated of another in relation to a third. In this mode a third entity is required prior to the other two, to which they then both refer. Aquinas is clear that this mode of predication is not applicable where God is concerned. Quite simply, there is no entity prior to or more simple than God. The second mode involves only two entities and the one simply has reference to the other. This concept is much more appropriate to God and maintains his priority within the hierarchy of beings.

However, there is a central distinction within this second mode of analogical predication which shows that the mode is not simply a matter of proportion or degree. That is, it is not simply the case that if the words 'good' or 'wise' are used of God, then they are to be understood in the sense of goodness or wisdom in greater degree than would be meant in relation to human beings. Aquinas makes a distinction between 'proportion' and 'proportionality' in relation to analogical predication. Part of the difficulty in establishing Aquinas' understanding here arises from the fact that he sometimes uses the words interchangeably, thus confusing the issue considerably. However, it is the case that there are two main concepts, whatever they may be called on different occasions. Let us outline these two main concepts of analogy in order to enable further clarity here.

First, 'proportion' or *proportio*. This involves there being a continuing likeness or relation between the two things concerned. Within the relation the same qualities are borne by the one as by the other, even if not to the same degree. In the *De Veritate* Aquinas says:

> We find something predicated analogously of two realities according to the first type of agreement when one of them has a relation to the other, as when being is predicated of substance and accident because of the relation which accident has to substance, or as when healthy is predicated of urine and animal because urine has some relation to the health of an animal (Aquinas 1952 p.113).

The first type of analogical predication lies essentially in the relation between the two things and is concerned with the degree to which each possesses what is spoken of them.

The second type of analogical predication is called 'proportionality' or *proportionalitas*. This, by contrast involves only a similarity of proportions. Thus, as six is the double of three, four is the double of two and the similarity of proportions lies in the fact that each is a double. Likewise, as Aquinas says, 'sight is predicated of bodily sight and of the intellect because understanding is in the mind as sight is in the eye' (p.113). The main problem with this second type is that it gives us no essential point of contact between the two things concerned. It is only like saying that the finite is to the finite as the infinite is to the infinite, or that the goodness of man is to man as the goodness of God is to God. Although this may be the case, there is no way of knowing, from this second type of analogical predication, that it is the case.

On some occasions Aquinas rejects the first type of analogical predication as a possible way of understanding human language about God and on some occasions he rejects the second. On other occasions, he can be more positive. For example, he says of the first mode, *proportio*, that 'nothing can be predicated analogously of God and creature according to this type of analogy; for no creature has such a relation to God that it could determine the divine perfection' (p.113). He then says, more positively, of the second mode, *proportionalitas*, that 'no definite relation is involved between the things which have something in common analogously, so there is no reason why some name cannot be predicated analogously of God and creature in this manner' (p.113).

In the *Summa Theologiae*, Aquinas gives us a more concise definition of the distinction, inverting the order given above and contradicting his view that analogical predication of the 'proportion', *proportio*, type is inadequate. He says there that:

> When we say one thing is in proportion to another we can either mean that they are quantitatively related - in this sense double, thrice and equal are kinds of proportion - or else we can mean just any kind of relation that one thing may have to another. It is in this latter sense that we speak of a proportion between creatures and God, in that they are related to him as effects to cause and as the partially realized to the absolutely real; in this sense it is not altogether disproportionate to the created mind to know God (Aquinas 1964c p.7).

There are, then, contradictions in Aquinas' discussions of his two types of analogical predication. This has led to disagreements as to which one lay at the centre of his thinking. Cajetan, to whom we have referred, interpreted Aquinas as upholding the 'proportionality' view rather than the 'proportion' view. This, however, is unfair to Aquinas' writings as we find them.

Concerning the relation between these two types, it is clear that without a basic analogical predication of the 'proportion' type, there could be no analogical predication of the 'proportionality' type. Without the similarity established in the cause-effect relation, there could be no similarity of the 'proportionality' type. However, we must not forget that Aquinas is not concerned to produce a 'theory of language'. His apparent contradictions arise from his engagement with the basic problem of speaking about God.

These apparent contradictions in Aquinas' understanding of language used of God, however, need not be read as incoherence or inconsistency at all. In fact, it is here that we come upon the heart of Aquinas' position. He is trying to maintain both views. R.L. Patterson says of Aquinas that 'it is clear that he was concerned to emphasize the incommensurability of the finite and the infinite, while insisting at the same time upon the legitimacy of analogous predication' (Patterson 1933 p.245). Patterson sees that Aquinas is trying to maintain God's infinitude, whilst at the same time claiming that language about God does say something real about him. The attempt to avoid purely univocal and purely equivocal predication is to the fore here. Aquinas is struggling to formulate a mode of understanding human language about God which is thoroughly responsible to its subject matter, God himself.

One final feature of Aquinas' discussion of analogy remains for our attention. Hill observed that 'analogy always retains a dimension of metaphor' (Hill 1987 p.704). Aquinas does discuss metaphor in relation to analogy but contrasts it with the literal and loses sight of the power of the most important feature of human language about God. Speaking of words used literally of God, in the *Summa Theologiae*, he says that 'these words have a bodily context not in what they mean but in the way in which they signify it; the ones that are used metaphorically have bodily conditions as part of what they mean' (Aquinas 1964c p.59). Thus, metaphor cannot be used in relation to God because it implies 'bodily conditions' in what is signified. Since God is incorporeal, metaphor can only be applied to him in a secondary sense.

Earlier in the *Summa Theologiae* Aquinas discusses whether or not our language about God should use metaphor and symbol at all. He says that,

> It seems that holy teaching should not use metaphors. For what is proper to a lowly type of instruction appears ill-suited to this, which, as already observed, stands on the summit. Now to carry on with various similitudes and images is proper to poetry, the most modest of all teaching methods. Therefore to make use of such similitudes is ill-suited to holy teaching (Aquinas 1964a p.33).

Aquinas stands in the tradition which rejected metaphor as cognitive, seeing it merely as a decoration which was to be contrasted with the literal. He is, however, positive about it as a decoration. In responding to the above point, he says that 'poetry employs metaphors for the sake of representation, in which we are born to take delight. Holy teaching, on the other hand, adopts them for their indispensable usefulness...' (p.35). In theology, therefore, metaphor can be useful, but is ultimately of less value than the literal. Metaphors, symbols and images generally are a decorative matter of secondary importance in theology. They are for the 'uneducated...who are not ready to take intellectual truths neat with nothing else' (p.35).

Aquinas' confusion over metaphor here prevents him from taking his insights into analogy further. We shall see that viewing human language in the light of the Chalcedonian Definition will show us how central metaphor really is.

Analogy and Chalcedon

We have traced two main features in the Christian tradition of speaking about God, the positive and the negative. These were crucial to the theology of Dionysius the Areopagite and were taken into the theological framework used by Aquinas. Aquinas responded to the problem in terms of analogical predication, but in fact stumbled up against the similar impasse of trying to articulate the continuity between human language and God alongside the discontinuities. His two types of analogical predication are closely related to the cataphatic and apophatic traditions which he inherited. The one drifts in the direction of affirming unity, whilst the other drifts in direction of affirming distinction.

In his study of the place of analogy in theology Battista Mondin clinches the importance for theology of both the apophatic and the cataphatic ways as follows:

The negative and the positive ways are rather like the wheels of a bicycle. As a bicycle cannot go if the two wheels don't go together, so too there cannot be any sound theology if the negative and positive ways are not used together. The positive way alone leads to anthropomorphism, to idolatry, to blasphemy. The negative way alone leads to agnosticism and atheism (Mondin 1963 p.98).

How are these two aspects to be kept together? We saw that for Jüngel the main concern of theology is to avoid the abuse of the word God and to secure a responsible use of theological language. A responsible use must hold together the two elements which are crucial in speaking of God. This responsible use can be secured by viewing human language about God in the light of the Chalcedonian Definition.

Aquinas does not discuss the relation between language and christology, but we have seen that there is a fundamental link here and that where one is neglected the other is likely to be inadequate. It is clear that the structures operating in the traditions about language parallel the structures operating in the two traditions of christology which we have considered, the Alexandrian and the Antiochene. These two come together in Chalcedon forming a dynamic structure of 'is and is not'. It will become clearer as we proceed that Aquinas' lack of an adequate balance in understanding the way human language about God operates, in spite of his articulating the fundamental dimensions of 'is and is not', is related to his not making an overt connection with christology.

If we do use the Chalcedonian Definition in this way, we shall have a single heuristic model of 'similarity and distinction' with which to focus our understanding of the way human language about God operates. Indeed, we can see that Aquinas' attempts to articulate the way human language about God works lend themselves to precisely this model, but that he does not achieve this through his notions of analogy alone. The two essential features are present in the one model from Chalcedon. The relational 'distinction in unity' found there serves to articulate the way human language about God operates in the same way that it served to articulate the relation between the human and the divine within the person of Christ.

That Aquinas does not find a balanced statement of the two essential elements results from his not exploring the link between language and christology. The use of Chalcedon shows Aquinas' notions of analogy to be inadequate. The two notions of 'proportion' and 'proportionality' can be seen in relation to the two central elements in christology, one affirming a connection within a relation, the other operating on a distinction. Although he has the two features, however, Aquinas does not bring them together satisfactorily. Where christology has been neglected, notions of language become inadequate.

Aquinas' notions of analogical predication require Chalcedon to enable the view of 'is and is not' for which he is seeking, to emerge fully. Linked to this, we may also note that notions of 'stretching' language, which lie at the heart of analogy, also leave a division between the language and that about which it speaks. Chalcedon sheds new light on these problems by its fine tuning of a 'distinction within unity' in the divine-human relation. Through notions of ὑπόστασις and φύσις the unity and the distinction are articulated. Chalcedon shows us, not only that the problems in Aquinas' notions of analogical predication could be reduced by reference to christology, but also that ultimately analogies as such do not lie at the heart of our language about God. The 'stretching' here is a step away from metaphor, to which it is related and which is in fact far more important.

We have already noted that a key feature of Aquinas' discussion of analogy is a contrast between the literal and the metaphorical. This misunderstanding of metaphor, however typical of his age, also contributes to his failure to formulate the two essential elements in human language about God in a single model. By using the Chalcedonian Definition we will show that human language about God is, in fact, understood more adequately as metaphorical. It is here in metaphor that language and christology come together most clearly. There are, however, different views of metaphor and we turn now, therefore, to an examination of these.

IV

METAPHORS AND MODELS

The Importance and Place of Metaphors

Human language is riddled with metaphors and models. Hardly a sentence passes without some use of these. The seventeenth-century poet Thomas Campion writes of his beloved, 'There is a garden in her face, | Where roses and white lilies grow' (Gardner 1972 p.162). T.S. Eliot, perhaps even more vividly, tells us that 'The yellow fog that rubs its back upon the window-panes, | ...licked its tongue into the corners of the evening' (Eliot 1969 p.13). Such language, however, is not limited to the realm of poetry. Even in the most banal circumstances in everyday life, we speak metaphorically and we speak on the basis of models. We 'upset the apple cart' or 'put the cat amongst the pigeons' and our friends, if we are lucky, are 'towers of strength'. More generally even than this, we 'attack' people's 'positions' and call them 'half-baked'. We shall see that metaphors and models are very closely related and that they permeate not only our language, but also our very processes of thinking. It is important, therefore, to try to establish how they work.

We have seen that Thomas Aquinas makes a distinction between the literal and the metaphorical. In this sense he stands in a long tradition of theologians and philosophers who have seen metaphor as a secondary and primarily decorative feature of human language. This tradition has dominated western thinking about metaphor until very recently. In recent years, however, there has been a complete reversal of this view and metaphor is enjoying a popular role in theories of music, literary criticism, philosophy, theology and the sciences. In theology, for example, we are becoming more aware than ever that when we speak of God as a 'rock', a 'mighty fortress' or a 'consuming fire', we are speaking metaphorically. Within this renewed popularity, however, there is a variety of different views as to how metaphors achieve their meaning. McFague's emphasis upon 'metaphorical theology' and upon the importance of metaphor in human talk about God, prompts us to look at this phenomenon more closely.

McFague is clear that whilst she rejects an 'incarnational' christology, she nevertheless sees the 'is and is not' view of theological language as crucial. This 'is and is not' view of language forms the root of her 'metaphorical theology'. Although she frequently affirms the centrality of the 'is and is not', we have seen that the dissociation of language and christology in her thinking renders her understanding of theological language less than adequate. It is important to note that whilst metaphor may be understood as containing these crucial elements of human language about God, it is possible, nevertheless, to operate on an inadequate understanding of such elements. That is to say that the 'is and is not' dimensions of metaphor could be understood as merely a meaningless ornament or decoration with no content. We must turn now, therefore, to examine metaphor in order to show that some concepts of metaphor are inadequate, especially in human language about God. We shall subsequently turn to look at models in order to illustrate the case. Once again, we shall take our insights from Chalcedon with us in order to establish the most adequate notion of the most important aspect of the way we speak.

Literal and Metaphorical

The most appropriate place to begin an examination of the nature of metaphor is with the distinction between the literal and the metaphorical. In its contemporary colloquial sense metaphor is still contrasted with the literal. We think of truth only as what is 'literally true' and if something is 'only metaphorically true', it fails as a candidate for truth altogether. It is normally maintained that whereas the literal can be verified and checked as either true or false, it is inappropriate to attempt to verify the metaphorical in such a way. This common distinction arises from the long tradition in western philosophy of which we have spoken. We shall examine this in some detail shortly. Here it serves to raise the most basic and most difficult question of all: What is a metaphor?

The obvious way of answering this question is by way of illustration. The statements 'Herod is a fox', 'that man is a wolf' or 'Juliet is the sun' are clearly false at one level. Herod is not a fox, a particular man is not a wolf and Juliet is not the sun! As we shall see later, the 'literal' falsity of a metaphor is, in most cases, important. What, however, is meant by the word 'literal'? This is as difficult to establish as the meaning of the word 'metaphorical'. Owen Barfield comments that 'we call a sentence "literal" when it means what it affirms on the face of it, and nothing else' (Barfield 1960 p.48). Similarly, George Caird says that 'words are used literally when they are meant to be understood in their primary, matter-of-fact sense' (Caird 1980 p.133). We may say, therefore, that the 'literal' meaning of language is its 'primary' meaning, what it means 'on the face of it'. Suffice it to say at present that the way in which metaphorical expressions have their meanings is of a different order from the literal. It would be absurd for someone to attempt to verify such an expression as 'There is a garden in her face', by trying to see if this were literally the case. By contrast, statements used literally, such as 'the cat sat on the mat', or, 'there is a tree in the garden', mean what they mean 'on the face of it'. Thus, the metaphorical and the literal senses of language are different. Caird redresses the balance in the popular misunderstanding of the relation between metaphorical and literal when he says that 'any statement, literal or metaphorical, may be true or false, and its referent may be real or unreal' (p.131).

The word 'metaphor' comes from two Greek words μέτα (meta: across) and φέρειν (pherein: to carry). Together they mean 'to carry across' in the sense of a transference. Although metaphor is quite difficult to identify and define, the sense clearly has to do with the 'carrying over' of one thing into another. The immediate problem here is that it is sometimes very difficult to know what it is that is being 'carried over' in a given instance, whether words or meanings or both. The situation is complicated further by the fact that even though metaphors constitute a figure of speech, they exist in a complex web of associations and not all parts of the transference are necessarily verbally present at once. Finally, the family of figures of speech constituted by metaphor, simile, analogy and other tropes makes close definition of metaphor especially difficult. Ingolf Dalferth has referred to one hundred and twenty-five definitions of metaphor and at the present time there are probably many more [8]. The fact that the word is itself a metaphor does not assist clarity here!

There are obvious limitations with developing a 'theory' of metaphor and each case of metaphor is either successful or unsuccessful on its own merits. This does not mean, however, that there are not some basic characteristics and that of the various views of metaphor some are not more adequate than others. Let us begin our investigation with Aristotle. His comments on metaphor occur mostly in his two works the *Poetics* and the *Rhetoric*. In the *Poetics* he says that 'metaphor consists in giving the thing a name that belongs to something else; the transference being either from genus to species, or from species to genus, or from species to species, or on grounds of analogy' (1457b). This element of transferring (*epiphor*) is central, although Aristotle himself is not always clear how he understands it. He did not treat metaphor systematically enough and focused too much on individual words [9]. This impoverished his understanding somewhat and resulted in a tendency to see metaphor as decorative.

The business of using a term of something when it really belongs to something else, however, does lie at the heart of metaphor. It is related to bringing together two elements and referring to them as one. Thus, Herod and the fox or Juliet and the sun are identified in a particular way. Bringing the two ideas together and speaking of them as one is crucial here. Mary McCloskey captures this element in her definition of metaphor when she says that 'when we use a word metaphorically, we apply a word which is usually applied to one sort of thing to another sort of thing' (McCloskey 1964 p.215). Colin Turbayne thinks of metaphor in terms of Gilbert Ryle's 'category mistake' and refers to 'sort-crossing' as a characteristic of metaphor [10]. The important thing to note here is that even though we may have a view of metaphor which sees it as using a term which is usually applied to one thing, of another thing, we are still left with the question of whether this is merely a decorative or ornamental action or whether it encapsulates something which cannot be said in any other way. In terms of human language about God, this question is crucial.

Metaphor as Ornament

Even though it may be clear that a metaphor consists of speaking of one thing in terms of another, it is by no means obvious that a metaphor is anything more than a decoration of what could be said in literal language. The western philosophical tradition, as we have noted, has maintained that metaphor is just that. Only the 'literal' sense of language is important where truth is concerned. Umberto Eco summarizes the basic options for metaphor when he says that:

> either (a) language is by nature, and originally, metaphorical, and the mechanism of metaphor establishes linguistic activity, every rule or convention arising thereafter in order to discipline, to reduce (and impoverish) the metaphorizing potential that defines man as a symbolic animal; or (b) language (and every other semiotic system) is a rule-governed mechanism, a predictive machine...with regard to which the metaphor constitutes a breakdown, a malfunction, an unaccountable outcome (Eco 1984 p.88).

We shall now briefly examine the second concept here. This is the view of metaphor which has predominated in the western tradition.

Let us trace a path backwards from the present time to Aristotle in order to observe what the main emphasis has been. At the present time it is clear that the overwhelming trend is in the direction of Eco's first sense above, that is that metaphor is fundamental to human speech. The western tradition, however, has seen it, to use the words of I.A. Richards, as a 'happy extra trick with words' (Richards 1936 p.90). Metaphor in this view is a 'breakdown' of language. The predominant view here has been Eco's second sense above. The root of the problem has undoubtedly been the analytic approach to language which has associated meaning in language with the single word. Aristotle saw metaphor as fundamentally associated with the individual words we use and this was part of his contribution to the rather negative view we now have. Paul Ricoeur in his discussion of the 'decline of rhetoric' summarizes succinctly the features which characterize this tradition:

A whole series of postulates is at work between the point of departure - the primacy of the word - and the final outcome - metaphor as ornament. Step by step, they bring together the initial theory of meaning, whose axis is naming, and a purely ornamental theory of tropes, which finally proclaims the futility of a discipline that Plato had long before placed among the 'cosmetic arts' (Ricoeur 1978 p.45).

The stress on the single word, the 'tyranny' or 'hegemony' of the word, as Ricoeur calls it, sits naturally with the view of metaphor as ornament, because of its empiricist roots. The concentration on the narrow identifiable unit tends in an empiricist direction and reduces the power of figurative language. James Barr has recently affirmed the poverty of this approach in his work on biblical semantics [11] .

A step backwards from the present day to the period of the European Enlightenment exposes even more clearly the location of the problem of the 'decline of rhetoric'. First, in John Locke's work *An Essay Concerning Human Understanding*, Book 3, chapter 10, we find a passage which is a *locus classicus* of the attitude to figurative language which we are discussing. Locke says that:

Since wit and fancy find easier entertainment in the world than dry truth and real knowledge, figurative speeches and allusion in language will hardly be admitted as an imperfection or abuse of it. I confess, in discourses where we seek rather pleasure and delight than information and improvement, such ornaments as are borrowed from them can scarce pass for faults. But yet if we would speak of things as they are, we must allow that all the art of rhetoric, besides order and clearness, all the artificial and figurative application of words eloquence hath invented, are for nothing else but to insinuate wrong ideas, move the passions, and thereby mislead the judgement, and so indeed are perfect cheats, and therefore, however laudable or allowable oratory may render them in harangues and popular addresses, they are certainly, in all discourses that pretend to inform or instruct, wholly to be avoided; and where truth and knowledge are concerned, cannot but be thought a great fault, either of the language or person that makes use of them. What, and how various they are, will be superfluous here to take notice; the books of rhetoric which abound in the world will instruct those who want to be informed: only I cannot but observe how little the preservation and improvement of truth and knowledge is the care and concern of mankind; since the arts of fallacy are endowed and preferred. It is evident how much men love to deceive and be deceived, since rhetoric, that powerful instrument of error and deceit, has its established professors, is publicly taught, and has always been had in great reputation: and, I doubt not, but it will be thought great boldness, if not brutality in me, to have said thus much against it. Eloquence, like the fair sex, has too prevailing beauties in it to suffer itself ever to be spoken against. And it is in vain to find fault with those arts of deceiving, wherein men find pleasure to be deceived (Locke 1823 Vol 11 p.288).

This resounding statement of the deceit and fancy which is involved in figurative language sums up the whole attitude of the western tradition. Such things are 'perfect cheats' and are not related to 'things as they are'.

This view of metaphor is found also in another text from the same period. In Thomas Hobbes' *Leviathan* we find the view that speech is the vehicle which translates thoughts in the head into words. In relation to this, Hobbes speaks of several 'abuses' of words, one of which is metaphor. To use words metaphorically, according to Hobbes, is to use them 'in other sense than that they are ordained for; and thereby deceive others' (Hobbes 1985 p.102). Although the view here is not as hostile as that found in Locke, it is nevertheless in full agreement that such language is not a form of truth-telling. Metaphor is a deception.

If we pursue our line back to Aristotle, we find, as we have already indicated, a mixture of attitudes. Aristotle certainly has a positive attitude towards metaphor when he says that 'the greatest thing by far is to be a master of metaphor' and that 'a good metaphor implies an intuitive perception of the similarity in dissimilars' (*Poetics* 1459a). The general understanding of Aristotle's view of metaphor, however, has been that he saw it as decoration which must ultimately give way to the literal in the interests of truth. Janet Martin Soskice has recently defended both Aristotle and Quintilian against this accusation. She says of Aristotle that he 'shows his sensitivity towards the capacity of metaphor to name the unnamed' (Soskice 1985 p.9). The ambiguity here in Aristotle has, however, clearly fed the later tradition which sees metaphor in a negative light. The first occurrence of the word 'metaphor' is in Isocrates' *Evagoras* and is used in relation to a distinction between poetry and prose. Poetry uses metaphors, prose does not [12]. The tradition of seeing metaphor as decoration predates Aristotle, whatever his view, and this has dominated until the present day.

We can see clearly here that in the western tradition particularly since the Enlightenment, and especially as a result of concentration upon single words, rationalist and positivist views of language have dominated and metaphor, along with all figurative language, has been regarded with considerable distrust as an ultimately unnecessary decoration of literal language. As we noted earlier, the situation in the present day has changed. We now turn to a contemporary view which takes us a step forward in regarding metaphor as useful but which still ultimately leaves it relatively meaningless in terms of telling us new truths. This view is particularly associated with Donald Davidson.

Nudging into Noting

In his article 'What Metaphors Mean', Davidson exposes his (at first sight impossible) view that 'metaphors mean what the words, in their most literal interpretation, mean, and nothing more', and that 'a metaphor doesn't say anything beyond its literal meaning' (Davidson 1979 p.30). Davidson is not, however, maintaining that metaphors do not have a special character. He speaks, for example of the 'hidden power' of metaphor and of its usefulness in a wide variety of fields of knowledge (p.45). Indeed, he dissociates himself from those who would see it merely as an emotive, confusing and unnecessary element in language. On the other hand, however, he still operates with a separation of the literal and the figurative in language and is not prepared to admit that metaphor has any distinctively 'cognitive' content. The real meaning of metaphor for Davidson lies in its pragmatic impact. The meaning is in the use. It has its value in making a comparison between two things and in 'nudging us into noting' similarities between things which we might not otherwise notice (p.36). In many ways this view of metaphor looks hopeful, for it follows a middle path between the view which sees it as totally meaningless and the one which sees it as saying something which cannot be said in any other way. Davidson, therefore, is worth following closely.

Davidson's theory of metaphor is rooted in a distinction between meaning and use. That is to say that the heart of the difference that is made when a metaphor is used lies in what it does, rather than in a meaning inherent in the words or sentences. Here metaphor is seen as an essentially creative process whose meaning lies in its success in use. If it succeeds in drawing a comparison then it has done its job. It is worth underlining the fact that *within this context* it is the literal use of the words which is to the fore. There are no other dimensions to be found. A metaphor cannot be paraphrased because there is nothing in it to be paraphrased. What you see is what there is. The primary or original meanings of the words, what they mean 'on the face of it', are crucial to the way the metaphor 'works'. They are in fact all there is. Metaphors are not translatable for there is nothing there to translate.

Part of Davidson's discussion concerns the relation between metaphor and simile. Clearly these two aspects of speech are very closely related. In Davidson's view they are really the same thing. In each case the root of the matter lies in 'comparison' and there are many such devices within language which do this job. Here again Davidson emphasizes the need to take the words in a metaphor literally, saying how important it is that the literal sense be understood as a falsity. Once we have recognized it as a falsity, we can then search for the meaning intended by the user. The statement of falsity draws a comparison and 'nudges us into noting' something we would otherwise not note at all. In their comparative dimension both simile and metaphor enjoy their success through the effect they have upon their audience.

One of the most important reasons for raising Davidson's view is in order to observe its weaknesses and thus to see further into the meaning of metaphor. Soskice sums up the main shortcoming as follows: 'Part of the attractiveness of Davidson's theory is the insistence, surely correct, that metaphor cannot be simply a play with word meaning but is necessarily a matter of use. The shortcoming of his approach is that by so emphasizing use, semantic considerations seem banished entirely with some odd consequences' (Soskice 1985 p.29). Thus, Davidson is correct to emphasize the fact that the actual use of a metaphor is central to understanding its meaning. The problem is that he reduces metaphor to 'use' and nothing else. We are reminded here of Lindbeck's emphasis, inherited from the later philosophy of Wittgenstein, on meaning as use. The same problems emerge with Davidson as emerged with Lindbeck. Let us now pursue this shortcoming further.

Max Black, to whose work on metaphor we shall turn in due course, has responded specifically to Davidson's views on metaphor noting a number of fundamental flaws. These are all related to the main shortcoming identified already. Black's overall view of Davidson's work is that he has reduced metaphor to a 'comparison' view and thereby lost sight of its specific content. Black observes that by concentrating on the literal meaning of the words in metaphors and claiming that there are therefore no truth-claims involved, Davidson is left in a position of holding that metaphors are simply false statements meaning nothing at all. Black points out that words used in metaphor need not permanently change their meaning and in any case argues for a much more fluid concept of the words and meanings involved [13]. Davidson has given insufficient attention to how metaphors really work and has merely merged them with other tropes.

Davidson's merging of metaphor with simile is a symptom of the basic character of his approach. He does note that whilst similes are true, metaphors are false, indicating some semantic difference. It must be remembered, however, that such distinctions for Davidson remain at the level of language and use. It is still the case for him that metaphor and simile do not contribute any specific truth-claims and semantic dimensions are in fact still undermined. Davidson's failure to see the real power of metaphor is closely related to his separation of the literal and the figurative and then his merging of figures of speech. A more fluid approach to meaning and a tighter conceptualizing of the various figures of speech is in order here. Distinctions between the different figures of speech are important.

Although they may overlap and do a similar job at one level, simile and metaphor are distinguished by distinctive inner dynamics. That is to say, a simile is essentially characterized by its nature as 'comparison' whereas a metaphor has an element of tension arising precisely through its being partly false. Davidson is right that the words in a metaphor do have a false sense, but there is more to it than this. There is also the sense of identity which is absent from simile. Davidson does not take on board the possibility that there might be literal falsity at the level of language or sense, e.g. 'There is a garden in her face', and yet still be 'metaphorical truth' at the level of reference, that is, that such an expression might mean something which cannot be said in any other way.

Metaphor, especially but not only that of the 'A is a B' kind (for example, 'God is a rock'), preserves linguistically a semantic tension which is generally absent from the simile. In the statement that 'A is a B' there is an internal linguistic link which also retains the difference. Admittedly some metaphors as they move towards becoming models may lack the tightness of this tension and some particularly vivid similes may have such a tension. It is here that we are faced with a serious problem in the definition of metaphor. Part of Davidson's weakness is that he only discusses metaphors of the 'A is a B' type and then merges them with simile. Overall, the main distinction needed here between metaphor and simile lies in the fact that metaphor creates a greater impact than simile through the greater tension at its centre.

The fact that there are many different types of metaphor makes this matter extremely complex. Whatever the most appropriate way of solving the problems, Davidson has apparently seen nothing of the tension which is so fundamental to this sort of language. He specifically denies the claim of Owen Barfield that a metaphor 'says one thing and means another' and of I.A. Richards that there is an 'interaction' within the way a metaphor functions (Davidson 1979 p.44). Nor does he mention Richards' stress on the 'double unit' in metaphor to which we shall turn later.

These shortcomings on Davidson's part relate to our previous comments on the 'decline of rhetoric'. Commenting on Davidson's views, Black says that he is 'fixated on the explanatory power of standard sense' (Black 1979a p.191). This accusation implies that Davidson has fallen into the classic separation of the literal and the figurative. Whatever the reasons, we have here a case within the debate about metaphor which has the same shortcomings as Lindbeck's view of language in general. Black is much more aware of a rich reservoir of meaning in the semantic realm. He speaks of the 'tantalizingly elusive' nature of metaphor and, more importantly, he says that 'to say something with suggestive indefiniteness is not to say *nothing'* (p.192). Davidson has fallen into an easily identifiable and classic trap. We shall turn now more specifically, therefore, to the tradition associated with his critic, Max Black.

Interinanimation and Interaction

The strand in the debate to which we now turn is distinguished specifically by the general view that metaphor is not simply a decoration of what can be said more straightforwardly in literal language, but is a uniquely cognitive dimension of speech. This tradition, as we have made clear, is particularly modern, although Aristotle hinted at it. Its main proponents stand together in the view that with metaphor we are dealing with a dimension of speech which articulates truths which can be articulated in no other way. The main thrust in this area has come from literary critics, especially I.A. Richards, Max Black and Paul Ricoeur. The tradition finds its roots ultimately, however, in the nineteenth century in the writings of S.T. Coleridge.

The most positive aspect contributed to the debate concerning metaphors by Davidson was that the typical, and for him the only, function of metaphors was to be found in their use. Whatever the weaknesses of this view on the semantic level, the emphasis at least began to take context seriously. In his work *The Philosophy of Rhetoric*, I.A. Richards stresses this element particularly and takes things very much further. Richards is concerned from the outset to show that language and meaning are thoroughly contextual. Early on in the lectures which constitute this book Richards speaks of the 'proper meaning superstition', that is, the widespread belief that each word in a language has a 'proper meaning' which can be found in a dictionary and which is then considered to be 'the meaning' of that word (Richards 1936 p.11). We saw that Aristotle tended to concentrate on individual words. The idea that each word has an unchangeable meaning is still widespread in the western world today.

Richards was clear, however, that words did not simply name ideas, and that for a satisfactory concept of language to emerge, full cognizance must be taken of the past life of the language, that is, of its various past contexts. Richards thus speaks of the 'context theorem of meaning' (p.40) and says that 'we shall do better to think of a meaning as though it were a plant that has grown - not a can that has been filled or a lump of clay that has been moulded' (p.12). Within this growth, we can expect a good deal of fluidity and ambiguity which we must value. In the ancient school of rhetoric to which we have referred, figurative speech was seen as a decoration and a deceiver. Richards now exhorts us to a new understanding:

> The context theorem of meaning will make us expect ambiguity to the widest extent and of the subtlest kinds nearly everywhere, and of course we find it. But where the old Rhetoric treated ambiguity as a fault in language, and hoped to confine or eliminate it, the new Rhetoric sees it as an inevitable consequence of the powers of language and as the indispensable means of most of our most important utterances - especially in Poetry and Religion (p.40).

A crucial aspect of this new understanding is to acknowledge the interrelatedness of words with contexts and of words with each other.

Acknowledging his debt to Henri Bergson [14], Richards speaks of the 'interpenetration' or 'interinanimation' between words and other words, language and context and indeed 'everywhere in perception' (p.70). Thus, a note of music, a colour in a painting or the shape or size of an object only make sense in relation to other such phenomena in their contexts. Here, Richards reflects a thoroughly gestalt view of perception. There is no such thing as complete isolation or separate meanings. Indeed, to find the 'meaning' of language, we must take into account not only other words and context, but also actions and even unuttered and unarticulated dimensions.

In turning specifically to the question of the meaning of metaphor, it can be seen that here, no less than anywhere else, context, use, language as a whole, and even 'tacit' elements can and are likely to be relevant. The key thing here is to dethrone the view of metaphor which has dominated western philosophy and reduced the power of figurative language. Richards says that 'throughout the history of Rhetoric, metaphor has been treated as a sort of happy extra trick with words, an opportunity to exploit the accidents of their versatility, something in place occasionally but requiring unusual skill and caution. In brief a grace or ornament or *added* power of language, not its constitutive form' (p.90). By contrast Richards is concerned to emphasize figurative language, including metaphor, as part of the 'constitutive form' of language. This involves taking the emphasis off individual words and taking the whole context seriously.

We turn now to examine Richards' understanding of the internal dynamics of metaphor. Dr. Johnson's famous definition of metaphor provides a useful starting point for considering its internal workings. Johnson says: 'As to metaphorical expression, that is a great excellence in style, when it is used with propriety, for it gives you two ideas for one' (Richards 1936 p.93). This notion of 'two ideas for one' brings us close to the heart of metaphor. It stresses the double element in metaphor, what Richards calls the 'whole double unit' (p.96), and the expression retains the unity. The unfortunate element in Johnson's statement is that he clearly sees metaphor as a decoration and the 'two ideas' are brought together consciously in his view for 'excellence of style'. The view is basically one of comparison. Nevertheless, the expression itself 'two ideas for one' exposes something of the unified two dimensions of metaphor which are so important to its character.

Following Johnson's 'two ideas for one', Richards draws attention to the two elements in metaphor by calling them the 'tenor' and the 'vehicle'. The tenor is the 'underlying idea or principal subject' (p.97), that is, the subject of the utterance. The vehicle is the mode, figure or image. These terms can be misleading, however, and Richards is at pains to stress the 'whole double unit'. The important thing to understand in Richards' concept is that tenor and vehicle are not necessarily two terms of the verbal utterance itself. The utterance itself may actually only contain the vehicle, for example, whilst the tenor may be silent. Soskice notes that both Black and Ricoeur misunderstand Richards because they apparently miss his full intention here. Both think that the two terms refer to elements within the sentence concerned and do not appreciate that the whole context is crucial [15]. Richards' emphasis on interinanimation or interaction is not simply between two elements in a sentence, but occurs within the context of the whole utterance.

The 'two ideas for one' concept in Richards' thinking shows how these elements in metaphor are important both at the level of language and at the level of meaning. If we are to avoid a comparison view of metaphor, or a view which simply merges it with simile, we must be able to show how metaphor, whilst having two elements, only has one subject. Soskice says that 'the advantage of Richards's formulation is that it allows us to distinguish between the tenor and the vehicle of the metaphor without suggesting that the metaphor has two subjects' (Soskice 1985 p.46). Thus, a concept of metaphor is emerging in which something singular is spoken of within an interaction of a number of elements in the utterance. Although Soskice is clear that there are wide 'associative networks' involved in metaphor, it nevertheless remains a figure of speech which involves a number of elements within a single subject.

Soskice has some further comments which are illuminating in relation to this matter. In emphasizing the complete context for understanding how a metaphorical utterance produces its unique contribution, she says:

> The metaphor and its meaning (it is artificial to separate them) are the unique product of the whole and the excellence of a metaphor...is not that it is a new description of a previously discerned human condition but that *this* subject, this particular mental state, is accessible only through the metaphor. What is identified and described is identified and described uniquely by this metaphor. It is in this way that a metaphor is genuinely creative and says something that can be said adequately in no other way, not as an ornament to what we already know but as an embodiment of a new insight (p.48).

We thus see a view emerging which maintains metaphor as yielding new knowledge through a number of interactive elements rooted in a specific context but finding its articulation in speech. We now turn to look in more detail at the work of Max Black in order to shed more light on this element of 'two ideas for one' in metaphor.

In two important essays Max Black has provided us with a number of insights which enable us to see further into the function of metaphor. The first essay is 'Metaphor' in his work *Models and Metaphors*. The second, an updating of the views exposed there, is entitled 'More About Metaphor'. We shall agree with Soskice that there are serious problems with some of the things Black maintains and that although he is dependent upon Richards, he nevertheless misunderstands crucial elements in Richards' view. Dr. Johnson's 'two ideas for one' in metaphor is a convenient point of entry once again.

An important feature of Black's understanding is his distinction between the 'focus' and the 'frame' of a metaphor. In making this distinction he concentrates on one word in a sentence which makes that sentence metaphorical. Thus, the single word which is the 'focus' makes the utterance metaphorical and the sentence which surrounds that word is the 'frame'. The two elements are, of course, both crucial to the making of a metaphor. It is not the case that a single word is 'in itself' metaphorical. Rather, the context or 'frame' makes the word metaphorical. A change of frame may render the word non-metaphorical. Thus, Black avoids the 'proper meaning superstition' against which Richards' work was geared, and is, like Richards, concerned with context. For Black, both semantics and pragmatics are important in understanding metaphor. Like Richards, he emphasizes the importance of the complete context in which the metaphor is uttered.

Having thus set the scene for understanding metaphor, Black rejects two widespread views which tend to dominate the discussion. These are the substitution view and the comparison view. The substitution view is simply the view of metaphor as ornamental or decorative, a 'substitution' for literal language. The comparison view maintains that metaphor merely 'compares' two things, like simile. In moving away from both of these concepts of metaphor, Black offers us the possibility that metaphors are creative and cognitively unique. He says that 'it would be more illuminating in some of these cases to say that the metaphor creates the similarity than to say that it formulates some similarity antecedently existing' (Black 1962 p.37). It is in the light of this concept that Black then offers us his 'interaction' view in which he follows Richards' 'interinanimative' view. Black maintains that in a metaphor the two elements are interactive, that is they interact 'to produce a meaning that is a resultant of that interaction' (p.38). A key concept here lies in the use of the expression 'associated commonplaces' which is the same as Soskice's 'associative network' (Soskice 1985 p.50). By this Black means the web of things commonly associated with a certain category. So, to call a person a wolf is to bring together two networks each with its own commonplaces. By bringing such networks together we produce 'interaction', 'interillumination' and 'co-operation' which itself is creative of new meaning. Although on this understanding there can be seen to be ripples of metaphorical change throughout the web of associated meanings, Black nevertheless notes that the heart of the utterance lies in the key expression itself.

Thus, within a metaphorical statement we have two distinct elements which carry with them entire systems of meaning. When a metaphor occurs we have the application of one system of meanings or associations applied to another. The metaphor then functions as an organizing principle in which there are various shifts in meaning through the interaction of the networks. This is how new meaning is produced, in the formation of a new grid. Black points out that it is important to understand that there may indeed be metaphors which are straightforwardly comparative or simply a substitution for literal speech. The heart of the metaphorical process, however, is much more rich and complex.

Throughout the early essay, Black argues against both the substitution and comparison views. In this he is primarily out to show how we need metaphor to refer successfully to phenomena which cannot be clinched in so-called literal language. In the later essay the argument is made stronger and in the face of criticisms that have been made. A key development in the later article is that Black acknowledges a close relation between metaphor, models and analogy. He argues now that 'every metaphor is the tip of a submerged model' (Black 1979b p.31). Also, the question of whether and in what sense metaphor is a mystery comes to the surface. There are, of course, great difficulties with the use of the word 'mystery' in the study of metaphor, especially if it involves knowledge which would not otherwise have been achieved. Here, the concern is with adequacy and inadequacy rather than with truth and falsity.

Perhaps the most important development in the later essay relates to the specific function of metaphor. In the earlier essay it was suggested that metaphor 'creates the similarity' which lies at its heart. In the later essay, we learn that metaphors are 'cognitive instruments' which play a role in perception. As such, they discover existing connections, although Black is still very concerned to bring together meaning and use. Thus, he says that he wishes 'to contend that some metaphors enable us to see aspects of reality that the metaphor's production helps to constitute' (p.39). The role of the metaphor, therefore, is crucial in perception, but it is not simply a matter of discovering 'things as they are' so that truth and falsity might be established. Rather, metaphor proceeds *pari passu* with the perception of reality. It both reveals and creates 'the way things are'. Of course this is true only of some metaphors. It is still possible that a particular metaphor might be closer to a straightforward comparison or a substitution.

Black furthers our understanding of metaphor quite considerably in these two essays but there are still weaknesses. The main shortcoming is that he still thinks of metaphor as having its two elements within the sentence in which it occurs. The tendency is always to treat only metaphors of the 'A is a B' type and thus to drift into a comparison theory. When this occurs, the heart of the interaction theory is ultimately lost. Soskice's stress on the possible silence of part of the metaphor is important here and takes much more seriously the whole context of the speech act [16].

More positively, these views of metaphor as 'interinanimative' and 'interactive' have contributed a basic feature to our understanding of how metaphors work. The two elements in the metaphor which are brought together are very closely related to each other to the point of identity. The 'two ideas for one' concept focuses this relation. It is important to note that this metaphorical relation is not simply a comparison in which the two elements remain separate. They are united and yet distinct. Let us now turn to the work of Monroe Beardsley in order to elucidate this matter further.

The Controversion Theory

Monroe Beardsley has developed what he calls a 'controversion' or 'verbal-opposition' theory of metaphor. Here we have a theory which is close to Black's 'interaction' theory and which takes seriously the element of tension which is so crucial to how metaphor works. Beardsley's view has both strengths and weaknesses, but our main purpose in looking at it is to observe that, although he does emphasize tension, he nevertheless still tends in the direction of keeping the elements apart. In his *Aesthetics*, Beardsley says of this theory that:

> Its essential principle is that the speaker or writer utters a statement explicitly but in such a way as to show that he does not believe what he states, or is not primarily interested in what he states, and thereby calls attention to something else that he has not explicitly stated - 'If he wins, I'll eat my hat'. It is discourse that says more than it states, by canceling out the primary meaning to make room for secondary meaning (Beardsley 1958 p.138).

This cancelling out of the primary meaning revolves around the 'logical absurdity' which is part of how metaphor achieves its meaning. The logical absurdity is made up of a 'controversion' or 'verbal-opposition' and the utterance is one in which self-contradiction and falsity are important. At the heart of a metaphorical utterance lies a conflict of meaning.

There are various possible levels of meaning involved in an utterance. Beardsley calls these 'designation', 'denotation' and 'connotation'. For Beardsley, 'designation' concerns designating a category or class, for example, 'wolf', whilst 'denotation' concerns denoting particular individuals in that category which have the characteristics concerned. In addition to these, however, there are 'connotations' of characteristics that wolves are widely believed to have, such as 'fierceness, persistence, and predatory clannishness' (p.125). The important point here is that in metaphor there occurs a logical falsity at the level of 'designation'. Thus in the phrase 'the man is a wolf', we have literal falsity at the level of designation (clearly a man is not a member of the catagory 'wolf') but metaphorical meaning at the level of connotation, that is at the level of the meaning beyond the merely literal (he may be fierce and persistent).

Beardsley speaks of an utterance containing a subject and a modifier. Thus, in the phrase 'large dogs', 'dogs' is the subject and 'large' is the modifier. There are different types of usage and various relations within such expressions, but in metaphor we are concerned with a basic incompatibility between subject and modifier. There are different types of self-contradiction. Oxymoron is clearly one of them. When we say 'living death' or 'unkindly kind' we have a basic self-contradiction which enables new meaning to emerge. Likewise, in metaphor we have a basic contradiction, according to Beardsley, in which the modifier contradicts the subject in an internal semantic 'twist'.

Beardsley develops his theory further with the help of this concept of a 'twist' in the meaning of metaphor. Rejecting an 'implicit comparison' concept of metaphor, he says that 'this twist of meaning is forced by inherent tensions, or oppositions, within the metaphor itself' (Beardsley 1962 p.294). He adds that 'the opposition that renders an expression metaphorical, is...within the meaning structure itself' (p.299). Clearly we are dealing here with two levels of distinction, the semantic and the logical:

A metaphorical attribution, then, involves two ingredients: a semantical distinction between two levels of meaning, and a logical opposition at one level. Thus there is no question of 'spiteful', in a metaphorical context, denoting spiteful people and injecting them for the purpose of comparison; the price it pays for admission to this context is that it function there to signify only its connoted characteristics (p.299).

Thus, when metaphor occurs, as for example in 'a spiteful wind', we have a distinction at the level of designation and connotation and also at the level of the logical. The utterance is inherently self-contradictory and logically absurd.

Two criticisms of Beardsley's concept of metaphor must be noted. First, the concept is limited to the language and meaning structure. The logical absurdity and the self-contradiction occur at the level of word and meaning and fail, as Soskice has observed, to take the full context of the utterance into account: 'The central idea remains that the metaphoricalness of metaphors stems from a conflict of meaning in the terms themselves' (Soskice 1985 p.34). This limitation of pragmatic and contextual factors obviously limits the full force and scope of a metaphorical utterance. Indeed it also limits the full scope of the tension which arises within the whole context of the utterance.

Secondly, later in his work *Aesthetics* in which this 'controversion' theory is laid out, Beardsley discusses the possibility of translating metaphor into literal language in order to check its empirical truth. So, e.e. cummings's sonnet 'Chimneys', with its reference to 'Cambridge ladies', is discussed. 'The Cambridge ladies who live in furnished souls' (Beardsley 1958 p.431), Beardsley maintains, might be checked by the 'literal' translation, 'Cambridge ladies still have the same political, social, religious, and moral beliefs that their parents and grandparents had' (p.431). Beardsley is uneasy at certain points in the discussion concerning the translatability of such metaphors into literal language. However, later in the book when he discusses the possibility of the paraphrase of poetic metaphor he seems clear that this is possible. If we wish to translate 'Napoleon is a wolf' into non-metaphorical language, according to Beardsley, we can still use 'wolf' non-metaphorically, as in 'Napoleon is cruel, and the cruelty of Napoleon is like the cruelty of a wolf'. Beardsley is aware that such translations might result in an endless circle of other metaphors, but thinks that, 'this difficulty is only apparent' (p.435). This tendency of Beardsley to allow paraphrase, leads Douglas Berggren to conclude that Beardsley's theory is 'ultimately unsatisfactory' because it fails 'either to accept or to apply the full tension theory'. For Berggren, Beardsley 'refuses to accept the irreducibility of vital poetic metaphors' (Berggren 1962-63 p.250).

Beardsley's 'controversion theory' takes us a long way towards understanding metaphor, but it has serious limitations. If it fails to maintain the inner tension which it is trying to emphasize, then its basic insight is lost. It looks as though, for Beardsley, metaphors remain at the level of comparison. The two ideas within the metaphor drift apart and the essential 'twist' is lost. A similar thing happens when metaphor is seen in terms of 'ambiguity'.

Metaphor and Ambiguity

In discussing the views of Richards we noted that he lamented the fact that ambiguity has had such a bad press in the western tradition. He asserted that we must treat this more positively at the present time. He is, of course, correct. The concern at this point is with whether metaphor may usefully be understood in terms of ambiguity. In holding that it may not, we shall focus further on some crucial elements in finding the true nature of metaphor.

Some have maintained the view that metaphor is essentially ambiguous and finds its nature in ambiguity. Both William Empson and Israel Scheffler have treated metaphor as a type of ambiguity [17]. There are of course many views of ambiguity. Basically, it is either a vagueness or a case of double meaning. These are, of course, related. If something is vague, it is unclear. If we are dealing with double meaning, we have an 'either/or' dynamic. With both vagueness and double meaning we are dealing with at least two meanings, either of which may be the case. This tension may be resolved when the meaning is clarified. In metaphor, on the contrary, we have a double meaning whose tension must not be resolved if the intended meaning is to be maintained. Eva Feder Kittay sums up the difference usefully when she says that '...in the case of ambiguity, the two (or more) thoughts expressed are independent of each other and each reflects conventional uses of the term, while, in metaphor the thoughts depend on and are motivated by each other' (Kittay 1987 p.16). The important point here is that the two elements in ambiguity are not interacting with each other. A statement is simply ambiguous and unclear. In metaphor, the two elements relate through transference and interaction into a single phenomenon. The meaning is not ambiguous or unclear, but metaphorical.

Epiphor and Diaphor

Another distinction within the debate about metaphor sheds light upon the basic issues. This is the distinction between 'epiphor' (ἐπιφορά: 'bringing to' or 'upon') and 'diaphor' (διαφορά: 'difference'). Basically, these are two sorts of metaphor, although Philip Wheelwright sees them both as essential to the overall impact of metaphoric creativity. When Aristotle spoke of 'transference' at the heart of metaphor (Poetics 1457b) he used the Greek word ἐπιφορά. Although clarity here as to what exactly is transferred is difficult to come by, the basic dimension is that of movement involving two elements, a 'bringing together' or 'carrying over'. The second type of metaphor is 'diaphor' and involves a 'carrying through'. Here the two elements are associated with each other but are different. They only have their significance within the context in which they are juxtaposed. Let us illustrate these two different types.

Epiphoric metaphor, or 'epiphor', is what we are basically maintaining metaphor to be here. It is a cognitive phenomenon enabling new insight. It operates in the coming together of images, in the bringing together of dissimilarities into similarity. Wheelwright speaks of a 'tensive vibrancy' which has a shock value (Wheelwright 1962 p.74). He quotes T.E. Hulme's 'Autumn' as an example containing epiphor:

A touch of cold in the autumn night
I walked abroad
And saw the round moon lean over a hedge,
Like a red-faced farmer.
I did not stop to talk, but nodded;
And round about were the wistful stars
With white faces like town children (p.74).

Although this is in fact simile, Wheelwright is of the opinion that the distinction between metaphor and simile at the grammatical level is unhelpful. Some similes are more tensive than some metaphors and it is this essential tensive quality which is the crucial feature.

Diaphoric metaphor or 'diaphor' on the other hand is basically a juxtaposition of images, one after the other. Wheelwright quotes an unpatriotic verse from an American magazine:

My country 'tis of thee
Sweet land of liberty
Higgledy-piggledy my black hen (p.78).

Here the point is that the tensive quality is created by the juxtaposition of the first two lines with the third. The first two lines alone are not tensive, nor is the third. Together they make diaphoric metaphor. Within the fabric of poetic creativity clearly both epiphoric and diaphoric metaphor contribute to tensive insight. The most interesting feature here, however, lies in the difference between these two types of metaphor, even if they do both contribute to an ultimate all-round tensive quality. The difference is that in the case of diaphor the tension is spaced out and the simultaneous 'is and is not' is lost. The 'tension' consists in a successive sense, 'carrying through', rather than the similarity and the dissimilarity occurring simultaneously as in epiphor. Clearly there can be a great deal of overlap between these elements but the important thing is the tensive quality which is produced [18].

Wheelwright is keen to sustain the essential tension within metaphoric creativity. In his earlier work he speaks of 'plurisignation' and says that 'the essence of metaphor consists in the nature of the tension which is maintained among the heterogeneous elements brought together in one commanding image or expression' (Wheelwright 1954 p.101). In fact, his overall view tends in the direction of separation or comparison and he does not always keep the 'tensive' quality fully in view. In his later work he says that 'to think or speak about reality is always to do so through one perspective rather than another' (Wheelwright 1962 p.170). The notion of 'alternating' from one perspective to another indicates that he has drifted in the direction of a separation of the elements where metaphor is concerned. Paul Ricoeur's notion of 'split reference' goes some way towards focusing the key relation here, although we shall see that similar difficulties arise even with this.

Split Reference

In attempting to articulate the central dynamics which lie at the heart of metaphor, Paul Ricoeur aims to take seriously the full context of the utterance in which a metaphor occurs, both its practical and semantic sides. Ricoeur is clear that metaphor has semantic significance. He says, 'by a semantic theory, I mean an inquiry into the capacity of metaphor to provide untranslatable information and, accordingly, into metaphor's claim to yield some true insight about reality' (Ricoeur 1979 p.141). By far the most important aspect in the way this 'true insight' is achieved is the notion of 'split reference'. W.B. Stanford has called this 'stereoscopic vision' and it reminds us of Wheelwright's 'plurisignation'. This concept of split reference focuses precisely upon the 'two ideas for one' element to which we have referred. The reason it is so important is that it attempts to articulate at once both the unity and the distinction within a metaphor.

In *The Rule of Metaphor*, in discussing the concept of 'split reference', Ricoeur draws attention to the importance of the Majorca storytellers' opening line *Aixo era y no era*, that is, 'It was and it was not'. He says that '...this notion of split reference...as well as the wonderful "It was and it was not"...contains *in nuce* all that can be said about metaphorical truth' (Ricoeur 1978 p.224). Thus, Ricoeur draws attention to the two elements in the metaphorical process - the 'is' and the 'is not' - and to the corresponding pitfalls which loom when one or other is undermined. He speaks of 'the inadequacy of an interpretation that gives in to ontological *naïveté* in the evaluation of metaphorical truth because it ignores the implicit "is not"' and of 'the inadequacy of an inverse interpretation that, under the critical pressure of the "is not" loses the "is" by reducing it to the "as if" of a reflective judgement' (p.248/249). So it is, in Ricoeur's view, that both the 'is' and the 'is not' are crucial to any understanding of the way metaphor works. It is precisely this feature which enables metaphor to yield unique knowledge and gives it its specific power.

The 'split reference' here lies specifically in the tension which is set up in the way the two dimensions relate to each other. The 'is and is not' element is the split reference. More specifically, the metaphor finds its dynamic structure in the fact that a metaphorical utterance is at once both a truth and a falsity. Clearly at the literal or primary level a metaphorical statement is usually false. The truth which it articulates exists at another level. Thus, the simultaneous truth and falsity operating together gives this dimension of speech the very thing which makes it different from other figures of speech, different from mere comparison or simile, and enables it to yield unique knowledge.

The 'tension' which is created in this 'split reference' is thus the mark of real metaphorical utterance. Ricoeur says that 'metaphor is the tension between epiphor and diaphor. This tension guarantees the very transference of meaning and gives poetic language its characteristic of semantic "plus value", its capacity to be open towards new aspects, new dimensions, new horizons of meaning' (p.250). So, the 'two ideas for one', the two dimensions of the metaphorical utterance, interact in a tension. This tension is the 'nerve centre' of metaphor and the heart of the metaphorical process. Ricoeur observes three elements which constitute the overall tensive make-up of metaphor:

(a) tension within the statement: between tenor and vehicle, between focus and frame, between principal subject and secondary subject;

(b) tension between two interpretations: between a literal interpretation that perishes at the hands of semantic impertinence and a metaphorical interpretation whose sense emerges through non-sense;

(c) tension in the relational function of the copula: between identity and difference in the interplay of resemblance (p.247).

Although there is a tendency to limit this theory of metaphor to the statement only, we nevertheless have here some absolutely crucial features of metaphor: tension, literal and metaphorical senses, identity and difference.

In metaphor the literal meaning gives way to the new metaphorical meaning, although of course the 'literal falsity' is important in this. There is an incongruence at the literal level but this is balanced by the congruence at the metaphorical level. There is thus both proximity and distance. Ricoeur speaks of paradox, suspension and negativity in the metaphorical process and, like Turbayne, alludes to Gilbert Ryle's concept of a 'category mistake' in which one thing is seen as another. Ricoeur sees the value in understanding the metaphorical process as 'interactive' but also claims that this does not really solve the problem of metaphor. The crucial concern in articulating metaphor is with the 'is and is not' of 'split reference'.

Ricoeur illustrates his concept of metaphor particularly well when he shows how we must move beyond the basic 'interactive' views into a view which makes clear the inner tension. Speaking of 'proximity' and 'distance' he says:

I think that the decisive problem that an interaction theory of metaphor has helped to delineate but not to solve is the transition from literal incongruence to metaphorical congruence between two semantic fields. Here the metaphor of space is useful. It is as though a change of distance between meanings occurred within a logical space. The *new* pertinence or congruence proper to a meaningful metaphoric utterance proceeds from the kind of semantic proximity which suddenly obtains between terms in spite of their distance. Things or ideas which were remote appear now as close (Ricoeur 1979 p.145).

The proximity and the distance are part of the 'is and is not' of 'split reference'. The tension is inherent in the process. Ricoeur speaks of the 'war between distance and proximity' (p.146/7).

As with some of the other views of metaphor at which we have looked, however, although Ricoeur contributes some crucial elements to the enquiry, there are still some problems. The emphasis on 'split reference' has the potential for separating the elements within metaphor and losing the 'tensive quality' it is trying to maintain. Soskice thinks that Ricoeur's notion of 'split reference' drifts into a comparison view of metaphor by involving two elements at the level of reference as well as two elements at the level of sense [19]. If it were maintained that there were two things at the level of reference, a comparison view would begin to emerge. Such a view then begins to truncate the notion that metaphor enables new meaning to emerge. Soskice says that Ricoeur's notion 'eliminates the possibility that a metaphor may be genuinely, even ontologically, novel' (Soskice 1985 p.90). Thus, although there are some crucial insights here, we must be careful once again to guard all dimensions which form the tensive and cognitively unique qualities of metaphor.

Sort-crossing

We have seen that Aristotle's main concept of metaphor is 'epiphor', by which he means some sort of 'transference'. This could be of words or meanings or both. It is certainly clear that this element is crucial to the way in which metaphors achieve their meaning. Colin Turbayne takes up Gilbert Ryle's notion of a 'category mistake' in order to throw light on this feature. For Ryle, a category mistake consists quite simply in mistaking a category. So, the visitor to Oxford or Cambridge who has seen a number of colleges, libraries, department buildings and such like and then asks 'But where is the University?' has not yet understood that the 'University' is not of the same category as the things already seen. Ryle says that such a mistake 'represents the facts of mental life as if they belonged to one logical type or category (or range of types of categories), when they actually belong to another' (Ryle 1986 p.17). Turbayne calls this sort of transference 'sort-crossing' and says that it is 'the first defining feature of metaphor' (Turbayne 1962 p.11).

Ricoeur maintains that 'it is tempting to say that metaphor is a planned category mistake' (Ricoeur 1978 p.197) and this notion does shed some light on how we are best to understand metaphor. Turbayne thinks that metaphor is a device which, using two categories and bringing them together, can either illuminate or deceive the hearer. A metaphor is certainly not a 'mistake', but achieves its meaning in a manner similar to a category mistake. For Turbayne, a key feature in a successful metaphor is an awareness that it is happening. We must know that it is going on. If we are not aware that there has been a crossing of sorts then we are confused and are used by the metaphor rather than our using it. Turbayne speaks of 'category-fusion' and 'category-confusion'. Category-fusion is the legitimate and conscious crossing of sorts, whereas category-confusion is 'taking a metaphor literally' or 'sort-trespassing' (Turbayne 1962 p.22). Attempting to strike a balanced view, Turbayne refocuses Dr. Johnson's dictum and says that metaphor, rather than giving us 'two ideas for one', gives us 'two ideas *as* one' (p.17).

As we have seen in a number of cases now, the positive contribution of a given thinker can shed a great deal of light on the mystery of metaphoric utterance. However, things invariably drift in the direction of unifying or separating the elements, or the underlying epistemology prevents the desired balance. In the case of Turbayne, the underlying epistemology renders his observations somewhat empiricist. His understanding of metaphor implies that the 'categories' which we use and the 'sorts' which we 'cross' are static and manipulable. The emphasis on awareness in using metaphor leaves the user in total control and the real power of metaphor is reduced. It is at this point that Ricoeur thinks that it is inappropriate to call metaphor a 'category mistake' and says that Turbayne's notion excludes the possibility of being 'seized' by the metaphor. Instead, the user of the metaphor is seizing and controlling the categories being manipulated. For Ricoeur, Turbayne's notion of metaphor is stuck in 'neo-empiricist' roots and has made no real progress (Ricoeur 1978 p.253).

Clearly, the important matter here in these various views of metaphor is to find an adequate understanding of 'is and is not' in order to control our notions of how the language works. We have seen in this chapter so far that even the views which see metaphor as irreducible can often drift in the direction of comparison and separation of the elements. Furthermore, even those who specifically set out to emphasize the 'tensive' quality of metaphor can often end up drifting in other directions. We have seen these problems arising in the theories of Richards, Black, Beardsley, Wheelwright, Ricoeur and Turbayne. It is now clear, however, that because of the inherent relation between language and christology, because of the importance of metaphor at the heart of human language and because of its fundamental 'is and is not' character, the 'is and is not' of Chalcedonian christology enables the most fruitful notion of metaphor to emerge. Chalcedon sustains the inner tensive quality in its christology and this controls the tensional nature of metaphoric utterance. If the metaphors we use of God are understood in the light of christology and within the context of revelation, the central tension will be kept in view and they will be allowed to carry their particular significance. Problems of confusion and separation of the elements will be controlled. The tensive relation between the human and the divine will be sustained. Notions of metaphor will be guided by Chalcedonian christology.

Models

We turn now to a consideration of the role of models in both theology and the sciences. In both areas it is clear that we speak using metaphors and models and that these are closely related. Thus, in theology, we may speak of God using the model 'father', of Jesus using the model 'saviour' or of the church using the models 'servant' or 'institution'. In the sciences, we may speak of the behaviour of gas using the model 'billiard-balls', of light using the models of 'waves' or 'particles', or of the human brain using the model 'wordprocessor'. In each case we have an example of the employment of some sort of model in order to clarify or assist progress in relation to what we are trying to say or find out.

Although the use of models in theology has been generally acknowledged, there has been a reluctance to accept their use in the sciences. The popular position is that models in theology are fluid and expressive, whilst the language of the sciences is rigorous and 'objectively' true. Models in theology are a necessary part of human expression in religion, whilst the language of science concerns permanent truths. Its language is, therefore, static and unchanging. This makes it difficult to acknowledge that scientific language uses models, which may by definition become useless or inadequate. Recent developments in the philosophy of science, however, have revolutionized this attitude towards language in the sciences and acknowledged that in all areas models are used to help articulate what we are trying to say. We maintain here that in both theology and in the sciences, models are indispensable in the way human language and knowledge work.

In turning from metaphors to models we must observe the relation between these two crucial phenomena. It is clear that models are another member of the family which includes analogies, metaphors and symbols. Models are, in fact, especially related to metaphors and are to some extent extensions of metaphors. McFague says that 'a model is, in essence, a sustained and systematic metaphor' (McFague 1983 p.67) and Barbour follows Black in treating models as 'systematically developed metaphors' (Barbour 1974 p.43). Our definition of a model will obviously depend a great deal on what we understand a metaphor to be in the first place. Soskice is keen not to mix up models and metaphors, pointing out that a metaphor is always a matter of speech, whereas a model need not be associated with speech at all. However, although she considers it better to keep the two things separate, she does say that 'metaphors arise when we speak on the basis of models', thus admitting that there is a crucial link (Soskice 1985 p.101).

The main concern here is to show that models operate in essentially the same manner as metaphors. They are fundamentally related in the way they operate. The essential 'is and is not' which lies at the heart of metaphor also characterizes the way models operate. Although there are many different views of metaphors and models, we shall find that once again Chalcedonian christology will assist us in maintaining an adequate view of human speech about God and about the world.

Models in Theology

When we speak of God, in metaphors and on the basis of models, we are speaking in human language of one who is essentially different from us and yet known to us. The first thing to note is that models do pervade theological discourse at its most fundamental level. Just as our ordinary language involves metaphors and models more than we often realize, so theology is saturated with such usage, even though we are often unaware of this. A large part of the difficulty we have in acknowledging our use of metaphors and models in theology arises from the positivism which prevails in our notions of language. The widespread assumption is that theological language functions always in its primary or literal sense. However, in all areas of theology, of speaking about God, we speak on the basis of models.

When we speak of God as 'father' or of God 'sending his son', the metaphors operate on the basis of the model of 'father'. The same model is at work when Christians are spoken of as 'sons of God'. In the New Testament, Paul speaks of the new relationship 'in Christ' in terms of δικαιοσύνη (dikaiosune: 'righteousness' or 'justification'). Here the forensic metaphors he uses arise out of the basic model which he takes from the Jewish law courts. In the same way, when Paul speaks of the freedom brought about in the death of Jesus, the metaphor of being 'set free' is used [20]. This metaphor, frequently used in the Christian tradition for the death of Jesus, is based upon the model of slavery and freedom which formed such an essential part of Greek and Roman experience. We continue to speak of basic religious experience on the basis of such models, whether it is of baptism as a 'washing' or the eucharist as a 'sacrifice'.

One area of theological reflection in which the use of models has been acknowledged much more recently is that of ecclesiology. Avery Dulles has reflected on the use of models in relation to revelation and in relation to ecclesiology. For example, he discusses models of the church such as 'institution', 'servant', 'sacrament' or 'herald'. Dulles' comments upon the centrality and extent of such models are worth noting:

> ...the Church, like other theological realities, is a mystery. Mysteries are realities of which we cannot speak directly. If we wish to talk about them at all we must draw on analogies afforded by our experience of the world. These analogies provide models. By attending to the analogies and utilizing them as models, we can indirectly grow in our understanding of the Church (Dulles 1988 p.9).

He later adds that 'the method of models is applicable to the whole of theology, and not simply to ecclesiology' (p.12). Dulles is aware of the centrality of models in all theological understanding. He notes the importance of the relation between models or images and epistemology. He is aware also of the limitations of such figures in trying to articulate what is essentially mysterious. Models for Dulles are exploratory and heuristic in addition to being really explanatory.

In his discussion of the nature of models, Dulles refers to the one who did a great deal in the middle years of the present century to increase our appreciation and understanding of the role and meaning of models in theology: that is, the theologian Ian Ramsey. It was Ramsey who, in his *Models and Mystery* and elsewhere, spoke of 'cosmic disclosures' and underlined the use of models in our articulation of the mystery of God. Ramsey associates models very closely with metaphors and maintains that they work in essentially the same way. There are, of course, different sorts of models in theology as there are in science, but the overall aim is broadly the same. Models are to do with articulating the unknown.

According to Ramsey, the concern in theology is to articulate the 'mystery' or 'disclosure' which we call God. In this sense metaphors and models are 'born in insight' (Ramsey 1964 p.48,50). Because they are essentially about religious disclosures, they are about 'odd' situations and experiences and therefore demand 'odd' language if they are to be spoken of adequately. This articulation in metaphors and models maintains the mystery and Ramsey speaks of the need to acknowledge the permanence of the mystery which is articulated [21]. This is done through the use of 'qualifiers'. These are words which qualify the sense of the model in use. So, words like 'infinite' and 'perfect' in the expressions 'infinite wisdom' or 'perfect love' qualify the basic models of wisdom and love which are human models. Such qualifiers, according to Ramsey, are 'an absolute *sine qua non*, declaring the inadequacy of all models' (p.60). Although Ramsey is concerned to keep a balance in his notion of the way metaphors and models actually operate, we shall see later that he does not in fact achieve this. Thus, although Ramsey contributes a great deal towards our understanding of models, his view, like some views of metaphor which we have examined, is imbalanced.

In Sallie McFague's discussion of models in theology, as in her discussion of metaphor, we find a clear determination to acknowledge both their necessity and also their limitations. Models are necessary for theology to operate, but they are not pictures of reality and they should not be taken literally. They are an essential part of articulating the human-divine relation, but thay have their limitations. It is the central tension which characterizes metaphor which is also crucial to models. The basic 'is and is not' must be sustained. However, in McFague's overall system, there is the same tendency to impoverish the actual content which a model provides that we found in her view of metaphor. Thus, although she does allude to both dimensions of models, she often speaks of them as implements for 'ordering' experience rather than for discovering reality. In one summary of her view, she says that 'the function of theological models is comprehensive ordering rather than discovery' (McFague 1983 p.107). As with Ramsey, McFague's view of models ends up inadequate through being too subjectivist. Her view of models is, of course, continuous with her view of metaphors.

It is clear from all of those who have written on the place of models in theology that such phenomena are absolutely central to articulating the relation between human beings and God. Models are central to all theological activity. Ramsey is close to striking the required balance when he speaks of the need both to articulate the divine by use of a model and also to preserve the mystery of that which is disclosed. McFague has the unsatisfactory ambiguity which we have noted in relation to her view both of metaphor and of model. Clearly a balance of 'is and is not', of the tensive element which we saw is so central to metaphor, needs to be struck here. The use of Chalcedonian christology is as appropriate in the case of models upon the basis of which metaphors arise, as it was in the case of metaphors themselves. Let us now turn to the ways in which models have been viewed in the sciences.

Models in Science

In the past, various views have been taken as to the extent to which such figures as metaphors and models are needed in the sciences. Some have claimed that these are absolutely unnecessary to the pursuit of knowledge in science. They are unnecessary additions to, or decorations of, what can be stated literally. Others have acknowledged that the sciences do use metaphors and models in their work but have either claimed that these, once they have done their job, can be disposed of and literal or rigorous language can take over, or that such figurative language is used only to popularize what the professional scientist knows even more clearly in non-figurative language. At present, however, scientists are increasingly acknowledging the use of figurative language within scientific pursuit, the need for such language and its irreducible status [22]. The view of language in the sciences as literal, narrowly positivistic and empiricist is rapidly declining in some areas.

The main contribution to this turn-around in the understanding of how the sciences operate has come from T.S. Kuhn's work *The Structure of Scientific Revolutions*. The effect of this work has been to begin to dethrone the objectivism which has dominated the sciences. Rather than seeing the language of science as static and objective and the knowledge it produces as permanent and unchanging, Kuhn's work acknowledges that there have as a matter of fact in the history of the sciences been a number of very significant 'paradigm' changes. There have been many interpretations of what Kuhn means by 'paradigm' and of the extent to which his views have become subjectivist and relativistic. However, it is clear enough that there are various levels of paradigm and that there is a close connection here with models. Kuhn says that 'one sense of "paradigm" is global, embracing all the shared commitments of a scientific group; the other isolates a particularly important sort of commitment and is thus a subset of the first' (Kuhn 1974 p.460). 'Paradigm', therefore, may be taken in the sense of 'worldview', that is, an entire way of understanding the universe, as with Newtonian or Einsteinian physics. It may also mean a lesser element within an overall framework. Kuhn calls these lesser elements 'exemplars'. It is clear here that a model operating within a particular scientific endeavour functions as an exemplar or 'paradigm'. The interest here is in how these models operate.

In his work on models in the sciences, Ian Barbour maintains that models must be taken 'seriously but not literally' (Barbour 1974 p.7). This expression clinches perfectly the double-edged element of truth and falsity which operates when we use a model in order to speak about the world or advance our knowledge of the world. Clearly a model cannot simply be identified with what it models. At the simplest level, a map of the world cannot be identified with what it models. It is clearly not the world itself, but models the world. In the sense that it models the world it has both a truth and a falsity. If a map were literally even the same size as 'the world' it would be useless! Once again we find ourselves on the borderland between literalism and meaninglessness. Once again, the need is to strike a balance.

It is important to note that the word 'model' itself operates in a number of diverse ways in the sciences. Barbour identifies four types of model. First, the 'experimental' model. Such a model is a smaller reconstruction in the laboratory, of the actual thing. A good example of this sort of model would be the model of an aeroplane or of an electrical system. This is the most basic form of model and we can see immediately that there are senses in which the model is and is not what it models. However, there are more complex forms of model.

Secondly, Barbour refers to the 'logical' type of model. Here mathematical models are the prime example. The mathematician forms a model of a geometric type, for example, in order to deal with an abstract phenomenon, mathematical and theoretical. Thirdly, and very closely related to the second type, we have mathematical models *per se*. These are more specifically mathematical in that they do not necessarily reflect the structure of the phenomenon of which they are models at all. Thus, equations may be used as models expressing certain statistics in relation to economic or political life. Fourthly, and most characteristically, Barbour refers to 'theoretical' models. He says that 'these are imaginative mental constructs invented to account for observed phenomena. Such a model is usually an imagined mechanism or process, which is postulated by analogy with familiar mechanisms or processes...its chief use is to help one understand the world, not simply to make predictions' (p.30). Barbour goes on to say that a model of this sort is 'not a literal picture of the world', but a 'symbolic representation' whose origin is founded in 'a special kind of creative imagination'(p.30).

In each case it is clear that the model is a representation of the thing modelled, but is not identical with it. There is a relation to the actual phenomenon, but the actual phenomenon is not reducible to the model. Rom Harré has made the distinction between the 'source' and the 'subject' of a model [23]. The source is the phenomenon upon which the model is based. The subject is whatever it is that is modelled. In the case of a model aeroplane, of course, these would be the same. In the case of using a theoretical construct, like the billiard-ball model for gas, leading to the kinetic theory of gases, the source of the model is the billiard-balls, whilst the subject is the gas. In both cases, however, the function of such models hangs upon a 'likeness' and an 'unlikeness'. It is this tension which characterizes the model as a model and enables it to function.

Soskice articulates this distinction by calling the models in which source and subject are the same 'homeomorphic' and those in which they are different 'paramorphic'. She then observes that:

> The models used by the sciences for theoretical purposes are primarily paramorphic models, for while a homeomorphic model may have certain applied uses (a model aeroplane may be used in a wind tunnel to test the aerodynamic properties of its source), the task of theory construction itself is customarily the task of constructing models to explain better what we do not yet fully understand, rather than that of building models of states of affairs whose nature is clear to us (Soskice 1985 p.103).

Thus, in the sciences, it is commonplace to use paramorphic models for the discovery of what is not yet known. If we now take seriously the view that such models are both like and unlike the phenomena of which they *are* models, we see that they operate as tools or aids to understanding the world and not as mere predictions of what is the case.

Thus, in the sciences, models operate with a flexibility and fluidity. They are characterized by a number of features. Barbour observes that models in science are to be understood analogically and speaks of positive and negative sides of the analogy. The point here is that as a model functions, there will be some features which are appropriate to the subject and some which are not. Thus, in the billiard-ball model, gas is seen as particles colliding. Billiard-balls obviously do the same. However, the colour of billiard-balls is of no significance. Once again, the model is only of partial use and the discovery of which bits are, and of which bits are not, will be a matter of trial and error.

This 'trial and error' feature is further drawn out by Barbour's observation that 'models contribute to the extension of theories' (Barbour 1974 p.33). A model has the capacity to contribute to the development of a theory and to its modification. A model, as Mary Hesse has noted, has an 'open texture' or a 'surplus meaning' (Barbour 1974 p.33) which enables it to function in a suggestive way and never to be thought of as static or exhausted. Stephen Toulmin notes that 'it is in fact a great virtue of a good model that it does suggest further questions, taking us beyond the phenomena from which we began, and tempts us to formulate hypotheses which turn out to be experimentally fertile' (Barbour 1966 p.161). The model is something which is used in relation to reality for the furtherance of knowledge about the world. It is not a picture of reality. It remains a model in that it is not finally reducible to the phenomenon itself. Thus, there is room for freedom and novelty, for trying out different ways of using a model, for seeing what it will yield to us about the world. Barbour says that 'Models are not advanced as guaranteed truths; they are used to generate plausible hypotheses to investigate. They are a source of promising theories to test' (Barbour 1974 p.34). In that testing, however, they have their roots in reality, of which they become a dialectical articulation. In that testing, the models will be found to be both like and unlike what they model.

We have observed that there has been a significant change in the way in which the sciences understand language to operate. Whereas in the past this has been understood to operate literally, many areas of science now acknowledge the use of figurative language, and especially metaphors and models, in their activities. Such models are increasingly seen to have value precisely because they are not 'fixed' or 'final', but rather have a fluidity and flexibility which allows experimentation towards a more adequate understanding of the world. Barbour's claim that models in the sciences should be taken 'seriously but not literally' points us once again to the fundamental 'is and is not' which lies at the heart of human speaking even in areas in which 'objective certainty' has been thought to have pride of place. Berggren says that 'the truth of the paradigms and theories of science must be just as irreducibly tensional as is the truth of poetic metaphors' (Berggren 1962-63 p.462). We can see here that we are dealing in exactly the same currency when we deal with models as when we deal with metaphors. The 'tensive' element is present in both and we can see once again that Chalcedonian christology is of considerable value in coming to a fuller understanding of how human language works.

The Tensive Quality of Metaphor

It is now time to focus our view of the way in which metaphor works. At the heart of metaphor lies a 'tension', a 'distinction in unity'. In the two elements which comprise metaphor we are dealing with an essential tension which affirms both unity and distinction. To speak of Juliet as the sun, of Herod as a fox, or to speak of God as father, is to speak of one thing 'in terms of' another. Indeed, to speak of God at all requires that we speak of one thing in terms of another, thus rendering the heart of human language about God metaphorical. The 'tension' which arises from the revelation of God in the world gives rise to the need for an essential tension in language about God. The 'inner logic' of metaphor consists in its ability to sustain this tension and not to slip into literalism or mere comparison. Berggren says that 'metaphor constitutes the indispensable principle for integrating diverse phenomena and perspectives without sacrificing their diversity' (Berggren 1962-63 p.237).

We have seen that there are various views of the way in which metaphors work. Amongst those who have maintained that metaphor is cognitive and enables new insights, there has obviously been the rejection of some of the concepts which we have discussed. Metaphors are not to be taken literally; they are not mere ornaments or decorations which can be translated into literal language; they are more than practical instruments which 'nudge us into noting'. On the contrary they are cognitive phenomena in which we find an 'interaction' between two elements. This interaction must then be articulated in a coherent way. It is not simply the two elements side by side in an ambiguity. This would involve 'either' one thing, 'or' another. Nor is it a juxtaposed tension as in 'diaphoric metaphor'. Even 'epiphoric metaphor' might leave a chink of light and slide into comparison. Rather, the two elements, whether they are both present in a sentence or not, are both present in the interaction producing the simultaneous integration in diversity.

The essential feature of metaphor is its maintenance of unity and diversity, its ability to secure dissimilarity within similarity. The appreciation of this has been called 'stereoscopic vision' by Bedell Stanford and 'plurisignation' by Wheelwright. Some of the views of the relation between the elements in a metaphor even though they speak of a 'tension' and of 'is and is not', nevertheless fail to keep these two sides clearly in view. Even Wheelwright's 'plurisignation' is sometimes suspect. He underlines the need to see the double dimension of metaphor but fails to keep the two elements in focus when he speaks of metaphor as an alternation between perspectives or slips into a 'comparison' view. Berggren is much clearer when in discussing the two elements in metaphor he says that '...if the initial differences between the two referents were not simultaneously preserved, even while the referents are also being transformed into closer alignment, the metaphorical character of the construing process would be lost' (p.243). The tension is thus a simultaneous occurrence of 'unity and distinction' and lies at the heart of the nature of metaphor.

It is clear from this that we have here in metaphor exactly the same patterns as we outlined in christology. The essential 'is and is not' must be preserved if real justice is to be done to both the language and the christology. If the elements are separated, the reality is lost. If the elements are identified, the reality is also lost. Once again, we are on the borderlands between idolatry and meaninglessness. The language and the christology, as we have seen, are integrally connected and Chalcedonian christology can be of assistance in both areas. In conclusion, therefore, we must once again underline these connections.

Metaphor and Christology

We have seen that human language is fundamentally metaphorical. Even in speech about the empirical world and in more rigorous scientific activity, models and metaphors play an indispensable role. This is even more true of the language we use about God. The language we use in worship, the language of religious texts and the language we use to describe experiences of God abound in metaphor. Metaphor is a figure of speech which is especially appropriate to talking about God because it cuts through the purely literal and enables insights into the nature of things which would not otherwise be available to us. We are aware that the language finite creatures use of an infinite God does not operate in a straightforward way. Images, analogies, metaphors and symbols are all used in order to speak of the one who is beyond us and yet known. Thus, we call God 'Father' and Jesus 'Saviour' or 'Lord'. We speak of being 'justified' by faith or of the death of Jesus as a 'defeat of the devil'. Religious language is especially metaphorical, and it needs to be. It needs to be because we speak of one who is known as unknown. We speak of one whose reality is not simply at the level of empirical fact and who, therefore, needs to be spoken of 'in terms of' something else. If human language of God is inescapably metaphorical, how are we to understand metaphor?

We have seen that there are various views of metaphor and that, although the western tradition has maintained a rather negative view of metaphor, there are discussions today which are considerably rehabilitating it and recognizing its power to name the unnamed. We return now specifically to our concern with Chalcedonian christology. We have seen that there is a fundamental relation between language and christology and that a change in one area is often associated with a change in the other. We have seen that metaphor lies at the very heart of human speaking, especially about God. It can now be seen clearly, therefore, that metaphor and christology are fundamentally related. This is in fact very clear from the patterns which have emerged in our discussion of the different views of metaphor. Many of these patterns are paralleled in views of language in general and are subject to the same strengths and weaknesses. We saw some of these outlined earlier by Lindbeck. More important, however, is the fact that the patterns which emerged in the debates concerning metaphor are exactly paralleled in christology. Once again Chalcedonian christology can guide notions of language. Let us now focus the main links.

The view of metaphor as contrasted with the literal, or as essentially decorative or ornamental, constituted the point of entry into this debate. This view was shown to be typical of the western tradition and was particularly associated with an analytical approach to language, concentrating on particular words and searching after 'the truth' in the style of rationalism and empiricism. Metaphors were 'perfect cheats' according to Locke and should be dismissed in favour of finding the rational truth about the way things are. This approach, still very much the dominant one in our own day, is based on a separation of literal and figurative language. It is based on an understanding which separates the rational element from the emotional element in the way we speak. The view found in Davidson, which saw metaphor as 'nudging into noting' was similarly based on a separation of language and meaning. These ways are essentially of the same type as Lindbeck's 'cognitive-propositionalism' and are subject to the same weaknesses. In christology this separation is paralleled either by the undermining of one element in the union, as in Apollinarianism, or by the separation of the natures as in Nestorianism. In both cases the natures are separated, either because they are kept apart or because one is ignored. It is clear here once again that as language and christology are so fundamentally related, if Chalcedon enabled balance in relation to patterns in christology, it can enable it in relation to language and especially metaphor.

In the subsequent views of metaphor, the ones which acknowledged its cognitive content, we saw that the aim was always to articulate how the two elements actually related within the utterance. Thus, in the 'interactive' views the 'two ideas for one' were seen to interact with each other securing new insights. In our brief look at 'ambiguity' we found that the relation between the two elements was all-important. Separation of the elements, however, was to be avoided in favour of a tensive relation. Finally, Ricoeur's concept of 'split reference' and Turbayne's 'sort-crossing' again focused the importance of this tensional relation between the two elements. It can be seen clearly now that all of these concerns are exactly paralleled in christology. The attempt to articulate the two elements in the person of Christ exactly parallels the attempt to articulate the relation between the two elements in metaphor. If Chalcedon can enable balance in the one area it can enable it in the other, especially as metaphor is so fundamental a part of human language about God.

If we consider the various views of metaphor in the light of Chalcedon, we shall see that it shows us how to balance the elements involved and that it enables a theory of how human language about God operates. We are not claiming that the most appropriate view of metaphor can only be found through Chalcedonian christology. This is clearly not the case. Exactly the same inner dynamics as those in Chalcedon have been articulated in relation to metaphor without any reference to that document. Indeed, Berggren and Bedell Stanford have articulated a 'Chalcedonian logic' in their notions of metaphor. We are claiming, however, that the relation between humanity and divinity articulated in this document enables an adequate christological notion of theological language and that this can be seen especially in relation to the pitfalls which arise for an understanding of metaphor.

A consideration of metaphor in the light of Chalcedon shows the separation of elements within metaphor to be misguided. It shows that in articulating the relation between the two elements which are brought together, care must be taken that the unity and the distinction are properly balanced. It shows that such notions as 'nudging into noting' and 'ambiguity' are inadequate for understanding metaphor. Such concepts see the two elements as alternatives which are separate, a sort of 'linguistic Nestorianism', rather than really united. It shows also that such notions as 'split reference' and 'sort-crossing' can easily lead to or are based upon dualist or empiricist tendencies. Also, taking metaphor 'literally' or purely at face value, drifts into unifying the elements, a sort of 'linguistic Apollinarianism' and the real power of metaphor is again lost.

Furthermore, the Chalcedonian Definition shows how the view of metaphor which is now so widespread and which is sought after by so many writers whose views nevertheless drift away from it, that is the view emphasizing the 'is and is not' feature, is exactly the one which is articulated when we work with Chalcedon. The simultaneous 'is and is not' kept together in tension lies at the heart of both metaphor and of the Chalcedonian Definition. It is clear, then, that this Definition coheres with and epitomizes our understanding of the way human language about God operates. The next step is to turn to a consideration of various notions of symbols in order to see how these fare in a Chalcedonian climate.

V

SYMBOLS

The Importance and Place of Symbols

At the heart of all religious experience and of all religious traditions lie symbols. These constitute part of the very experience of that which is holy, transcendent or divine. Both in the awakening of religious consciousness and in the nurturing of religious life, symbols play a fundamental role. There are many different types of symbols: those within particular religious traditions; those within religious texts; those used in worship; those peculiar to a specific culture or society. Symbols extend, of course, beyond the narrowly religious: human beings, even in the most secularized societies are symbol-makers. Symbols are so foundational to human consciousness and experience that they cannot be overlooked in a consideration of the nature of human language about God.

Most religious traditions are epitomized by a symbol: the Star of David in Judaism, the Cross of Christ in Christianity, the Crescent in Islam. These play their role in the worship and in the scriptures of the religions concerned. Some symbols, however, are so foundational to human experience that they may be called 'archetypal'. Elemental symbols such as fire, water and air, or others such as animals, blood or wine, have played so powerful a part at the heart of so many religious traditions in all ages as to be called universal. In more secular terms it is also the case that symbols lie at the heart of human experience. The flag of a nation, or the symbol of a particular political group, for example the swastika, 'sum up' the ideology of that nation or group and in many cases lie at the interface of experience and reality shaping the experience of those who use them. The point of overriding importance here is the centrality and power of symbols in human experience and especially in human experience of God.

When asked to define a symbol, however, we soon run into deep water. As with analogy and metaphor and as with all language used of God, symbols do not lend themselves to narrow definition. To produce a 'theory of symbols' would be to run the risk of draining the effect of their power. Their power lies essentially in evocation and expression in the context of religious experience and worship. In this sense they defy narrow and purely intellectual definition. We are able to observe symbols, however, and to attempt to articulate the way they behave within the context of experience and worship of God. In this sense we can reflect upon them and articulate views which are adequate or inadequate.

It is important at this point to expound the relation between symbol and metaphor. These are very much of the same family. Their ways of meaning overlap considerably and indeed in some ways they coincide. This latter depends upon context and medium. Metaphors are essentially linguistic, that is, they are verbal or spoken. Symbols on the other hand, may exist within the narrative of a text, for example the vine or the shepherd in John's gospel, but they may also be objects such as a statue, or a piece of clothing or furniture, or an event such as a meal or an historic occurrence. In short, symbol is predominantly non-verbal metaphor and operates, as we shall see, in a very similar way. The presence of two elements in unity is fundamental to both. The 'symbol', from σύν (sun: with) and βάλλω (ballo: I throw), is a 'throwing with', that is a throwing of two things together. The symbol, however, is a more sustained image than a metaphor. When a metaphor is used repeatedly it may become a symbol. Philip Wheelwright puts this succinctly when he says that symbols are 'extensions and stabilizations of metaphorical activity' (Wheelwright 1962 p.128). Symbols are thus continuous with and operate in essentially the same manner as metaphors. We turn to them here, therefore, as equally important phenomena in the search for an understanding of human language about God.

Even though we may acknowledge the importance of symbols in human experience of God, however, we are still faced with the question of how their power actually works. Theories of how symbols operate in religious experience have been numerous and diverse. Are they merely expressive of human religious emotion or are they in some way unified with the divine life itself? As with metaphors in the western tradition, symbols have frequently been treated as decorative and the distinction between the merely 'symbolic' and the 'true' has become commonplace. As with any language about God, symbols may be viewed in 'experiential-expressivist' terms or in 'cognitive-propositionalist' terms. We may drift, as McFague put it, into 'meaninglessness' or 'idolatry'. There have, however, been theories of symbols which have contributed to striking a balance. Both Paul Tillich and S.T. Coleridge in the modern period are crucial examples of such contributions. Furthermore, we shall see that there are also significant links in their theology between symbols, christology and Chalcedon.

The concern, once again, therefore, is to show that an aspect of human language about God, in this case the symbol, can most helpfully be understood in relation to Chalcedonian christology. We shall find that the 'inner logic' of the symbol exactly parallels the 'inner logic' of Chalcedonian christology. Given the close links that exist between christology and language, it is clear that the sort of pitfalls into which we might fall in understanding the way religious symbols operate can be avoided by reference to Chalcedonian christology. This is the case, as with analogy and metaphor, because human language about God is rooted in his self-revelation. In viewing symbols in the light of Chalcedon, we shall establish even more solidly the relation between language and christology.

Paul Tillich's Concept of Symbols

Concepts of the symbol have been fundamental to the thinking of many theologians in the Christian tradition for reasons which we have stated above. Dionysius the Areopagite saw the union of the 'apophatic' and 'cataphatic' ways as lying within 'symbolic theology' [24]. We turn to the theology of Paul Tillich, however, because he has been one who has spoken more than anyone else in the twentieth century of the symbolic nature of human language about and knowledge of God. For Tillich, the nature of the symbol lay at the heart of all theology and religion. More importantly than this, however, we turn to Tillich because of the interesting relation in his theology between christology and language. His understanding of the place of Christ is related to his understanding of how religious language and symbols operate.

Tillich stands in the tradition of Schleiermacher in that he rejects the Chalcedonian Definition of the Faith. He speaks of the 'inescapable definitive failure of the councils e.g. of Nicaea and Chalcedon, in spite of their substantial truth and their historical significance' (Tillich 1978b p.142). Tillich's ideal for Protestant christology is that it 'must try to find new forms in which the christological substance of the past can be expressed' (p.145). The interest here is not so much in the new roads which christology might take, in Tillich's view, but in the fact that he rejects the concepts of the councils. Speaking of the 'shortcomings of the Chalcedonian formula' (p.145), he rejects this christology primarily because of its use of the word 'nature'. He says that 'the doctrine of the two natures in the Christ raises the right question but uses wrong conceptual tools. The basic inadequacy lies in the term "nature". When applied to man it is ambiguous; when applied to God, it is wrong' (p.142). The reason behind this rejection by Tillich is predictable: he sees 'nature' as static. He says that he wishes to replace the expression 'divine nature' by such expressions as 'eternal God-man-unity' or 'Eternal God-Manhood' (p.148). He adds that:

> The uniqueness of this relation is in no way reduced by its dynamic character; but, by eliminating the concept of the 'two natures', which lie beside each other like blocks and whose unity cannot be understood at all, we are open to relational concepts which make understandable the dynamic picture of Jesus as the Christ (p.148).

These two static natures lie beside each other 'like blocks' and according to Tillich are, therefore, unrelated and unrelatable. We have seen in our discussion of φύσις that this is not the only way of understanding the word. In fact, it is in its original sense much more to do with fluidity, relationality and movement.

The key feature of interest here, however, is that because christology and language are so fundamentally related, we may expect a problem in relation to Tillich's concept of language. The interesting thing is that Tillich does not reject Chalcedon outright. He speaks of its 'substantial truth' and of it 'raising the right question' (p.142). He intends to keep the central interests of Chalcedon in focus, but in fact misunderstands Chalcedon and therefore rejects it. This in turn affects his understanding of symbols in the sense that, although he makes some of the most balanced statements concerning the nature of symbols, his overall view has been accused of drifting into a form of idealism or mysticism. Let us examine this relation between christology and language in Tillich' s thinking more closely, before looking specifically at his work on symbols.

Tillich's work in christology constitutes an attempt to reinterpret the significance of Christ in terms of the existentialist categories of Martin Heidegger. He thus uses a different conceptual and ontological scheme from the traditional one. This is the first element in his rejection of Chalcedon. He attempts to do in modern existentialist categories what the Fathers of Chalcedon did in the categories available to them. Thus, he is not simply rejecting Chalcedon, but attempting to reinterpret it. He is fully aware of the dangers which loom in christology:

> The two dangers which threaten every christological statement are immediate consequences of the assertion that Jesus is the Christ. The attempt to interpret this assertion conceptually can lead to an actual denial of the Christ-character of Jesus as the Christ; or it can lead to an actual denial of the Jesus-character of Jesus as the Christ. Christology must always find its way on the ridge between these two chasms, and it must know that it will never completely succeed, inasmuch as it touches the divine mystery, which remains mystery even in its manifestation (p.142).

In spite of this awareness, however, it is widely recognized, and Tillich himself is clear enough about some aspects of this, that the 'Jesus-character' of his christology is undermined, in spite of all his concerns to discuss this and to do justice to it.

This feature of Tillich's christology is easily illustrated from his discussions concerning the significance of historical studies concerning Jesus of Nazareth. He is concerned that these be taken seriously, but his conclusion is that matters of this order, that is the historical, cannot ultimately affect belief in Jesus as the Christ. He discusses this in relation to his concepts of the Cross and Resurrection as symbols:

> The attempt has been made to describe both events, the Cross and

the Resurrection, as factual events separated from their symbolic meaning. This is justified, in so far as the significance of both symbols rests on the combination of symbol and fact. Without the factual element, the Christ would not have participated in existence and consequently not have been the Christ. But the desire to isolate the factual from the symbolic element is...not a primary interest of faith. The results of the research for the purely factual element can never be on the basis of faith or theology (p.154).

The final comment here gives the impression that there is a chink of light between the two things Tillich is trying to unite: faith and history. It is perhaps clearer when he says that 'no historical criticism can question the immediate awareness of those who find themselves transformed into the state of faith' (p.114). The point is that Tillich's Christology drifts into an undermining of the humanity of Christ and of the historical dimension of faith.

The concern here is whether this also happens in Tillich's understanding of language or, more particularly, symbols. As with his christology, there is every attempt to avoid this. Most of the time his statements concerning the way we should understand symbols balance the elements of the human and the divine extremely well. Once again, however, there is a tendency to undermine the empirical element, in order to avoid idolatry, and to drift into Platonism. Let us now examine Tillich's understanding of symbols in some detail, with this weakness in mind.

For Tillich, symbols are firmly rooted in and arise out of the revelation of the infinite in the finite. He calls the tension which arises within this revelation 'correlation' and speaks of the 'principle of correlation' [25]. It is because of this tensive element at the centre of the relation between God and humanity that symbols are required. They are demanded by the inner relation between God and humanity and arise out of it. This tensive relation results in the need for tensive language. The tensive language is constituted by symbols. Thus, for Tillich, symbols lie at the heart of all theology and experience of God. Although he changed his mind during his life as to whether there could be any non-symbolic language about God, he was never in any doubt that there must be symbolic language in relation to God [26].

Tillich's various discussions of symbols by no means leave us with a watertight theory. We have observed that this is not really what is required. However, he does contribute many shafts of insight which illuminate the way symbols work. In his short work *Dynamics of Faith*, Tillich's view of symbols is exposed at its best, although of course it permeates his thinking in all of his works, especially in the *Systematic Theology*. His understanding of religious symbols has its background in his understanding of symbols in general and in *Dynamics of Faith* Tillich outlines six characteristics of the symbol, all of which revolve around the crucial and yet confusing distinction between a symbol and a sign. This distinction, therefore, forms our point of entry into Tillich's understanding of symbols. According to Tillich, the symbol and the sign are radically different and yet they have one fundamental thing in common. This common element, which forms the first characteristic of symbols, is that they both 'point beyond themselves to something else' (Tillich 1957 p.41). After this, however, symbols and signs part company.

The distinction between sign and symbol is basically that signs are conventional whilst symbols are natural. That is to say that whilst signs get their meaning through convention and agreement within society, the symbol tells us more because it 'participates in that to which it points' (p.42). This forms the second characteristic of symbols and Tillich's key example is the national flag. A traffic sign, for example, points beyond itself, but is only successful as a sign in so far as its use is agreed upon by those in the society in which it operates. Furthermore, the traffic sign can be changed by agreement and another sign, meaning the same thing, put in its place. This can occur, in Tillich's view, without any change of reference. The thing pointed to, the reaction which is provoked by the road sign remains the same. The flag, on the other hand, not only points beyond itself to the nation, but also participates in the nation, as is illustrated by the fact that an assault on the flag comprises an assault on the nation. The only way in which a national flag might be changed is through a national catastrophe, but that would in any case constitute a change in the reality of the nation symbolized. Thus, Tillich says, 'Decisive is the fact that signs do not participate in the reality of that to which they point, whilst symbols do' (p.42).

Tillich's third and fourth characteristics of symbol form the two sides of a coin, one subjective, the other objective. First, a symbol 'opens up levels of reality which otherwise are closed for us' (p.42). Secondly, the symbol, and indeed all the arts, 'unlocks dimensions and elements of our soul which correspond to dimensions and elements of reality' (p.42). Here we see, on the one hand the rootedness of the symbol in the realm of the reality in which it participates and on the other hand its rootedness in the perceiver. The final two characteristics of the symbol also hang together. First, 'symbols cannot be produced intentionally...they grow out of the individual or collective unconscious...' (p.43), and secondly, '...symbols cannot be invented. Like living beings, they grow and die' (p.43). It is clear from these final characteristics that Tillich believes that symbols have a life of their own and in this sense we can see once again the contrast with the sign which does not.

It is clear that outside Tillich's system the words 'sign' and 'symbol' are frequently used interchangeably. In mathematics, for example, the word 'symbol' is often used for what Tillich would want to call only a sign. Aristotle uses 'symbol' to mean simply a pointer without participation, whilst Aquinas uses 'sign' to indicate participation in the thing signified [27]. Whichever word is used, the key thing here is that there is a distinction relating to the way these phenomena actually work. Tillich's contrasts between signs and symbols are based on the conviction that whilst symbols have a power of their own, are specific and cannot be replaced, signs are conventional, arbitrary and can be replaced.

In his work *Theology of Culture*, Tillich makes this point emphatically, stressing also that each symbol is unique and irreplaceable. He says:

Every symbol has a special function which is just *it* and cannot be replaced by more or less adequate symbols. This is different from signs, for signs can always be replaced. If one finds that a green light is not so expedient as perhaps a blue light (this is not true, but could be true), then we simply put on a blue light, and nothing is changed. But a symbolic word (such as the word 'God) cannot be replaced. No symbol can be replaced when used in its special function. So one asks rightly, 'How do symbols arise, and how do they come to an end?' As different from signs, symbols are born and die. Signs are consciously invented and removed. This is a fundamental difference (Tillich 1959 p.57).

Thus, Tillich uses the words 'sign' and 'symbol' in these ways in order to make the central distinction.

These elements of Tillich's understanding of general symbols as opposed to signs bring us more specifically to the question of the way in which religious symbols operate. All that has been said about symbols in general, of course, remains the same. Religious symbols participate in what they symbolize, open up levels of reality and so on. With religious symbols, however, we are specifically concerned with opening up levels of ultimate reality or of 'being-itself'. This makes the symbol the primary mode of religious language. Whereas it is true for Tillich that all statements made outside the context of 'ultimate concern' are meaningless, it is also true that all statements about 'being-itself', because they are about the ultimate, are symbolic.

In his article 'The Religious Symbol', Tillich draws attention to a number of characteristics of specifically religious symbols. First, they have a 'figurative quality', that is, something is symbolized by and in them. Second, they have 'perceptibility', that is, something invisible is made perceptible by the symbol and is given objectivity by the symbol. Third, it has 'innate power'. This is the most important characteristic of the religious symbol, distinguishing it, as it does, from the sign. Once again we are reminded that any symbol participates in what it symbolizes. Finally, the religious symbol has 'acceptability', that is, it is rooted in and supported by the social situation in which it functions. It is important to note that in the context of the society in which a symbol functions, the meaning and the status of an object, word or concept as a symbol, belongs together with its acceptance as such. It is not the case that a thing is first a symbol and then gains acceptability. Rather, symbols arise through use and common acceptance. They come into common currency and are then acknowledged as symbols. The acceptance of symbols and their status as symbols run together. This, of course, is not so true of a symbol like the cross which has been of central significance from the beginning of Christianity, although certainly where that symbol has ceased to be accepted as a symbol, it no longer is one.

Because it is concerned with 'being-itself' or 'the ultimate', theology needs symbols in order to be able to speak about the infinite at all. Purely literal articulation of the ultimate is not adequate and it is here that we encounter the heart of what it is that Tillich claims concerning religious symbols, namely that the symbol is able to articulate something which the sign and ordinary or literal language cannot. Symbols articulate the ultimate more adequately because they are able to avoid literalism and idolatry. Religious symbols, therefore, are the locus of special articulation of the ultimate and are also, therefore, the locus of revelation. Anything, in principle, could be a symbol of being-itself, although it is important to stress that God's action is, for Tillich, an important part of the creation of a religious symbol. Tillich is somewhat unclear here as he sometimes indicates that symbols emerge from within humanity, from the collective unconscious, and at other times he implies that God's action is crucial in the establishment of a symbol. God is the 'Ground of Being' and everything participates in God so that there is a unity here between being-itself and the human creative unconscious. In any case, the symbol is the medium through which all articulation of the divine must be made.

This emphasis on the importance of the symbol and its rootedness in what it is speaking of or articulating, brings us to our particular point of interest. It is here that Tillich himself relates his understanding of the symbol particularly to christology. In symbols of 'being-itself' he is clear that there must be an inherent tensive quality if justice is to be done. He says that 'one can only speak of the ultimate in a language which at the same time denies the possibility of speaking about it' (Tillich 1957 p.61). The symbol, therefore, finds its identity in the fact that it speaks both positively and negatively of the ultimate. It is an assertion and also a denial of that about which it speaks. This tensive element in the symbol means that we are never to view a symbol about the ultimate as actually being the ultimate. We are never to reduce the ultimate to the symbol of the ultimate. The ultimate can never become purely finite or empirical. Tillich says that 'a real symbol points to an object which never can become an object. Religious symbols represent the transcendent but do not make the transcendent immanent. They do not make God a part of the empirical world' (Tillich 1962 p.303). By this, Tillich does not mean that the symbol does not make God known in the world. Rather, he means that the symbol does not reduce God to the empirical order.

It can be seen that we have here the exact parallel to our patterns in christology and, as we have said, Tillich links his understanding of symbols especially with his christology. The main symbol of all for Tillich is the cross of Christ. This is obviously a religious symbol in that it qualifies in all the ways of which Tillich has spoken. It points beyond itself, participates in what it symbolizes and so on. It is here that we have the symbol of all symbols, however, because of its inherent dynamic. More than other symbols it is a simultaneous affirmation and denial. The cross negates its finitude and yet remains finite. That is, on the cross, Jesus' self-denial is also an affirmation by God. For Tillich, being-itself is manifest on the cross and has sacrificed its own finitude. Mondin puts the matter succinctly when he says that for Tillich 'the cross has two outstanding characteristics, maintenance of unity with God and complete self-denial' (Mondin 1963 p.135).

The question of balance here is obviously crucial. It arises in Tillich's discussions in terms of 'adequacy' and 'idolatry'. These two features are central to Tillich's concept of the truth or falsity of religious symbols of which the cross is typical. The criterion of 'adequacy' maintains that a symbol must in fact open up levels of reality, otherwise it has ceased to be a symbol. A religious symbol must open up the ultimate, being-itself, if it is to be acknowledged as a religious symbol at all. We have seen that religious symbols may grow and die and the possibility with religious symbols is that they will, with the passage of time or the change of culture, become dead symbols. Tillich argues that:

The relation of man to the ultimate undergoes changes. Contents of ultimate concern vanish or are replaced by others. A divine figure ceases to create reply, it ceases to be a common symbol and loses its power to move for action. Symbols which for a certain period, or in a certain place, expressed truth of faith for a certain group now only remind of the faith of the past. They have lost their truth, and it is an open question whether dead symbols can be revived. Probably not for those to whom they have died! (Tillich 1957 p.96).

The point here is that in certain circumstances symbols might die. Their test of life is that they remain adequate to 'being-itself' by sustaining the tensive quality. The cross of Christ maintains this tensive element most adequately.

The question of 'idolatry' is even more central to Tillich's understanding of symbols and is continuous with 'adequacy'. If a religious symbol becomes inadequate, for whatever reason, then it will have been treated as an idol and will have 'died'. When a symbol functions as an idol, the situation is one of the utmost seriousness. The symbol retains its innate power even when it is used in an idolatrous manner. When this occurs, the symbol has become demonic, an inversion of its true nature. Idolatry arises when the symbol is regarded as the ultimate, or to put the matter differently, when the ultimate has been reduced to the symbol. Tillich draws attention to Calvin's comment that 'the human mind is a continuously working factory of idols' (p.97). He is well aware that the line between faith and idolatry is extremely thin and that there is always a tendency in all religion to slip into idolatry. This tendency in religion to invert the real nature of the symbol has the effect of subverting the ultimate and unleashing the demonic. Adequacy and idolatry are related in that the symbol must always be seen as both an affirmation and a denial. Tillich says:

> Every type of faith has the tendency to elevate its concrete symbols to absolute validity. The criterion of the truth of faith, therefore, is that it implies an element of self-negation. That symbol is most adequate which expresses not only the ultimate but also its own lack of ultimacy (p.97).

Mondin draws attention to the threats which arise when symbols are misused. These are idolatry and mysticism. He says:

> The evil of idolatry is so common because symbols, by participating in that to which they point, have the tendency to replace that to which they are supposed to point and to become ultimate in themselves. All idolatry is nothing else than the absolutizing of symbols of the Holy and making them identical with the Holy itself (Mondin 1963 p.141).

and later, on mysticism:

> Mysticism criticises the demonically distorted symbols by devaluating every medium of revelation of the ground of being and by trying to unite the soul directly with the Holy, to make it enter the mystery of God without the help of any finite symbolic material (p.142).

Thus, the use of a religious symbol has become idolatrous when the 'symbolizandum', or the thing symbolized, in this case God or 'being-itself' has been reduced to the symbol. The symbolic has given way to the mystical when it is thought that the symbol is no longer necessary in knowing and speaking of God. The entire project, therefore, in the use of religious symbols, is to find a balanced use and understanding which keeps the balance of affirmation and denial, of unity and distinction. Where this has been lost, the divine itself has been lost.

The concern here is with just how successfully Tillich avoids these two elements of idolatry and mysticism. It is true that on most occasions he is overwhelmingly concerned to achieve a balanced understanding. Statements such as the following seem adequate:

> There can be no doubt that any concrete assertion about God must be symbolic, for a concrete assertion is one which uses a segment of finite experience in order to say something about him. It transcends the content of this segment, although it also includes it. The segment of finite reality which becomes the vehicle of a concrete assertion about God is affirmed and negated at the same time. It becomes a symbol, for a symbolic expression is one whose proper meaning is negated by that to which it points. And yet it also is affirmed by it, and this affirmation gives the symbolic expression an adequate basis for pointing beyond itself (Tillich 1978a p.239).

and:

> Religious symbols are double-edged. They are directed toward the

infinite which they symbolize *and* toward the finite through which they symbolize it. They force the infinite down to finitude and the finite up to infinity. They open the divine for the human and the human for the divine (p.240).

On other occasions, however, the balance does not seem so adequate and Tillich seems to drift into a tendency to underestimate the concrete element. Indeed, he has often been accused of mysticism and Platonism. This is perhaps most obvious when he is attempting to stave off idolatry. He says:

Holiness cannot become actual except through holy 'objects'. But holy objects are not holy in and of themselves. They are holy only by negating themselves in pointing to the divine of which they are the mediums. If they establish themselves as holy, they become demonic. They still are 'holy', but their holiness is antidivine. A nation which looks upon itself as holy is correct in so far as everything can become a vehicle of man's ultimate concern, but the nation is incorrect in so far as it considers itself to be inherently holy. Innumerable things, all things in a way, have the power of becoming holy in a mediate sense. They can point to something beyond themselves. But, if their holiness comes to be considered inherent, it becomes demonic. This happens continually in the actual life of most religions. The representations of man's ultimate concern - holy objects - tend to become his ultimate concern. They are transformed into idols. Holiness provokes idolatry (p.216).

The element throughout Tillich's discussions of 'pointing beyond', alongside the constant intention to avoid idolatry suggests that there is an overall 'drift' here into undermining the empirical element.

In conclusion, there are two essential points. First, Tillich's understanding of religious symbols is fundamentally linked to his understanding of christology. The link which we have seen to be so crucial elsewhere is once again extremely important. The link in Tillich's case involves a weakness. The tendency to undermine the historical and human aspects in his christology is linked with a tendency to do the same in his view of language. This is not something which Tillich does constantly, but is a drift of his whole system. The rejection of Chalcedonian christology is typical of this. Secondly, Tillich's discussions of symbols show that he has articulated very clearly on many occasions the central tensive quality which is crucial if justice is to be done to what is being symbolized. The aspects of unity and distinction or of affirmation and denial are exactly what we find in the Chalcedonian christology. It is clear, therefore, that the symbolic language we use of God, as with analogy and metaphor, has to do with the same features which we find in christology. It has to do with the relation between humanity and divinity. Because of this central connection we can see that viewing symbols in the light of Chalcedon will enable the most adequate notion of religious symbols to emerge.

We have seen that Tillich's discussion of symbols provides us with some fundamental insights into the way 'symbolic' language about God works. His contribution in pointing to the simultaneous 'is and is not', the unity and yet the distinction between the symbol and the symbolized, is absolutely crucial and is fully continuous with the 'inner logic' of metaphor which we saw earlier. Once again, we have seen that language and christology are thoroughly related. The weakness in Tillich, however, lies in his tendency to drift, in both his christology and his notion of symbols, into mysticism or Platonism. Where there are problems with Tillich's views, the situation can be improved in the light of Chalcedonian christology. With this in mind, let us now turn to consider the contribution of S.T. Coleridge in order to illustrate the case even further.

Coleridge's Understanding of Symbols

In turning to Coleridge, we turn back to the source of much modern thinking on the symbol. J.S. Mill, in the nineteenth century, called Coleridge 'the most systematic thinker of our time' (McFarland 1969 p.xxvi) and we shall find in his thinking a great deal to underline the connection which we have already observed between language and christology. For Coleridge, 'symbol' is a word used specifically in relation to language in general and not to empirical objects as in Tillich. Although he does not overtly refer to Chalcedonian christology in relation to symbols, Coleridge's view of symbols is, nevertheless, centred on the finely balanced 'reconciliation of opposites' and on the notion of the 'translucence of the eternal in the temporal'. Coleridge is concerned with the relation between the human and the divine and the links between language and christology are once again clear. Furthermore, in Coleridge's contribution, the roots of the links between human language of God and human knowledge of God are laid bare.

Coleridge does not develop a consistent 'theory' of symbols. The references to symbols in his works are diverse, fragmentary and incomplete. In spite of this he frequently puts his finger on the nerve centre of the symbolic nature of the human speaking and knowing processes. In this sense he is thorough and consistent. It is interesting that Coleridge himself was reared in the tradition which rejected metaphor as a decoration of the literal. His concern, however, was to rid us of such distinctions. In a letter to William Godwin in 1800 he wrote: '...I would endeavour to destroy the old antithesis of *Words and Things*, elevating, as it were, Words into Things, and living Things too' (Griggs 1956 p.626). It was in his understanding of symbol that he articulated this 'elevation of Words into Things' or, as he also called it, the fusion of opposites. In the *Biographia Literaria* he uses a word which epitomizes his view. From the Greek words εἰς ἕν πλάττειν (eis hen plattein: to shape into one), we find the Coleridgean word 'esemplastic' (Coleridge 1907 I,X,p.107), signifying the activity of the human mind as it unifies the diversities of its experience through perception and speech. It is this 'esemplasticity' which lies at the heart of Coleridge's understanding of symbols. They 'shape into one' what is also diverse.

In the *The Statesman's Manual*, in relation to a proper understanding of scripture, Coleridge makes the following distinctions and says what he understands a symbol to be:

It is among the miseries of the present age that it recognizes no *medium* between literal and metaphorical. Faith is either to be buried in the dead letter, or its name and honours usurped by a counterfeit product of the mechanical understanding, which in the blindness of self-complacency confounds symbols with allegories. Now an allegory is but a translation of abstract notions into a picture-language, which is itself nothing but an abstraction from objects of the senses; the principal being more worthless even than its phantom proxy, both alike unsubstantial, and the former shapeless to boot. On the other hand a symbol (ho estin aei tautegorikon) is characterized by a translucence of the special in the individual, or of the general in the special, or of the universal in the general; above all by the translucence of the eternal through and in the temporal. It always partakes of the reality which it renders intelligible; and while it enunciates the whole, abides itself as a living part in that unity of which it is the representative (Coleridge 1853 p.437).

This general principle of what a symbol is lies at the heart of all of Coleridge's utterances about the symbolic. As with Tillich, we have the emphasis on 'partaking of the reality which it renders intelligible'. This basic unity is the most important element of the symbol. Coleridge's use of the word 'translucence' here, however, is even more important. It is not simply a case of having unity with the thing symbolized. That unity is one of 'translucence'. This word captures, as does Coleridge's other word 'fusion', the essence of his concept of symbol. It is a merging of two elements into a single duality. However, we are not to think here of 'fusing' into one reality, but of the uniting of two distinct elements which remain distinct within the unity. The element of 'unity in distinction' is preserved in these words 'fusion' and 'translucence'.

We cannot understand Coleridge's concept of Symbol without fully taking into account his notion of the make-up of our perceptive faculties. We shall look at this in detail in our section on knowledge in Part Three. However, we need to lay the foundations here in order to understand what he says about symbols. It is because the symbol is rooted in these knowing processes that it is so crucial. Here in the symbol, in fact, knowing and perceiving are one. Coleridge's overriding concern was with the relation between the subject and the object in the human knowing processes. He was concerned, therefore, above all, with the business of the unity and reconciliation of opposites or of diversity within our perception. For him, the main concern was with the relation between the 'many and the one'. For Coleridge, man's place in nature, made as he is in the image of God, is one of both participation in nature and distinction from nature. The relation between these two elements and the search for the relation between the 'many and the one', therefore, constituted a large part of Coleridge's search for truth and it is with the balancing of these elements that so much of his writing is concerned.

Coleridge was convinced that although man contributes to what he knows in the world, yet he does truly know things as they are in themselves and as they come to him. In his poem 'The Eolian Harp', he speaks of the 'one life within us and abroad' (Coleridge 1912 p.101). Stressing the unity of human perception, he speaks of the interplay between Understanding, Reason, Ideas and Imagination. The understanding is that faculty of the mind which arranges and sorts phenomena in relation to sense-perception. It is what we now mean by 'reasoning' and for Coleridge has the characteristic of clarity, but is lacking in depth. Reason, for Coleridge, is related to understanding but also distinct from it. Reason is a unifying element, distinguishing us from the animals. It is not discursive like understanding, but unifies experience at the spiritual level. Moreover, reason is closely identified with the soul, with the divine, with God. Here we find an extremely close relation between the human and the divine. Here is the crucial link between the processes of human knowing and God himself.

Ideas, for Coleridge, are closely related to reason. These too are unifying elements. It is through ideas that the mind truly knows things in the world. Ideas are not merely regulative, but are creative phenomena which also tell us about things in themselves. The 'idea' also has unity with God. It is part of the crucial link between God and his creation. There is a congruence and affinity between God and humanity within these processes of perceiving and knowing. Basically, the ideas which men have are 'fused' with the supreme idea or reason which is God. God and humanity are 'fused' into unity through reason or the Λόγος. Here is the crucial link also with christology, the relation between humanity and the Λόγος.

It is when we turn to the imagination in Coleridge's thinking, however, that we find the heart of his notion of perceiving and knowing. It is in the imagination that the unifying elements in the whole process come together. Coleridge says that the imagination is 'a repetition in the finite mind of the eternal act of creation in the infinite I AM' (Coleridge 1907 I,XIII,p.202). The imagination is the key unifying element with which humanity recreates the creation in imitation of God. This faculty of knowing unifies the other dimensions and unifies the knower with the known. For Coleridge it is 'the living Power and prime Agent of all human Perception' (p.202).

The imagination, then, is that faculty of the mind which forms the heart of the way we know things. It is unifying in the sense that it brings into unity the diverse elements of experience. Through the imagination the many are brought into unity in the one. Thus, Coleridge says that the imagination 'reveals itself in the balance or reconciliation of opposite or discordant qualities: of sameness, with difference; of the general, with the concrete; the idea, with the image; the individual, with the representative...' (Coleridge 1907 II,XIV,p.12). It is the faculty which unites the diverse features of our perception and fuses the 'many into the one'. Human perception, active and passive as it is, produces imitations of the divine through the imagination. These imitations are places of revelation and form the basis of the concept of the symbol in Coleridge's thinking.

It is into this context that Coleridge's notion of symbol falls. Only through looking at his notion of the way human knowledge works can we fully appreciate what he means by 'symbol'. For Coleridge anything, even nature herself, could be said to be a symbol. This takes us to the heart of the importance of this notion for Coleridge. The same thing was true for Tillich. For both men, the creation itself as the place of the revelation of God could be said to be a symbol, if by symbol we mean that which 'partakes in what it symbolizes'. For Coleridge, apparently diverse aspects of experience could be said to be symbols. Nature herself, the biblical narrative, mathematics or geometry, art and the whole of language. These all qualify as symbols because of the one general principle which gives them their identity, that is that they are the places where the diversity of our experience becomes unified into a single whole. They are features of experience which are 'characterized by a translucence of the special in the individual, or of the general in the special, or of the universal in the general' (Coleridge 1853 p.437). This, more than any fuller theory of symbols, is Coleridge's overriding insight.

For Coleridge the symbol is the highest possible form of perceiving and knowing because it is continuous with God himself. He says that 'an IDEA, in the *highest* sense of that word, cannot be conveyed but by a *symbol*' (Coleridge 1907 I,IX,p.100). The symbol is a conductor of the unity which exists between God and the world. In this context it is important to note that the symbol, as in narrative or in art, is not a copy of nature, but an imitation or a presentation of the unity between God and the world. This distinction is crucial. A 'copy' loses the unity between the original and the copy. The imitation is the vehicle of continuity. The symbol for Coleridge sustains the essential unity and in this sense 'presents' that unity.

The place of symbols as the unifying element of all perceiving and knowing clearly puts them at the heart of Coleridge's concept of speaking about God. Where the 'translucence' or 'fusion' or the balance between the two elements has been lost, then we have no symbol and we certainly have no speaking about God. It is important, however, that we are clear as to Coleridge's intention when he speaks of 'translucence' and 'fusion'. Clearly the two words have the sense of duality in unity. They retain the sense of a distinction even after the unification has occurred. In Coleridge's poem 'The Destiny of Nations', he speaks of the freedom given to us when we see God through the sensible world. The divine reality is seen 'effulgent, as through clouds that veil his blaze' and we learn the 'substance from its shadow' (Coleridge 1912 p.132). We are not to turn away from the shadow in order to find the substance, but we learn the 'substance from its shadow'. The view here is clearly that God is known through the world of the senses, through the creation. The unifying mind, through its creative and symbolic perception, perceives the divine through 'a translucence of the Special in the Individual'.

A further illustration of how Coleridge unites his concepts of the human and the divine can be found in his attitude to faith and history. We saw that Tillich ultimately drifted in the direction of separation of the elements here and that, for all his talk of tension in symbols, he let go of the concrete or historical in relation to the historical Jesus. Coleridge was more successful. In his *Aids to Reflection*, in relation to the Genesis account of the Fall of Adam, the question is raised as to whether this can be understood as history as well as symbol. Coleridge's reply is that it must be both at once because a symbol is 'a sign included in the idea which it represents; that is, an actual part chosen to represent the whole' (Coleridge 1853 p.270). The point here is clear: that Coleridge is concerned to see history as an essential part of what a symbol is and how it has its meaning. In this, his concern is indeed to unite the otherwise diverse elements and he achieves this where Tillich did not.

A final point is of particular interest to us. Coleridge does not explicitly relate his notions of the symbol to Chalcedonian christology, although of course later in his life he rooted such notions in the relations of the Trinity. It is interesting, however, to note his use of two specific words here: 'consubstantial' and ὁμοούσιος. He says of symbols that they are 'harmonious in themselves, and consubstantial with the truths of which they are the conductors' (Coleridge 1853 p.436). Furthermore, on one occasion, in his unpublished Notebook 35, an interest in the word ὁμοούσιος arises. Coleridge speaks of the 'dear lucky *homoousios*, that had set all Christendom by the ears' (J.R. Barth 1977 p.11). He does not make the links that we are making here overtly, however, and the use of such words as 'consubstantial' and ὁμοούσιος can signify a potential drift into pantheism unless they are properly checked. Once again, however, our case here is supported. Chalcedonian christology exposes the issues more fully and secures a balanced relation of the elements.

We can now see that in Coleridge we have a prime example for our case. The links between christology and language are once again appearing. Here we have the 'translucence of the eternal in and through the temporal'. The language is based in the relation which also lies at the heart of the christology. The christology allows a balanced understanding of symbol which is itself thoroughly part of the christology and is constituted by translucence, fusion and a 'distinction in unity'. It seems clear from this that, in a very positive way, we have firm support for the argument: the Chalcedonian Definition, articulating as it does the unity of the human and the divine, and yet their simultaneous distinction, can enable a much more adequate understanding of human language about God.

Symbols and Christology

There are many concepts of 'symbol'. We have seen that the key aspect of symbol is the coming together of two elements into unity. Human language and experience are made up of symbols and we are inherently symbol-makers in every realm of our lives. Religious consciousness is especially saturated in symbols of different sorts. Clearly symbols lie at the heart of human talk about God and knowledge of God. The concern here has been to discern a way in which the pitfalls in understanding human language about God might be avoided. The problems articulated by Lindbeck and McFague have been especially in mind. We would avoid seeing symbols either as mere expressions of human emotion or as objects of worship which we treat ultimately as idols. We have found, through our brief study of symbol in Tillich and Coleridge, that the two elements which are 'thrown together' in a symbol relate in a certain 'tensive' way. The symbol is in union with what it symbolizes, but there is also a distinction.

The conclusions here are twofold. First, that symbols operate on an inner dynamic which contains both unity with, and distinction from, the reality which they symbolize. Tillich's emphasis on the 'double-edged' nature of symbol and Coleridge's more finally balanced 'translucence' or 'fusion' of the two elements, constitute the 'inner logic' of the symbol. This now confirms the argument that human language about God is best seen in the light of the Chalcedonian Definition. Through use of this christology, the essential features of the religious symbol are guarded. Secondly, and supporting this, it is the case that the 'fine tuning' of a notion of the symbol was related in both Tillich and Coleridge to christology. Tillich's rejection of Chalcedon was symptomatic of his drift into Platonism and mysticism. A reassessment of Chalcedon would certainly improve things here. Coleridge's emphasis on the 'translucence of the eternal in and through the temporal', especially supports the case that because language and christology are so fundamentally related, the Chalcedonian Definition provides an appropriate central paradigm for understanding both symbols and human language about God generally.

Christology and the Inner Logic of Language

At the end of Part One we saw how the christology of Chalcedon forms a highly appropriate manner in which to view human language about God. The link between christology and language was clear enough. What was required was a view of language which held on to the ontological roots which Lindbeck had lost and which gave the language the objective rootedness which McFague had let go. We saw that the 'is and is not' which McFague rightly acknowledged as the heart of theological language could be found in the christology of Chalcedon. The two models of unity and distinction had come together to form the 'inner logic of christology', that is, its essentially tensive inner quality. Furthermore, we saw that both christology and language were rooted in the revelation of God.

In Part Two we related this 'inner logic of christology' more specifically to language. Three crucial phenomena in human language, difficult to define, but nevertheless forming the most important aspects of theological naming, are analogy, metaphor and symbol. We examined these phenomena and noted the inner workings of them all. When human beings speak about God, it is clear that there are essential differences between such language, on the one hand, and language about phenomena within the world, on the other. With God we are dealing with a reality which is not a phenomenon within the world. There are, therefore, bound to be differences. When speaking of God we are 'speaking of one thing in terms of another'. We do, however, genuinely speak of God and we do so in analogies, metaphors and symbols common to our general language use. Herein lies the central tension within the human-divine relation.

In examining these three ways we found that Chalcedonian christology was crucial in ironing out problems at the very heart of things. In relation to Aquinas' notions of analogy, we saw that the two views, proportion and proportionality, never came together adequately in his thinking. He did not relate his notions of human language specifically to his christology. However, Chalcedonian christology enabled us to see how these two need to be brought together if the essential tension, which Thomas is indeed attempting to identify, is to be allowed its full significance. Thus, the *proportio* notion of analogy is characterized by likeness, similarity and continuity. This is essentially the positive element, or the feature stressing unity. The second notion, *proportionalitas*, involves only similarity of proportions and into this is built ultimate distinction or difference. Chalcedonian christology, however, brings these together into the tensive 'difference in unity' pattern which characterizes the christology to which human language about God is inherently related.

The examination of metaphors and models showed that these lie at the heart of human language, especially language about God. Discussions of metaphor have not been carried out in relation to christology and for most of the western tradition the real power of metaphor has been almost completely overlooked in philosophy. Metaphors have been seen merely as the 'perfect cheats' of the rhetorical tradition. However, we found that in metaphor especially there is the inner tension of 'is and is not'. There are of course still many views of metaphor but we have found that Chalcedonian christology enabled us to identify just how adequate these views were. Thus, views which stressed only the decorative or the functional role of metaphor could be seen to be slipping into some of the very problems we have been trying to avoid.

In finer detail also, views which see metaphor as 'comparison' or as 'ambiguous', or which tend to separate the two elements in metaphor or unite them, have been seen to be lacking. Even those who have attempted to bring out the very tensive element which is so central have sometimes failed to sustain their case. Chalcedon, however, has enabled us to focus on the essential tension within metaphor: that is, the *simultaneous* 'distinction in unity' of the elements. Similar value was found in Chalcedonian christology when we came to discuss models. Again, it provided the required 'is and is not' dynamic, giving models their ontological rooting in addition to their revisability. Because language and christology are inherently continuous with each other, Chalcedon has enabled us to come to a more satisfactory notion of how theological language works.

Finally, in relation to symbols, which can be either solid objects, events or language within narrative, we found exactly the same 'inner logic'. Tillich's discussion of symbols has both insights and weaknesses. His basic insight that the symbol has both negative and positive features, that it negates its own positive significance and must do so if idolatry is to be avoided, provided us with some essential insights into the nature of symbols. His attempt is to articulate the basic tension of which we are speaking. However, although Tillich does relate symbols to the cross, it is important to note that his dissatisfaction with Chalcedonian christology leaves his notion of symbols and language tending in the direction of idealism. It was with Coleridge, for whom the notion of symbol comprises our basic language, produced from the realms of the imagination, that we found the most balanced notion of symbol. Coleridge speaks of the 'reconciliation of opposites', of the 'translucence' of the two elements and of the 'fusion' of the mind with the reality which it knows. It is the symbol which comprises the unity of the 'many in the one' for Coleridge and all of these features constitute the 'inner logic' of the symbol.

In all, we have found in this section that the Chalcedonian Definition enables a notion of 'unity and distinction' in the elements within theological language, to emerge clearly. The ontological rootedness within the revelation of God is combined with the 'human' side, acknowledging inadequacy and openness to change. Where these elements are already articulated, as for example in Tillich's notion of symbol, Chalcedon enables the ironing out of inadequacies. The inherent 'is and is not' which lies at the heart of Chalcedonian christology lies also at the heart of human language about the God who is revealed in Jesus Christ. Chalcedonian christology, therefore, offers the most fruitful light in which to view human language about the God whom we know in revelation, but who is also hidden from us in that revelation. We have now seen this in relation to analogy, metaphor and symbol.

In Part One we noted that the problem of human language about God brings with it problems relating to human knowledge. Any view of language presupposes or implies an epistemology. We turn now, therefore, in Part Three to an examination of the epistemology which lies within the Chalcedonian notion of theological language which we have developed in Part Two.

Part Three:
The Inner Logic
of Knowledge

'Where is the wisdom we have lost in knowledge?
Where is the knowledge we have lost in information?'
 T.S. Eliot, *Choruses from 'The Rock'*.

VI

LANGUAGE AND KNOWLEDGE

Introduction

The opening question in Part One concerned the problem of how we are to speak about the God who is both known to us and yet also hidden from us. We noted how Dionysius the Areopagite pointed out the difficulties which arise when we try to speak of one who is both incomprehensible and yet also known to us. Dionysius observed that, although God is incomprehensible, we do in fact name him in a riddle. He cited the Sinai theophany in which God is known in revelation and bears the name 'I am that I am'. We have stressed that within the context of the revelation of God in Jesus Christ, there is an inbuilt tension which demands that we speak of God in such riddles. We have seen that the most adequate language for speaking about God is metaphorical language. We have traced the 'inner logic' of both christology and language and have shown them to be inherently connected. We have illustrated how, if fundamental changes are made in one of these areas, there will be very significant changes brought about in the other. Thus, we have seen that in the patristic and the modern debates concerning the person of Christ, language and christology are inherently connected. We have also seen the need for a greater emphasis on christology in Aquinas' discussion of human language about God.

We have seen that the problems raised in christology are concerned with the relation between the human and the divine. The Chalcedonian Definition of the Faith, viewed through Ephraim of Antioch's understanding of ἐνυπόστατος provided a way of articulating the relation between the two elements in christology. We have argued that this Definition also provides a way forward for understanding theological language. The initial question, however, concerned both speaking about and knowing the God who is different from us. Karl Barth made the point that 'christology is the touchstone of all knowledge of God in the Christian sense, the touchstone of all theology' and went on to say that here in christology all things become 'bright or dark' (Barth 1949 p.66). As with language, so with knowledge, we find that christology is central in that the divine-human relation is once again of paramount importance.

Knowledge, language and christology, then, are inherently related. Indeed, for Christian theology they are inseparable. We approached the question of language first because of its more general and immediate nature. Gadamer has emphasized the intimate relation which exists between language and thought and it is clear that behind all views of language there are notions of knowledge. All language presupposes and implies a view of knowledge and this is certainly true in relation to language about God. The question of knowledge or epistemology must, therefore, now be examined. We shall see that knowledge generally and especially knowledge of God, operates in a manner which is well in tune with the 'inner logic' of Chalcedon.

The concern in epistemology, as in christology and language, will be to identify specific 'patterns'. We shall find that patterns exactly parallel to those in the other areas operate also in the realm of epistemology. Once again the basic concern is with the relation between the human and the divine. In terms of epistemology this will be approached in relation to the 'knower and the known', that is, the knowing human mind and the phenomenon it knows. Once again we shall find that concepts of knowing have been dominated by dualisms or 'distinctions' between the two elements. We shall also find, however, that the pattern of 'unity' or of clear and distinct knowing has played a dominant part. The interesting feature here is that the two patterns with which we have been concerned throughout, that of unity and that of distinction, have often coincided, but in a totally inadequate manner. Distinctions between knower and known, and between mind and body, have combined with absolute unity or 'clarity' concerning the object known. Whilst this combination has brought the patterns together, it has usually had the effect of turning the epistemology which we now seek to examine 'inside out'.

In order to expound the epistemology which lies behind a Chalcedonian understanding of language, we must emphasize, once again, that we are dealing here with the relation between the human and the divine. We have stressed the tensive nature of both language and christology and their inherent relation. We shall now show how the combinations of unity and distinction which have dominated western epistemology down to the present day need to be inverted. Rejecting the objectivism and dualism which we find in the major contributions to epistemology, we shall show that the human mind operates in a manner which is fully in tune with its dominant form of language, that is, metaphor. Through its use of metaphorical language, the mind reveals the basic features of its knowing capacity, the imagination. The processes of knowing can then be shown to involve the union of the knower with the known and yet also their distinction. This 'distinction in unity' is a personal knowing which involves the mind in a 'heuristic conversation' with that which is known. It is clear already that this notion of the human knowing processes is continuous with the notion of language which we have encouraged here. Because of the inherent relation between these areas, Chalcedon can shed light on both.

Colin Gunton has recently characterized modern western Enlightenment epistemology as revolving around three basic features: 'individualism', 'spatial distance' and 'foundationalism' [1]. Working with these terms, he shows how knowledge has come to be viewed as possessed by the 'individual', who is 'spatially distant' from what is known and whose knowledge is based upon some sort of 'foundational' axioms. These three features stem from and combine in a number of important Enlightenment thinkers. They are accompanied by another, double-sided feature which permeates the entire western tradition. This is the relation between the 'active' and the 'passive' in the processes of knowing. The epistemology of the Enlightenment philosophers is characterized by a separation of the active mind and the passive perception [2]. These four features together sum up the Enlightenment legacy in relation to human knowledge. Furthermore, they epitomize so well the contemporary climate in notions of knowledge that they provide an important point of departure.

We must not forget that, as in the discussion of language, so here in the discussion of knowledge, we are dealing with the problem as it arises in the context of revelation. The primacy of that revelation in enabling knowledge is as important here as it was in relation to understanding language. Certainly Chalcedonian christology requires that we take seriously the divine reality which we seek to know. The Enlightenment philosophers whom we shall consider here, did not proceed in this way. We shall say more about this in the third section of this chapter. Suffice it to say at present that the epistemology which we seek to examine must take seriously the God we seek to know, both revealed and hidden.

The first concern now is to trace Gunton's epistemological elements in representative thinkers and note the inadequacies of the overall view. The legacy of such thinkers as we shall consider is well summed up by the third of Gunton's basic features of epistemology, that is 'foundationalism'. We shall, therefore, consider them under this general heading.

Foundationalism

The modern western notion of human understanding has arisen upon the bases laid down by the philosophers of the Enlightenment. Although Plato broods over this entire tradition, Descartes, Locke, Kant and the philosophers of science, typified by Bacon, epitomize the epistemology which lies at the heart of what modern philosophers have called 'foundationalism'. Ronald Thiemann says that:

> The foundationalist claim runs as follows: Ordinary knowledge rests upon that intricate web of inferential beliefs we call a conceptual framework. Knowledge is justified true belief, and justification consists in tracing the pattern of inference supporting the belief in question until we find those true beliefs on which the questioned belief rests. If we accept those beliefs to be true, and if the pattern of inference is valid, then we can assert the belief in question to be a justified true belief. But, the foundationalist adds, we are not *theoretically* justified in bringing our inquiry to an end until we have discovered a self-evident, non-inferential belief, i.e., a belief that must

be *universally* accepted as true (Thiemann 1985 p.45).

This search for secure, certain and 'universally true' bases upon which all other beliefs should stand if they are to be taken seriously as candidates for truth, is the heart of the Enlightenment legacy in relation to knowledge. D.Z. Phillips characterizes this basic feature more succinctly when he says that 'foundationalism is the view that a belief is a rational belief only if it is related, in appropriate ways, to a set of propositions which constitute the foundations of what we believe' (Phillips 1988 p.3). Indeed, any 'foundation' which allegedly provides a base upon which everything else stands or falls is essentially of this type. Some foundationalist views will be broader than others. We are concerned here with the foundationalism of the Enlightenment which has been predominantly rationalist and empiricist.

The modern western understanding of knowing anything is characterized through and through by what Richard Bernstein has recently called 'Cartesian Anxiety' (Bernstein 1983 p.l6f). This anxiety, in its most extreme forms, is a peculiarly modern phenomenon. Although it stems from the roots of the western philosophical tradition in Plato, it flowered especially, as Bernstein's tag implies, in the philosophical system of Descartes. The anxiety is caused by the desire for absolutely clear and distinct objective knowledge. Its aim is to find an Archimedean point from which to observe neutrally everything it seeks to know and thus arrive at value-free, once-for-all, permanently true facts. It is this concept of knowledge which lies behind what Lindbeck called the 'cognitive-propositionalist' view of language: if something is once true, it is always true. We shall now trace briefly the development of this ideal of knowledge, noting its centrality in a number of areas of western epistemology. We begin with Plato.

Plato's theory of knowledge is rooted in his doctrine of Forms. All things experienced in the world partake in an absolute 'form' or 'idea' which is the object of human knowledge. The route to absolutely certain knowledge, as opposed to Heraclitean 'flux', belief or opinion, is through the mind to the forms. There is here a radical dualism between the intellect and the senses. Because the world of matter and the senses is clearly a world of flux, the world of permanence lies in the abstract, that is, in ideas. For Plato, the world of the 'really real' is the world of the intellect and true knowledge can only be achieved by the rigorous discipline of turning the mind away from the world of the tangible to the world of the Forms. For example, Plato makes his distinction between these two realms in his *Theaetetus*. Countering Protagoras' tendencies towards relativism, Socrates makes it clear that sense-perception 'has no part in the attainment of truth' (186). Truth is equated with permanence, the tangible is played down and perception is predominantly passive.

There are of course many interpretations of Plato's concept of knowledge and the extent of his dualism. It is certainly true that, generally speaking, Neo-Platonism was much more negative than Plato himself about the sensible world and this contributed considerably to the subsequent predominance of dualisms in western notions of knowledge. Nevertheless, the basic dualism between mind and matter permeates Plato's writings and provides a blue-print for the way things were to develop subsequently. This basic separation of mind and matter, T.S. Eliot's 'dissociation of sensibility' (Eliot 1921 p.111), finds its greatest exponent by far, in Descartes. Once again, it is true that there are different interpretations of Descartes' contribution and that it was the 'Cartesianism' which followed Descartes himself which opened up further the dualisms which he had espoused. Nevertheless, it is in Descartes that we find the basic blue-print for knowledge which was to govern western thinking down to the present time. It is to Descartes, therefore, that we turn now.

It is especially in Descartes' search for absolute knowledge that the 'Cartesian Anxiety' of which we have spoken finds its roots. His fundamental separation of the knowing mind from the known object and from the body which contains that mind, forms the greatest influence upon the desire for permanent truth in western consciousness. For Descartes, the road to truth lay through mathematics and logic. The instrument was the mind and the method was doubt. Descartes strengthened the mistrust of the senses which was so prominent in Plato, turning even more radically to abstract certainty, now based within the mind itself. His bifurcation of the individual thinker (*res cogitans*) and the outside world (*res extensa*) gave rise to his conviction that the only certain truth which could be had was that which could be established firmly and clearly by the mind. Once established, such knowledge was of permanent value. The establishment of knowledge lay in the method of doubt. Only by systematically doubting everything that he had until that time thought to be knowledge, could he find a point of absolute certainty from which he could then proceed to establish further knowledge. In the fourth *Discourse*, he says, '...I wished to give myself entirely to the search after Truth...and to reject as absolutely false everything as to which I could imagine the least ground of doubt, in order to see if afterwards there remained anything in my belief that was entirely certain' (Descartes 1967 p.101). That point of absolute certainty was, of course, his consciousness of being a 'thinking thing': *cogito ergo sum*. This formed the Archimedean point from which all subsequent certainties could flow. It brought with it, however, some epistemological features which constitute its essential weakness.

Descartes' system of doubt proceeded by asking what things could be known to be clearly and distinctly true. In the third *Meditation* he says that '...all things which I perceive very clearly and very distinctly are true' (p.158). In his *Principles of Philosophy*, he outlines his notion of clarity and distinctness as follows:

I term that clear which is present and apparent to an attentive mind, in the same way as we assert that we see objects clearly when, being present to the regarding eye, they operate upon it with sufficient strength. But the distinct is that which is so precise and different from all other objects that it contains within itself nothing but what is clear (p.237).

This notion of clarity and distinctness brings into focus some of the major features of Descartes' epistemology. The isolated and attentive mind, clear objects distinct from other objects, and the beholding eye. These features, of the objectivism of what is known, spatial distance between things known and between the mind and the thing known, and the subjectivity and passivity of the knower, are all results of the 'Cartesian Anxiety', the basic desire to 'know' once and for all the truth concerning things.

In Descartes, then, we already find the basic features of western epistemology as characterized by Gunton: 'individualism', 'spatial distance' and 'foundationalism'. The search for an Archimedean vantage point in knowledge brings with it the separation of the knower from the known, alienating the two in the process [3]. In the search for 'objective' knowledge, the knower becomes 'subjective' and a basic dualism emerges. The world becomes 'object' and knowledge of it becomes manipulation of data. This basic subject/object divide brings with it an active/passive divide. For whilst it is true that Descartes' mind is rigorously active in its methodical doubting and sifting of data, and that the mind possesses innate ideas, it is, nevertheless, essentially passive in that it contributes nothing to what it knows. The search is for 'value-neutral', 'objective' data.

These central epistemological features can also be found in the philosophy of the so-called 'British Empiricists'. John Locke, the founder of a great deal of supposed British 'common sense' in relation to the things we are discussing, typifies this tradition, although there are of course differences between him and the other representatives of this school, Berkeley and Hume. It was Locke, it will be recalled, who rejected metaphors as 'perfect cheats'. Although different in many ways from Descartes, especially in turning from the rational to the sensible as the route to knowledge, there is a key continuity between Descartes and Locke in that the basic dualism between knower and known prevails in both men's views. Locke strengthens some of the elements of epistemology which we have noted. For him, the human mind is essentially a 'container' of knowledge. Once again, we have an 'epistemology of spatial distance'. Let us examine how Locke understands knowledge to come to the human mind. In his work *An Essay Concerning Human Understanding,* he rejects the basic idea found in Plato and Descartes that knowledge is separated from perception through the senses. In fact for Locke, knowledge comes to us ultimately through our senses. He says:

> Let us then suppose the mind to be, as we say, white paper, void of all characters, without any ideas; how comes it to be furnished? Whence comes it by that vast store which the busy and boundless fancy of man has painted on it, with an almost endless variety? Whence has it all the materials of reason and knowledge? To this I answer, in one word, from experience: in that all our knowledge is founded, and from that it ultimately derives itself (Locke 1823 Vol.1 p.82).

The mind, then, is a sheet of white paper and the sensible experience of the knower paints things upon it.

Locke spends the first part of the *Essay* claiming that there are 'no innate principles in the mind' (1:11). This basic notion that the human mind is totally empty at birth and then has ideas fed into it through sensible perception in experience, lies at the heart of his philosophy. Here, once again, we find the Cartesian separation of the knower and the known. For Locke the mind is a *tabula rasa*, an empty cabinet, which, through perception, comes to contain knowledge. He says:

> The senses at first let in particular ideas, and furnish the yet empty cabinet; and the mind by degrees growing familiar with some of them, they are lodged in the memory, and names got to them: afterwards, the mind, proceeding further, abstracts them, and by degrees learns the use of general names. In this manner the mind comes to be furnished with ideas and language, the materials about which to exercise its discursive faculty (p.21).

From these ideas it can be seen that, for Locke, perception is an essentially passive matter based in the senses. In so far as it is active, this lies in sifting the knowledge that comes to it via the senses, thus filling an otherwise empty container. The key element of interest in both Descartes and Locke is the dualism between the knowing mind and the known ideas. In Descartes the ideas are innate but separated from the shadowy world. In Locke, they come from the world, but into an empty mind which merely sifts them. In both cases the mind-world dualism is strong. The mind is active, but the process of perception is passive.

It is interesting to note the continuity of these patterns in the other British Empiricists. By and large, David Hume continued the view he had inherited from Locke. For Hume the mind was active only in sorting out and making sense of the data which it received passively. Hume's understanding of causality which awoke Kant from his 'dogmatic slumber' is a fine example here (Kant 1977 p.5). A stone breaking a window is really only two separate events within our perception. We add the notion of 'cause' and link them together, actively ordering them as we receive them passively. In this way, Hume opened up Descartes' gap between knower and known even more. George Berkeley also perpetuated these dualisms but in a slightly different way. His attempt at least was to show that perception is rational and that there is a fundamental link between the human mind and the known world. His attempt to move beyond Locke's empiricism, however, still left him with a basic understanding of this rational perception as passive, the mind ordering the material it receives as it comes in.

It was Immanuel Kant who attempted a synthesis of the rationalism of Descartes and the empiricism of Locke. In raising the question of the very possibility of metaphysics, he was attempting to secure a unity between the two approaches. In the opening sentences of his *Critique of Pure Reason*, Kant sets out the problem as he sees it. He observes that 'there can be no doubt that all our knowledge begins with experience....But though all our knowledge begins with experience, it does not follow that it all arises out of experience' (Kant 1933 p.41). Kant's aim was to establish knowledge which although it may be achieved through the experiencing subject, nevertheless had *a priori* status. Once again, however, we find that the same dualisms emerge as before. Kant's aim is to find certain knowledge, to know 'things in themselves'. In fact he drifts along with the others into a fundamental dualism between knower and known.

In the Preface to the second edition of his *Critique of Pure Reason*, Kant lays out his aim to bring about a 'Copernican revolution' in western epistemology. Copernicus had achieved a revolution in western science by claiming that instead of the earth lying still and the other planets encircling it, it is the sun which lies at the centre of the universe and the other planets encircle it. Thus, instead of lying still at the centre, the earth was in motion. The relation of that which is still, to that which is in motion is crucial here. Kant followed Copernicus' views and took them with him into his reflections on how the human mind knows the world. Is it the subject which moves, or the object? Kant says:

Hitherto it has been assumed that all our knowledge must conform to objects. But all attempts to extend our knowledge of objects by establishing something in regard to them *a priori*, by means of concepts, have, on this assumption, ended in failure. We must therefore make trial whether we may not have more success in the tasks of metaphysics, if we suppose that objects must conform to our knowledge. This would agree better with what is desired, namely, that it should be possible to have knowledge of objects *a priori*, determining something in regard to them prior to their being given. We should then be proceeding precisely on the lines of Copernicus' primary hypothesis (p.22).

Whereas in the past it had been maintained that the knowing subject moved about and the objects of knowledge were still, Kant now suggests that the objects of knowledge are dependent upon the still, knowing subject. After his Copernican revolution in epistemology, objects conform to the knowing mind. The aim, it must be noted, is to establish *a priori* knowledge.

For Kant, the world is divided into two levels, the world of appearances or 'phenomena' and the world of 'things as they really are', or 'noumena'. This distinction focuses Kant's basic epistemological pattern, for although we know the world as it comes to us through our perceptive faculties in experience, we do not have any sort of 'objective' or 'permanently true' perspective on that knowledge. It is important not to think of Kant's epistemology as subjectivist, however. It is the real world which comes to us in our experience, but it is our minds which shape that experience as we receive it, rendering it knowable only as perceived by the human mind. Thus, although, for Kant, we really do perceive an object, the 'categories' of the human mind sift the experience so that our knowledge is relative to those categories. We do not know the *ding an sich* or 'thing in itself'. We know only our experience of the object.

In his *Prolegomena to Any Future Metaphysics*, which was an attempt to present the content of the first *Critique* in a more concise and popular form, Kant is clear about the points we have stressed. He says, 'For sensuous perception represents things not at all as they are, but only the mode in which they affect our senses; and consequently by sensuous perception appearances only, and not things in themselves, are given to the understanding for reflection' (Kant 1977 p.34). He later adds:

And we indeed, rightly considering objects of sense as mere appearances, confess thereby that they are based upon a thing in itself, though we know not this thing as it is in itself but only know its appearances, viz., the way in which our senses are affected by this unknown something. The understanding therefore, by assuming appearances, grants also the existence of things in themselves, and thus far we may say that the representation of such things as are the basis of appearances, consequently of mere beings of the understanding, is not only admissable but unavoidable (p.57).

Thus it is for Kant that there really are 'things in themselves' but the human mind is incapable of knowing such things. It knows only in the mode in which it receives things and shapes them in the mind. This 'turn to the subject' in Kant's philosophy can be seen to bring with it some of the basic features of Enlightenment epistemology which we have been emphasizing. There is the search for absolutely certain knowledge and the individual knower who is ultimately separated from what is perceived. In this case the subject/object divide has worked differently from that in Descartes. For Kant the mind is active in shaping what it knows and it certainly contributes to what it knows. This is true to such an extent, however, that it has lost its rootedness in objective reality.

Even though these basic patterns of subject/object and active/passive and their relations to the three basic features to which Gunton drew attention, vary in the ways in which they come out in a given thinker, they nevertheless characterize the problems with which we are most concerned here. The search is for the correct and balanced understanding of the relation between the knower and the known. We are especially concerned with how human knowledge of God operates. In the philosophical systems which we have considered, the epistemology governs the notion of God which emerges and we can see here the crucial inner relation between epistemology and theology. The question concerns the relation of the human and the divine. The search for clear, distinct and foundational knowledge of God, by an isolated individual thinker who is spatially distant from what it is he knows, is not the recipe we need for producing the theological epistemology which lies behind a Chalcedonian view of language. In each case we have considered, the notion of God follows the epistemology. God might be portrayed as 'objective' and 'certain' or as 'objective' and 'unknowable'.

These epistemological patterns have been established in western thinking not only by those thinkers we have already looked at, but also by notable philosophers of science. Francis Bacon's epistemological programme in many ways brings together the worst of Descartes and Locke. F. Copleston remarks that 'men like Francis Bacon and Descartes were thoroughly persuaded that they were making a new start' (Copleston 1958 p.1). This new start involved attempting to sweep away completely whatever had been thought in the past and start with a clean slate. Descartes had his method of doubt. Bacon rejected the 'bookishness' of the ancients and 'turned to nature' for knowledge. He attempted to work out a system which would begin from scratch and build up objective knowledge untouched by the theories, values and presuppositions of human minds. His method was to be 'inductive', that is, establishing general principles from examples of observed data and proceeding neutrally, allegedly without presuppositions. In his *Novum Organum*, Bacon says that his aim is to proceed more like the bee than the ant or spider (Bacon 1905 p.288). That is, unlike the ant who merely collects and the spider who merely spins what he already has, Bacon aims to extract the material and to shape it.

Thus, in the same work Bacon says that his aim is to 'prepare a Natural and Experimental History, sufficient and good; and this is the foundation of all; for we are not to imagine or suppose, but to discover, what nature does or may be made to do' (p.307). His aim is to establish a system in which he collects data from the natural world and then weighs them in the attempt to establish what can be known for certain. Neutral and value-free examination of the world will yield ultimate and foundational truth which lies in the world waiting to be uncovered. His ideal is to produce secure knowledge, free from the perceptions of the collector. Bacon's ideal for human knowledge is exactly the one articulated by Pierre de Laplace in his *Traité de Probabilité*. The all-knowing mind would know at a single moment

> ...all the forces by which nature is animated and the respective situation of all the beings who compose it...would embrace in the same formula the movements of the greatest bodies of the universe and those of the lightest atom; for it, nothing would be uncertain and the future, as the past, would be present to its eyes (Polanyi and Prosch 1975 p.105).

This comprehensive vision of the nature of human knowledge was based upon the supposed possibility and necessity of assessing the past, present and future conditions of all atomic data in the universe if real knowledge was to be established. Once such information had been secured, it would be logically possible to determine all future possible states of affairs in any situation whatsoever and therefore to have complete knowledge. The basic assumption was that all knowledge was graspable in this way and that once such knowledge had been achieved, there would in principle be nothing more to know. Its basic assumption, therefore, was that all knowledge was reducible to observable, value-free atomic data. The epistemology operating in Laplace is the one with which Bacon set out to collect his knowledge of the world. As with the Enlightenment philosophers, the pattern of attempted objectivism and the active mind contributing nothing to what it knows, dominates the views of Bacon and Laplace.

In the philosophy of science, the 'inductive' method of Bacon has been challenged most significantly this century by Karl Popper. Here in Popper's 'deductive' method we find the ideals of Bacon and Laplace turned upside down. Instead of attempting to proceed neutrally and without theories or presuppositions, Popper proceeds by acknowledging that our knowing processes and theories are value-laden and that such theories proceed tentatively and may be mistaken. According to this notion, we proceed using a theory which we have taken up and test that theory in relation to the world. The process is one of 'falsification' of existing theories, rather than an attempt at total objectivity. A theory for Popper operates somewhat similarly to a Kuhnian 'paradigm'.

Central to what is often called Popper's 'evolutionary epistemology' are his 'three worlds'. World 1 is the world of objective and material things. World 2 is the subjective world of individual minds. World 3 is the world of objective structures and abstract ideas produced by minds. These three worlds interact at a fundamental level. World 3, although it is man-made, interacts with the others and, although it deals in knowledge, it is open and incomplete. Rather than being a *tabula rasa* as Locke thought, the human mind is more like a torchlight for finding out about the world. For Popper, the human mind is not passive, waiting for the world to impress itself upon it, but is rather active and creative in its relation to knowing the world. Popper's 'evolutionary epistemology' has a number of strengths in that it aims to articulate a non-foundationalist notion of human understanding which cuts through some of these basic dualisms. Popper says:

> The empirical basis of objective science has thus nothing 'absolute' about it. Science does not rest upon rock-bottom. The bold structure of its theories rises, as it were, above a swamp. It is like a building erected on piles. The piles are driven down from above into the swamp, but not down to any natural or 'given' base; and when we cease our attempts to drive our piles into a deeper layer, it is not because we have reached firm ground. We simply stop when we are satisfied that they are firm enough to carry the structure, at least for the time being (Popper 1959 p.111).

Here we have in a nutshell Popper's 'fallibilism', that is, his view that knowledge in the sciences proceeds tentatively and always operates upon a structure which might collapse and which will need reassessing constantly. Popper is adamant that the search for knowledge is not the search for 'absolute' knowledge or *episteme*. It is a tentative, searching quest. 'We do not know', he maintains, 'we can only guess' (p.278).

In the patterns which emerge from the comparison between Bacon and Popper we can, once again, note certain features. The objectivism of Bacon is clear enough and he stands well within the tradition carrying Gunton's three basic features. With Popper, however, things are not so clear. On the face of it he has an epistemological programme which counteracts much of the objectivism which we have encountered. His aim is in a direction away from foundationalism. He acknowledges the personal, the dynamic and the changing elements within the human knowing processes. It is here, however, that we face the perennial problem of finding a balanced understanding of knowing. Popper, in rejecting the sort of objectivism we have found in Descartes and Bacon, is in danger of slipping into idealism in attempting to construct a foundationless concept of knowledge. The difficulty which arises, can be found already in Kant and in the notion of 'paradigm' in Kuhn's philosophy of science. Whatever may be the intentions of a particular philosopher, the tendency to drift into idealism or into objectivism is extremely strong. For example, Popper's notion of 'deductive' method can so easily lead into a form of foundationalism in which the theory or paradigm, supposedly fluid, becomes solid.

The features of Enlightenment epistemology outlined here have come to dominate western thinking to such an extent that they have become the 'common sense' view of reality. The development and predominance of scientific method based upon these patterns has also contributed to this. The system of physics laid down by Newton and upon which Kant based so much of his thinking, was essentially deterministic. It saw the world as a system of inter-related causal laws which determined the way things worked. Again, the mind was seen as active and perception as passive. The predominance of this method of determinism and objectivism in the sciences linked with the limitation of all knowledge to that known through the senses, for example in logical positivism, brought about a situation in which rationalism and empiricism became the only recognized forms of knowledge.

In the continental and British schools of Logical Positivism, the reduction of knowledge to what could be known through the senses eclipsed the possiblity of meaningful theological, ethical or aesthetical talk. Edward Schoen, writing of the ideology of the logical positivist Rudolph Carnap, has drawn attention to the way in which this limited epistemology came to govern all knowledge. He says of Carnap, 'Not only was he convinced that scientific truth claims must stand in some relatively straightforward evidential relation to the course of experience, he went on to add that "this is the theory of knowledge in its entirety"' (Schoen 1985 p.10). In all of this, we find that western epistemology has developed a form of foundationalism which excludes knowledge of God. The basic elements of individualism, spatial distancing and foundationalism, proceeding as these do upon a subject/object divide, have led in the direction of reducing knowledge to a process of manipulation and to an experience of alienation [4].

We are concerned here to set out an epistemology which is in keeping with the Chalcedonian notion of language which we have developed. The patterns which we have observed in Enlightenment epistemology are exactly the ones which emerged in relation to christology and language. As with christology, so with epistemology, we are seeking a personal union of knower and known which does not tend into the total objectivism or subjectivism which we have seen so frequently. An epistemology in which knower and known are in personal union within a 'heuristic conversation' is continuous with Chalcedonian christology. If theological language is to be understood, the union of the two elements in the knowing process must be articulated. In short, we need to escape the narrow confines of the 'foundationalism' or 'Cartesianism' which we have discussed. An inversion of the patterns which we have observed is now necessary. As Marjorie Grene has observed, '...it is a renewal of epistemology that is needed if we are genuinely to overthrow our Cartesian inheritance' (Grene 1966 p.224). We turn, therefore, to examine more closely how the human mind must be thought to work, if the understanding of language which we have encouraged here is to be taken seriously. If human language operates predominantly metaphorically, then the key organ of knowing is the combining faculty of the imagination. The 'renewal of epistemology', therefore, will take place in relation to both these areas.

Metaphor and Imagination

We have seen that in the western tradition of reflection upon the nature of human knowing, there have emerged some very clear elements. Gunton summarized these succinctly as 'individualism', 'spatial distance' and 'foundationalism'. We considered all of these under the heading of 'foundationalism' as this word has come to typify the search in the western tradition for absolutely certain knowledge based upon secure foundations of some sort or other. Bacon, Descartes, Locke, Kant, Laplace and many others have contributed to this tradition which is only now really being challenged in a significant way. Having addressed the question of the problem of the relation between the knowing mind and the known object and having noted the inevitable reductionisms which occur in these paths of enquiry, we now begin to postulate an alternative notion of knowledge which is in line with a Chalcedonian approach to language and with a notion of language as essentially metaphorical. We turn first to observe the rootedness of metaphor in the human knowing processes themselves and then observe that the main faculty for knowing is the imagination.

It is now perfectly clear that a large part of human language involves metaphor. Clearly not all language functions in this way, but even our most banal utterances can contain metaphor. We have seen that analogy, metaphors and models, and symbols all behave in similar ways, sometimes adequately and sometimes inadequately where talk about God is concerned. The main feature which binds them together, however, and which is crucial to speaking about God is the 'essential tension' of 'is and is not'. Here in this affirmation and denial, in this partial falsity and partial truth, we find a way of speaking about the God who reveals himself in Jesus Christ. Even though it is now widely acknowledged that metaphor is a central element in human speaking, the fact that it also pervades processes of thinking is still not acknowledged enough. George Lakoff and Mark Johnson have drawn attention to the fact that a great deal of human thinking and perception of the world is carried out in essentially metaphorical terms.

Lakoff and Johnson maintain that it is not just the case that we speak using metaphor or that metaphor is cognitive and irreducible. They claim that human thinking processes function along metaphorical lines at a very basic level, to the extent that perception itself is 'metaphorical'. Even if we want to reserve the word 'metaphor' for a speech act, the point is still clear that thinking, perceiving and knowing processes are continuous with the processes which we have identified in metaphor itself. Briefly, the argument runs as follows. Speech is saturated with metaphor even at the most basic level, that is normally at the unconscious level. For example, the metaphor 'argument is war' determines the way in which we encounter our 'opponent'. We speak in terms of 'attacking someone's position', of 'demolishing' someone's argument, of claims being 'indefensible' and so on. Here we are not just using expressions of which we are probably unaware, but are perceiving the other person as an opponent to be dealt with in a certain way. We move about the world perceiving others as opponents in war.

Perhaps even more instructive are the less obviously metaphorical examples provided by Lakoff and Johnson. For example, what they call the 'conduit' metaphor. This can be seen to be functioning in almost everything we say, so frequently does it occur. The metaphor here concerns spatial distance. We say, 'It's hard to *get* that idea *across* to him', or, 'Your reasons *came through* to us' (Lakoff and Johnson 1980 p.11). Another example is the 'container' metaphor. We say 'I've had a *full* life', or, 'There's *not much left* for him *in* life', or, 'Live your life to the *fullest*' (p.51). Even more common, perhaps, is the 'ideas are food' metaphor. We say that we have the 'raw facts' or that someone's ideas are only 'half-baked' (p.109). By drawing attention to these metaphors, functioning as they do at a very basic level of language, these authors alert us to the fact that perception itself also runs along these lines.

Lakoff and Johnson follow the view that metaphor is speaking about one thing in terms of another. The new contribution is that this has to do with understanding and experiencing as well. They say that 'the essence of metaphor is understanding and experiencing one kind of thing in terms of another' (p.5). These very basic metaphors are indeed 'metaphors we live by' and they structure experience at the level of creative understanding. Although their contribution to this whole problem of the nature of metaphor sheds a great deal of light upon the way we speak about and know things, there is still a basic problem with which we are now familiar. Refuting both objectivism and subjectivism as impoverishments of ways of viewing human speaking and knowing, these authors still give the impression that it is the knowing mind which creates the whole metaphorical process. Thus, for example, they say that 'we give structure and significance to our activities, minimizing chaos and disparity in our actions' (p.234). The notion that *we* give the structure still leaves us with the basic problem which we encountered in Kant. However, there is still a great deal more to be taken from these authors as they do stress the creative and imaginative dimensions of metaphor in the speaking and knowing processes. Thus, they say that 'metaphor is a matter of *imaginative rationality.* It permits an understanding of one kind of experience in terms of another' (p.235).

This element of 'imaginative rationality' is not examined in detail by Lakoff and Johnson, but in referring to it they bring out an element which is of paramount importance. This leads us directly from the importance of metaphor as an element of speech and experience, to the centrality of its basic features in perception and knowledge. First let us establish the rootedness of metaphor in the human mind. We have seen that the essence of metaphor is the 'duality in unity', the simultaneous 'is and is not'. The activity of the human mind, furthermore, has to do essentially with connecting otherwise separate things in the formation of knowledge. In his *Philosophy of Rhetoric*, I.A. Richards, in speaking of metaphor and the tension involved in it, says the following in relation to the function of the human mind in comprehension:

> Let us consider more closely what happens in the mind when we put together - in a sudden and striking fashion - two things belonging to very different orders of experience. The most important happenings - in addition to a general confused reverberation and strain - are the mind's efforts to connect them. The mind is a connecting organ, it works only by connecting and it can connect any two things in an indefinitely large number of different ways (Richards 1936 p.124).

Here we see that the mind itself perceives through connecting and through the tensions which arise in that connecting. This insight into the functioning of the human mind underlines the dialectical processes of human knowing and can be seen to be continuous at the level of perception with the inner workings of metaphor. The same point is made by Ernst Cassirer, who maintains that in order to understand the different types of language that we use, we should begin with the 'nature and meaning of metaphor' and with 'metaphorical thinking' (Cassirer 1953 p.84).

The centrality of metaphor in the very processes of human thinking has also been stressed by Owen Barfield. In discussing the development of human consciousness and the emergence of language he stresses as absolutely crucial the two features of metaphor which we have brought out. He is worth quoting at length:

> In the whole development of consciousness...we can trace the operation of two opposing principles or forces. Firstly, there is the force by which...single meanings tend to split up into a number of separate and often isolated concepts....The second principle is one which we find given us, to start with, as the nature of language itself at its birth. It is the principle of living unity. Considered subjectively, it observes the resemblances between things, whereas the first principle marks the differences, is interested in knowing what things *are*, whereas the first discerns what they are not. Accordingly, at a later stage in the evolution of consciousness, we find it operative in

individual poets, enabling them (τὸ ποιεῖν) to intuit relationships which their fellows have forgotten - relationships which they must *now* express as metaphor. Reality, once self-evident, and therefore not conceptually experienced, but which can *now* only be reached by an effort of the individual mind - this is what is contained in a true poetic metaphor; and every metaphor is 'true' only in so far as it contains such a reality, or hints at it (Barfield 1984 p.87).

Barfield is concerned to see the language of poetry as a unification of the subjective and the objective. This is rooted in the human consciousness and was given to us in the birth of language. This metaphorical process is part of the process of perception itself.

The concern here is with the relation between this metaphorical speaking, experiencing, perceiving and thinking and the object known by the mind. It is possible, as we have seen, to maintain that metaphor is central but still to regard it as in some way ornamental and secondary. John Middleton Murry, for example, sees metaphor as crucial and yet still gives the impression that it is a matter only of the human mind. He says that 'metaphor is as ultimate as speech itself, and speech as ultimate as thought' (Middleton Murry 1931 p.1). Later, he adds that it 'appears as the instinctive and necessary act of the mind exploring reality and ordering experience' (p.2). Our interest here, however, is in how metaphor not only governs speaking and thinking and orders experience, but actually does tell us something about the world, God or whatever it is which is known through metaphor in a given case. Metaphor's rootedness in the human imagination provides us with the step we must take if we are to come to a full understanding of how, in the metaphorical 'play' of 'is and is not', we really do come to know as truth something more than we would without it. We turn now, therefore, to a consideration of the main features of the way in which the human imagination works in relation to knowledge.

According to Coleridge, the imagination at its primary level is 'the living Power and prime Agent of all human Perception' (Coleridge 1907 I,XIII,p.202) [5]. We turn now to this faculty of perception and the immediate question is one of definition. Although there is a clear line of philosophical reflection on the nature of imagination, there still remains the question of how best to conceive of it. In popular understanding in the West, the imagination has gone the way of its products, metaphors. That is, it is seen as contrasted with literal or scientific 'truth' and therefore viewed as decorative or ornamental. In terms of truth, it has come to be a term held in very low esteem. For Coleridge it was the main faculty of human perception. We have seen that language is inescapably metaphorical and it is clear that the imagination is the combining faculty which produces metaphors. The question here is: does the imagination tell us about the world, or is it purely an element for the ornamentation of knowledge?

Contrary to popular thinking, the imagination has been seen as central to human knowing from Aristotle onwards. Aristotle's word for 'imagination' means 'how the object appears' (Warnock 1976 p.38) and it is clear that with this faculty we are dealing not just with human perceptions, but with the way in which objects in themselves appear. We are concerned to show that here in the imagination there is the combining faculty which really does give us knowledge. For some for whom the imagination has been central, it has still functioned within an epistemology which reduces its knowledge-giving power. Indeed, this was the case, as we shall see, with Kant.

In all cases in which the imagination has been taken seriously as a powerful knowledge-giving faculty, it has been acknowledged to have an active, combining role. It has not always been seen as a good thing, however. David Hume in his *Treatise of Human Nature* sees the imagination as a creative, image-making, combining aspect of the human mind which joins together the ideas which come to us and thereby helps us to create coherent and continued sense of the world we experience. The human mind, for Hume, remembers things essentially through the imagination which 'images' things and helps us to have continued perception of things in their absence. Thus, we are provided with impressions which enter the mind and are then stored there by the imagination enabling us to join perception with the image when we next see the object. However, although this role is quite central to Hume's concept of human understanding, without which we would not be able to make continued sense of the world, he nevertheless has a rather low view of it and frequently calls it 'feigned' and 'fictitious'. The imagination turns out to be partly a lure into illusion, a false joining together of a really disparate world.

Hume is clear that the imagination is active and combining, rooted in the creative activity of the mind as 'image-maker'. It is Kant, however, who takes us further here. Indeed, it is Kant who contributes considerably to the tradition which Coleridge would later receive and reform. Kant uses the German word *Einbildungskraft* for 'imagination'. Once again this is to do very much with the power of making representations and images of things. Kant divides the human imagination into two levels, the 'empirical' and the 'transcendental'. The 'empirical' or 'reproductive' imagination is a general level of imagination and is to do primarily with 'association'. At this level, the human mind associates the things it receives as it makes sense of the world. This level of imagination will be different for each individual. The specific things which have happened to one individual and not to another will determine what that individual has associated and collected at this basic level. The key thing here, however, is that it does bring otherwise disparate things together.

The second level of imagination for Kant is the 'transcendental' or 'productive' imagination. This is a much more universal dimension of the imagination and is active in constructing basic perception of the world. The imagination at this level is unifying and synthesizing, making sense of basic experience of the world and bringing together the sensory and intellectual. Indeed, without it, no sense would be made of the manifold experiences which come to us:

> A pure imagination, which conditions all *a priori* knowledge, is thus one of the fundamental faculties of the human soul. By its means we bring the manifold of intuition on the one side, into connection with the condition of the necessary unity of pure apperception on the other. The two extremes, namely sensibility and understanding, must stand in necessary connection with each other through the mediation of this transcendental function of imagination, because otherwise the former, though indeed yielding appearances, would supply no objects of empirical knowledge, and consequently no experience (Kant 1933 p.146).

The imagination at this level, then, is the synthesizing aspect of the mind which makes sense of the data we receive in experience. In addition to these features of the imagination, we should also note the coming together of active and passive in the imagination. The active mind combines and makes images of the passively received data of sensory experience.

However, even though the imagination is the prime faculty of knowing for Kant and has the role of bringing together, unifying and making sense of the data received through sensory experience, it still cannot bring us knowledge which is free from the confines of the imagination. In discussing the relation between the categories of the human mind and sensory experiences for Kant, Mary Warnock affirms that the limitation which applies to the categories generally, also applies to the imagination. She says:

> These categories were devised by the mind to apply to the appearances of things. What things were *in themselves* was forever beyond our understanding to find out. And as understanding could not grasp laws which govern things in themselves but only those which govern appearances, and as ideas of reason lay beyond the world of appearance, so Imagination could not frame images of such ideas either (Warnock 1976 p.64).

In spite of the rich and active role of the imagination in all human perception, and indeed its total indispensability, it is, nevertheless, true that the imagination for Kant still yields limited knowledge. Clearly this is the condition of his entire epistemology.

Warnock observes that the line from Kant to Coleridge with regard to a notion of the imagination is 'relatively straight' (p.72). It is indeed true that in Kant many of the distinctions which are made can be found in similar form in Coleridge. With Coleridge, however, we are dealing with a different epistemological pattern. For Coleridge, inheriting in this respect rather from Schelling than from Kant, the imagination is the faculty which not only combines and synthesizes the elements which the mind receives. It also combines and synthesizes the mind with what it knows, that is the world and the infinite. Schelling had made the link between the ideas of the mind and the infinite ideas within creation. Coleridge later took this up in order to produce his theory of the way poetic language works in relation to the world.

We have already seen that symbols are crucial in Coleridge's understanding of language. We turn now to consider his view of the imagination, that faculty of the mind which actually produces symbols. Like Kant, Coleridge speaks of two levels or functions of the imagination, primary and secondary:

> The IMAGINATION...I consider either as primary, or secondary. The primary IMAGINATION I hold to be the living Power and prime Agent of all human Perception, and as a repetition in the finite mind of the eternal act of creation in the infinite I AM. The secondary Imagination I consider as an echo of the former, co-existing with the conscious will, yet still as identical with the primary in the *kind* of its agency, and differing only in *degree*, and in the *mode* of its operation. It dissolves, diffuses, dissipates, in order to re-create; or where this process is rendered impossible, yet still at all events it struggles to idealize and to unify. It is essentially *vital*, even as all objects (*as objects*) are essentially fixed and dead (Coleridge 1907 I,XIII,p.202).

These two levels of imagination are close to Kant's 'empirical' and 'transcendental' imagination. Coleridge's primary imagination is the general level of unifying and bringing together. The secondary imagination is that involved in the special activity of the poet, artist or man of genius. The two types are continuous and differ only in degree. The primary is a 'repetition in the finite mind of the eternal act of creation in the infinite I AM'. It is, therefore, fundamentally at one with the mind of God and the human imagination functions as a re-creation of the divine act of creation in the world. The unity between the knowing mind and the known world and the divine mind is here asserted. Let us now see how Coleridge understands this.

In his poem 'Dejection: An Ode', Coleridge speaks of a time when all his difficulties were diffused in joy. In a state of deep depression, he now considers his central creative drive to have sunk low under the weight of affliction. This creative drive is the imagination. It is associated with joy and was given him at birth. More importantly, it is the power of 'shaping' the perceptions. Speaking of his afflictions he says that '...each visitation | Suspends what nature gave me at my birth, | My shaping spirit of Imagination' (Coleridge 1912 p.366). This 'shaping spirit of Imagination' for Coleridge is given at birth. It is that faculty of knowing which combines images and constructs symbols. It has the power to induce deep feelings within us and to enable us to see universal significance in the particular. It is essentially the 'shaping' or 'esemplastic' power.

Imagination is distinguished, for Coleridge, from understanding, reason and ideas. As we have already seen, the understanding is the faculty which seeks clarity, abstraction and generalization. It is what we normally mean today by 'reason'. It is discursive and analytic, proceeding with step-by-step logic. Although it is necessary for knowledge, it is insufficient by itself because it provides 'clearness without depth' (Coleridge 1853 p.460). It is thus that faculty which reduces in order to categorize, but which is inadequate on its own. Reason is obviously closely related to understanding. It may be either speculative or practical, but is concerned with the eternal, the universal and the spiritual. It is a spiritual insight, having a relation to the spiritual similar to that which understanding has to the sensory. Ideas are the products of reason, or reason in its creative role. They are also part of creation. To have the idea of a thing is to know its essence. The idea has infinity and is linked with the mind of God. This is an essential part of the element of unity between the knowing mind and the known object. Thus it is that 'an IDEA, in the *highest* sense of that word, cannot be conveyed but by a *symbol*' (Coleridge 1907 I,IX,p.100).

It is, however, the imagination itself which is the prime unifying faculty. In the imagination the knowing mind is 'fused' with the known object, with the world and with the divine, in symbols. If understanding is concerned with discursive reasoning which analyses and separates, then imagination is primarily a poetic faculty unifying and shaping into one the disparate elements of perception. It is in the language of poetry that the imagination is especially active in such shaping, but this is also the prime function of the human mind as it makes sense of the world. In the *Biographia Literaria*, Coleridge describes the poet as the one who is able to bring about the unifying processes of true knowing. His description of the poet is also a description of the way poetic language works in relation to the world:

> The poet, described in *ideal* perfection, brings the whole soul of man into activity, with the subordination of its faculties to each other, according to their relative worth and dignity. He diffuses a tone and

spirit of unity, that blends, and (as it were) *fuses*, each into each, by that synthetic and magical power to which we have exclusively appropriated the name of imagination. This power, first put in action by the will and understanding, and retained under their irremissive, though gentle and unnoticed, controul...reveals itself in the balance or reconciliation of opposite or discordant qualities: of sameness, with difference; of the general, with the concrete; the idea, with the image; the individual, with the representative; the sense of novelty and freshness, with old and familiar objects; a more than usual state of emotion with more than usual order (II,XIV,p.12).

This is the role of the poet and indeed of the imagination. It is the coming together into 'esemplastic' unity of the manifold of experience. It is the 'reconciliation of opposites', fusing the many into one. The poet is the one in whom are combined in an unusual degree, the emotional and the intellectual. All of this combines in the faculty which Coleridge calls the imagination.

Coleridge was obsessed with the problem of the subject and the object, as can be seen in his overriding concern to unite these conceptually. Although his entire contribution to understanding language undermines any such division between knower and known, it is useful to maintain these terms for the two elements, as he himself did [6]. At the present time, as a result of the individualism and spatial distancing to which we have drawn attention, the terms subject and object are a particularly useful starting point. For Coleridge the relation between the human mind and the world is constituted by a dynamic unity in which the mind is active. We have seen that in the epistemologies of Descartes and Locke, the mind had an essentially passive role. Even in Kant, although the mind was active, it was so only in so far as it formed and shaped the data it received. There was a limit to what the mind could know. For Coleridge, on the contrary, the mind is fundamentally active in knowing the world in that it shapes as it knows, and it does truly know. That is to say that, for Coleridge, knowing is a form of 'making' and 'knowing' together. He says that 'to know is in its very essence a verb active' (I,XII,p.180). This is the 'esemplastic' power which knows as it makes. How, in more detail, does this work?

With Coleridge's notion of the imagination and with his concepts of the fusion of 'each into each' and his idea of the symbol as 'translucent', we have a very clear example of an epistemology which sees unity in distinction. The dualisms which we found earlier are brought together in Coleridge's understanding of knowing. For him the active process involves shaping and making as well as perceiving what is there. The subject performs its knowing within the object and any distinction is to be found within the unity. I.A. Richards has spoken of the 'coalescence of the Subject and the Object' in Coleridge's thought (Richards 1950 p.51). This coalescence is the activity of the mind making sense of its perception in unity with it and creating as it goes. It is a 'repetition in the finite mind of the eternal act of creation in the infinite I AM' (Coleridge 1907 I,XII,p.202). The close unity of the perceiver and the perceived is put succinctly by Richards when he says that 'the subject (the self) has gone into what it perceives, and what it perceives is, in this sense, itself. So the object becomes the subject and the subject the object' (Richards 1950 p.57). The internal unity of the knower and the known constitutes the very relation which enables perception to occur. However, care must be taken not to drift into idealism here. The distinctiveness of both knower and known need to be asserted, in addition to the unity. The creative process of the infinite in the finite produces re-creation in the human mind [7]. The 'translucence of the eternal in the temporal' and the 'fusion' of which Coleridge spoke, is the focus of the knowing processes of the human mind.

A final distinction will throw even more light on Coleridge's epistemology and upon the wider argument here. It is the distinction Coleridge makes between imagination and 'fancy'. Having outlined what he means by 'imagination', he says:

> FANCY, on the contrary, has no other counters to play with, but fixities and definites. The Fancy is indeed no other than a mode of Memory emancipated from the order of time and space; while it is blended with, and modified by that empirical phenomenon of the will which we express by the word CHOICE. But equally with the ordinary memory the Fancy must receive all its materials ready made from the law of association (Coleridge 1907 I,XIII, p.202).

This distinction between imagination and fancy is crucial as it once again brings us face-to-face with the issue of unity and distinction. The imagination is, as we have seen, the unifying faculty, but 'fancy' deals with things that are fixed, definite and, therefore, separate. Let us look at this more closely.

In his *Table Talk*, Coleridge makes the following distinction:

> You may conceive the difference in kind between the Fancy and the Imagination in this way, -that if the check of the senses and the reason were withdrawn, the first would become delirium, and the last mania. The Fancy brings together images which have no connection natural or moral, but are yoked together by the poet by means of some accidental coincidence....The Imagination modifies images, and gives unity to variety; it sees all things in one...' (Coleridge *Table Talk*, June 23rd, 1834).

Although these two are essentially different, they do need each other and both function in the mind together. At another point in *Table Talk*, he says that 'imagination must have fancy. In short, the higher intellectual powers can only act through a corresponding energy of the lower' (August 20th, 1833). So, although there are substantial differences between these two, they are related and to some extent need each other.

The crucial thing here is that these two types of activities of the human mind epitomize two types of epistemology. Everything we have said concerning imagination shows it to be a faculty of synthesis and unity. Fancy, however, although it does bring ideas together, keeps them apart in doing so. The reference to 'association' in the quotation from the *Biographia Literaria* on fancy, above, is a reference to a doctrine which Coleridge inherited from Hume and Hartley. It maintained that in perception the human mind merely associates the ideas it receives. Hume had attempted to show that the human mind supplies links and causes between events in the world. Hartley's doctrine affirmed the same. Coleridge came to reject this idea, attempting to find a way out of the dualisms into which it led. For Coleridge, the unity between the activity of the human mind and the world is paramount. Any suggestion of dualism is ruled out. Associationism, associating ideas but keeping them separate, was thus rejected. However, in his understanding of 'fancy', Coleridge affirms something very close to associationism. The ideas with which fancy deals are separate even when they are brought together in the mind. Richards says, 'Fancy, indeed, is the mind's activity in so far as Hartley's associationism seems to apply to it' (Richards 1950 p.77).

Richards formulates the difference between Imagination and Fancy in Coleridge very usefully as follows:

> In Imagination the parts of the meaning - both as regards the ways in which they are apprehended and the modes of combination of their effects in the mind - mutually modify one another.

> In Fancy, the parts of the meaning are apprehended as though independent of their fellow members (as they would be if they belonged to quite other wholes) and although, of course, the parts together have a joint effect which is not what it would be if the assemblage were different, the effects of the parts remain for an interval and collide or combine *later*, in so far as they do so at all' (p.86).

For Coleridge, then, the imagination blends and fuses ideas together, whilst the fancy simply plays with them as separate fixed entities. The key element here is, of course, the unity and the distinction. The human mind is a reconciling organ which is fused with the things it knows. It also makes distinctions. Both of these are central to human knowing.

In terms of the concern with epistemology, it can now be seen that in the various concepts of knowing which have come to dominate, namely in the philosophies of the Enlightenment, there has been an overemphasis on foundationalism, individualism and spatial distancing. These have all separated the knowing mind from the object known. In Coleridge we find a more adequate notion of the way the human mind is united with what it knows. This is, of course, rooted in his concept of 'symbol' and has very far-reaching implications for our understanding of the relation between language and God. In Coleridge the distinction between imagination and fancy sharpens this up. The mind engages in separation and distinction, but is characterized essentially by the fusion of the manifold into unity. If speech, perception and understanding are all fundamentally metaphorical, then it is the imagination which, as Coleridge saw, is the 'primary faculty of perception'. With its emphasis on 'distinction in unity', this notion of understanding is continuous with a Chalcedonian approach to human language about God. It is clear, then, that we are dealing in terms of 'imaginative rationality' when we speak about and know God.

So far, we have established that the business of human knowing is not an objective, passive matter. The knower in his or her 'imaginative rationality' is in unity with what is known. In the process of perceiving what is real, the knowing is also a 'making'. In interpreting Chalcedon, we followed Ephraim of Antioch's notion of ἐνυπόστατος. The emphasis was on the personal union or 'composite hupostasis' of the human and the divine, if the union was to be understood aright. Here also in theological epistemology, the union between the human and the divine must be seen in terms of the personal. The subject is in personal active union with the object. The process of knowing is also a process of making [8]. This 'heuristic conversation' is an active and personal seeking which speaks metaphorically and knows imaginatively. In these senses, christology is inherently linked with speaking and knowing. In view of this, we turn now to a more detailed consideration of the inner workings of 'personal knowledge'.

Personal Knowledge

The primary concern is with the relation between the knowing mind and the known object within the human act of knowing. Where knowledge of God is concerned we are once again dealing with the relation between the human and the divine. The insights of Coleridge, both in relation to the workings of symbols and of the human imagination, showed us how such unity could most adequately be conceived. The potential for dualism between the knower and the known is as great here in the realm of knowledge as it is in the realms of christology and language. The interrelation between these areas leads to exactly the same patterns of dualism emerging. Coleridge provided a way forward in speaking of the 'reconciliation of opposites' and of the 'fusion' of the mind and the world in knowing. For him, the human imagination was a 'repetition' of God's creative act. Finite ideas in the mind were essentially 'fused' with the infinite ideas of God in creation. Coleridge, however, although he was both poet and philosopher, did not produce a systematized exposition of this knowing in the philosophical sense. We turn now, therefore, to the philosophy of Michael Polanyi who does articulate, in very appropriate terms, that 'fusion' of which Coleridge spoke.

Polanyi's key work, *Personal Knowledge*, is an attempt to outline a 'post-critical philosophy'. As the title suggests, he is concerned to articulate the central role of the personal in all human knowing processes. The contribution of the knower to what is known is crucial to what we are ultimately able to know. As for Coleridge, so for Polanyi, knowing is a kind of doing or making. It is not simply a matter of knowing that something is the case. It is an active matter in which the contribution of the knowing person is all-important. Knowing and being are therefore unified in a single act. Also, where Kant failed, but Coleridge succeeded, Polanyi now expounds the inner workings of the unity between the rational and the empirical. Within this context Polanyi stresses that human knowing is a discovery-based skill which operates around 'indwelling' and 'tacit knowing'. It is a fiduciary and heuristic activity in which the mind, in its skill of knowing, makes sense of the world which it encounters.

The two concepts 'indwelling' and 'tacit knowing' are crucial to Polanyi's insights into knowing. We shall look at them in turn. Polanyi's notion of 'indwelling' is a reaction against the objectivism and passivity in knowledge which we have outlined. For Polanyi, the Copernican Revolution led to an idealism which has thoroughly alienated the knower from the known. In *The Study of Man*, he speaks of the 'ruthless mutilation of human experience' which results from the empiricism of modern science and of its 'violent and inefficient despotism' (Polanyi 1959 p.21). For Polanyi, the Laplacean ideal of objectivism has brought about the 'massive modern absurdity' (Polanyi 1958 p.9) under which we now live in the west. The 'scientistic Minotaur' (p.268) has separated the one who knows from that which is known, producing gross alienation in the process. It is the attempt at total objectivism in knowledge, stemming ultimately from Descartes and Plato, which Polanyi sees as such a threat to real knowledge. This attempted objectivism has eclipsed the personal from all knowledge, leaving us alienated from the very things we are attempting to know.

In order to redress the balance and in order to show how human knowledge really does operate, Polanyi says that we 'indwell' all our knowing processes. There is a fundamental unity of knower and known at the personal level. Even in what might be thought to be trivial matters and even in the most rigorous of the sciences, we 'indwell' what we know, contributing a personal dimension to all knowledge. This concept of 'indwelling' is part of Polanyi's view of human knowledge as a skill and as discovery-based. He uses several examples to illustrate this. On a number of occasions he invites us to consider our use of a hammer and draws attention to two important dimensions of our awareness during this activity. On the one hand, we are aware of the hammer hitting the nail. On the other hand, we are aware of the handle of the hammer hitting our palm. These two aspects of the process are central to the act of knowing. They form the two poles central to Polanyi's concept of knowing and show how the person using the hammer 'indwells' the tool which is used.

Even more frequently, Polanyi uses the example of the blind man and his stick in order to illustrate the same point:

> Let us think now of a probe instead of a hammer. A probe is used for exploring the interior of a hidden cavity. Think how a blind man feels his way by use of a stick, transposing the shocks transmitted to his hand and to the muscles holding the stick into an awareness of the things touched by the point of the stick. In the transition from hammer to probe we have the transition from practical to descriptive knowing, and we can see how similar the structures of the two are. In both cases we know something focally by relying subsidiarily on our awareness of something else (Polanyi and Prosch 1975 p.33).

By use of such illustrations we can see that human knowledge proceeds in a skilful manner, probing into the unknown, using a tool which is central to perception but which is not itself the thing perceived. We feel the object through the probing. Central to the knowing process is the active use of the skill. Polanyi frequently uses examples like swimming, cycling and playing the piano which illustrate this basic point that knowledge is a skill. Furthermore, too much concentration on a single element in the skill can be paralysing as when a pianist concentrates too much on a single note and then makes a mistake. It is the whole action which produces the knowledge.

The 'tacit dimension' is closely related to 'indwelling' and is also part of the personal aspect of the way the mind relates to the world. The 'tacit dimension' is summed up in Polanyi's well-known expression that 'we can know more than we can tell' (Polanyi 1967 p.4). Human knowledge is not simply a matter of objective knowledge at the fully conscious level. We bring personal knowledge to that which we know, in a mode which is 'tacit'. The fully objective or conscious level may be the least of the knowledge involved. The tacit dimensions are the realms in which personal knowledge feeds what it is that we know. In *The Tacit Dimension*, Polanyi refers to four central features of the structure of human knowing which will help us to define the inner workings of the process. These features are: the functional; the phenomenal; the semantic; and the ontological. Let us take these in turn.

The first, the functional, refers to what actually goes on when something is known. Polanyi emphasizes that knowing something has an essentially 'from/to' structure, that is, in knowing we attend from our 'subsidiary' or 'tacit' dimension to our 'focal' or articulate dimension. The two poles thus interrelate. So, when looking at a human face, we recognize the whole, but it is the particulars which make up that whole. We are subsidiarily aware of the particulars and focally aware of the whole. The functional aspect is thus to do with what is going on when we know something and it can be seen that this involves our awareness as well as the presence of the object. The second dimension is the phenomenal. This arises out of the functional. The phenomenal structure concerns the actual 'phenomenon' which is known in the process of knowing. As we attend from subsidiary awareness to focal awareness something is made known which is more than the sum of the parts. Human knowledge is to do with attending from subsidiary awareness to focal awareness.

The seeing of the whole, which is an active shaping of the data which come to us, has two fundamental poles, the subsidiary and the focal or the 'proximal' and the 'distal'. These two poles are inarticulate and articulate knowledge respectively. The subsidiary or proximal element is the part which is more than we can tell. This is not to be equated with the subjective or subconscious. Although they are, of course, not focally conscious, the subsidiary elements of awareness vary in degrees of consciousness. These two elements of knowledge are parts of a whole and interrelate with each other. In speaking of the proximal and distal terms, Polanyi says that 'we know the first term only by relying on our awareness of it for attending to the second' (Polanyi 1967 p.10).

This relation between the proximal and distal terms underlines the from/to structure upon which our knowledge is based. We operate, in knowing, from tacit awareness to the focal object. It is important to note that the knower is a central term in this relation. From this angle it can be seen that knowing has a triadic structure: the subsidiary awareness; the focal target or thing known; and the knower who holds these together in the act of knowing. The importance of this triadic structure of knowing, even though it may seem perfectly obvious, cannot be overemphasized in Polanyi's understanding of knowing. When a subject knows something, he integrates the subsidiary elements in the direction of the focal target. The focal aspect, however, is in many ways the least of what is known. The tacit dimension, or the unacknowledged subsidiary awareness is far more significant. Polanyi says that '...tacit knowing is in fact the dominant principle of all knowledge...its rejection would, therefore, automatically involve the rejection of any knowledge whatever' (Polanyi 1959 p.13). Concentration on the focal dimension alone eliminates the greater part of what is involved in knowing something. Also, if a subsidiary element becomes articulate or focal, then something different is known, or the whole process is paralysed.

The third dimension in the structure of knowing is the semantic. This concerns the meaning of the phenomenon known. Polanyi stresses here the intentional aspect of knowing, that is, that when something is known, we are engaging with a reality other than ourselves. Knowing is not merely a subjective matter. When something is known, the knowledge is grounded in the overall meaning which emerges from the phenomenon known in the integrating 'from/to' relation. The semantic structure is the meaning of that which is more than the sum of the parts. The thing known has a bearing or impact upon the knower. The business of knowing is rooted in the meaning of the thing known.

Finally, we have the ontological structure. This is clearly related to the semantic structure. The ontological structure has to do with the reality of the thing known. The phenomenon known in the 'from/to' relation is real. The claim is that when something is truly known, the process of knowing has a significant bearing upon reality. Here there is even more emphasis on the objective groundedness of the object known. Polanyi says that the ontological function tells us 'what tacit knowing is a knowledge of' (Polanyi 1967 p.13).

Polanyi's notion of 'personal knowledge' has provided us with some of the crucial elements which we need if we are to maintain an epistemology consistent with a Chalcedonian view of human language. The unity between the knowing mind and the known object is crucial and is grounded in both sides of the process. It is essentially personal in that the one who knows engages with that which is known by contributing to it. As for Coleridge, knowing is a making or a doing as well as a discovering of what is actually objectively real. It is also an activity which is engaged with as a whole and not merely in parts. It is an activity embarked upon in the belief that it is worthwhile. This element of 'belief' is pivotal to the whole process. The knowledge involved in a given activity is personal in that we are engaged in doing it. We take up the instrument before we actually have the knowledge it enables. We get on the bicycle before we actually have the knowledge of how to ride it. We believe before we know.

The question of whether we first believe and then know, or first know and then believe, makes all the difference to what we think we are doing. Barth's work entitled *Anselm: Fides Quaerens Intellectum* stands as a testimony to his reversal of the Enlightenment project in epistemology in precisely this respect. For Barth, as we have seen, it is the revelation of God in Jesus Christ which provides the starting point for all human knowing. Here in christology everything becomes 'bright or dark'. Barth reaffirmed the well-known dictum of Anselm: *fides quaerens intellectum*. The mainstream tradition of knowledge in Christian theology has been founded upon this basic principle that faith precedes understanding. Since the Enlightenment, that principle has been reversed. We have demanded to know before we believe. Barth stands in complete opposition to this Enlightenment ideal. Polanyi also sees the great weakness of the Enlightenment to lie in the supposition that we can know without believing. It is this basic difference which cuts through the various approaches to knowledge at the present time.

The search for objective knowledge, in the style of the Enlightenment philosophers at whom we have looked, is characterized by the desire first to understand and then to make sense of or 'believe' in what is understood. Its value-neutral idealism concentrates on establishing certain knowledge as a basis for proceeding further. Only when the subject 'knows' can he legitimately act. On the contrary, the programme laid out by Polanyi has as a fundamental tenet the ideal that we first believe and then we understand. He says that 'according to the logic of commitment, *truth is something that can be thought of only by believing it'* (Polanyi 1958 p.305). Only by engaging in what is essentially an active matter can the subject really come to know anything really worth knowing. The subject must take up the implement and use it if he is to find the knowledge which it yields.

If we are truly to know anything, we must engage first with the process of knowing. Polanyi favours *fides quaerens intellectum* over its opposite, *intellectus quaerens fidem*. It is Augustine, rather than Anselm, however, whom Polanyi cites as his mentor. In the *De Libero Arbitrio* (Book 1, par. 4), Augustine cites his own mentor, Isaiah the prophet (Is.7:9): 'The steps are laid down by the prophet who says, "Unless ye believe, ye shall not understand"' (Polanyi 1958 p.266). This maxim, *nisi credideritis, non intelligitis*, forms the basis of Polanyi's concept of personal, active, discovery-based knowledge. Polanyi says:

> It appears then that traditionalism, which requires us to believe before we know, and in order that we may know, is based on a deeper insight into the nature of knowledge and of the communication of knowledge than is a scientific rationalism that would permit us to believe only explicit statements based on tangible data and derived from these by a formal inference, open to repeated testing' (Polanyi 1967 p.61/62).

Thus, knowledge is found through engaging first with the tool in an active venture. Polanyi is clear that this is the way knowledge operates even in the most rigorous exercises in the sciences. As we have seen, the place of metaphor and models in the sciences underlines this view.

It is important to note that 'commitment' is central to the way knowledge works. Polanyi speaks of a 'framework of commitment' (Polanyi 1958 p.311). This is obviously part of indwelling and part of personal knowledge. Polanyi stresses that in all human knowledge we first commit ourselves and then we come to know. He says that 'every act of factual knowing has the structure of a commitment' (p.313). He links this with his concept of 'universal intent' which is the desire that something be true. Here we come upon a combination of concepts which are crucial to the wider argument. Once again the tension arises out of the desire for absolutely certain truth. It is linked, however, with the realization that we may not have such certainty. Polanyi asks the question which stands at the heart of his main work. In *Personal Knowledge*, he says, 'The principal purpose of this book is to achieve a frame of mind in which I may hold firmly to what I believe to be true, even though I know that it might conceivably be false' (p.214). The problem of holding these together really only arises for a totally objectivist epistemology, or 'cognitive-propositionalism'. If we are operating within a system of personal indwelling the two elements will automatically be held together [9].

Within the pursuit of knowledge, then, there must be commitment, universal intent and the genuine possibility of error. Pursuing something as true even though I know it may not be so, must involve the possibility that it might in every sense be false and have to be abandoned. It is this which forms a crucial part of pursuing knowledge in the sciences. The realization that commitment may be based on a mistake, or that, if it is not, the knowledge it yields might be indeterminate, is part of the very real conditions of finding knowledge at all. Polanyi speaks of 'intellectual daring' as part of this dynamic of knowing (p.317). We move forward tentatively, searching with particular implements, in order to discover knowledge. The language, models and metaphors used in all realms of human knowledge operate in this way.

Thus, our knowledge will be essentially of the sort described by Polanyi. It will be personal. We shall 'indwell' what we know and believe so that we may understand. We shall take up the implement and use it so that it may yield the knowledge it makes available. This process of probing with the stick in a personal, heuristic activity is typical of the epistemology which lies behind a Chalcedonian approach to human language. Indeed, in this entire approach, the view is that we are involved in a dynamic 'conversation' with what we know.

Knowledge as Conversation

We have been seeking to articulate the epistemology which lies behind a Chalcedonian view of theological language. We have seen that parallels and pitfalls are the same in language, christology and knowledge. The patterns which arise out of 'Cartesian Anxiety', be they objectivist, subjectivist or coincidences of both of these, lead us into the same dilemmas in knowledge which they led us into in the other areas. The move in western philosophy at the present time is decidedly away from the Enlightenment tradition we have been describing. The limitations of foundationalism are at last being acknowledged and alternative paradigms are being put forward. We have seen some of the key elements in alternative ways of understanding human knowledge in the concepts provided by Polanyi. We seek now to move further into the heart of an epistemology which is continuous with a Chalcedonian understanding of language.

At the heart of Chalcedon lies the unique relation between the human and the divine elements in Christ. This relation is centred on the 'distinction in unity' or the 'is and is not' structure, which we have found to be so central to the way human language about God works. Any reduction of this 'tensive' element removes one side of the crucial dynamic which is centred in the revelation of God. The notions of imagination which we have traced, especially that in Coleridge, show us that the prime activity of the mind also has this central tension. Coleridge spoke of 'fusion' and 'translucence', speaking thereby of a duality in unity or a 'multeity in unity'. The mind in its relation to the world, just as the human in its relation to the divine in Chalcedon, operates in a combining capacity, fusing and unifying the duality. The dynamic element here is essentially a 'conversation' between the two elements.

Much of what has been said in recent philosophy concerning the nature of knowledge is in line with a 'Chalcedonian epistemology'. That is to say that the paradigms which are now emerging for understanding knowledge are based on principles of tentativeness, fallibility, relationality and the personal. The 'is and is not' structure of Chalcedon is continuous with modern non-foundationalist epistemologies. In some quarters in modern philosophy, the move has been away from the notion of, and sometimes even the word, 'epistemology'. Maintaining that the very word carries with it the search for 'foundations' of some sort, philosophers such as Richard Rorty have sought to replace 'epistemology' with 'hermeneutics', or 'phronesis', that is 'practical knowledge'.

For the most part, Rorty follows the insights of Hans-Georg Gadamer. Rorty's case against epistemology is that it has produced a concept of the mind which attempts to 'mirror' the world exactly. The 'glassy essence' of the mind is seen as a mirror in which exact copies of the world are produced. This concept of the mind has bred the sensation that in knowledge we are dealing with 'confrontation'. The object 'confronts' the mind and is thus perceived in a process of mirroring. This is Gunton's 'epistemology of spatial distance'. In its place, Rorty wishes to see the notion of hermeneutics or conversation. It is essentially a two-way matter in which 'certainty' in any foundational sense is discarded: 'Once conversation replaces confrontation, the notion of the mind as Mirror of Nature can be discarded. Then the notion of philosophy as the discipline which looks for privileged representations among those constituting the Mirror becomes unintelligible' (Rorty 1980 p.170). For Rorty, such a 'holistic' approach to knowledge along the lines he suggests will provide 'a conception of philosophy which has nothing to do with the quest for certainty' (p.171).

This notion is based in the philosophical hermeneutics of Gadamer in which 'conversation' is the main concept. Gadamer deals essentially with the interpretation of texts, but his epistemology has a great deal to contribute to the mind-world relation with which we are concerned here. Rorty uses the notion of 'conversation' to show that knowledge is not to do with finding the 'essence of a thing', but with living in relation to the thing and believing, as Polanyi has shown, in what is to be known. Rorty says:

> If we see knowing not as having an essence, to be described by scientists or philosophers, but rather as a right, by current standards, to believe, then we are well on the way to seeing *conversation* as the ultimate context within which knowledge is to be understood (p.389).

Rorty's critique of 'epistemology', and thereby most of western philosophy, turns, therefore, on the rejection of any concept of unrevisable or objective knowledge. He offers a new programme for philosophy. Instead of proceeding in the style of foundationalism, it proceeds as a conversation between mind and world, knower and known. Rorty calls traditional western foundationalist philosophy 'systematic'. It involves an 'epistemological', 'representational' and 'constructive' approach which seeks to construct and establish foundations. By contrast, Rorty calls the sort of procedure he envisages, an 'edifying' philosophy. This is 'hermeneutical', 'conversational' and 'reactive'. Thus, Rorty speaks of 'philosophy without epistemology' (p.357) and uses the term 'edification' by which he means the attempt at 'continuing a conversation rather than at discovering truth' (p.373). It is a holistic activity in which the significance of words and language is very much in their use, rather than in what they allegedly mirror.

In his concept of 'edification', Rorty has taken over Gadamer's notion of *Bildung*. For Gadamer this is essentially to do with culture and education. It is a multifaceted phenomenon whose essential feature is 'shaping'. It has the sense of natural or physical shape as well as developing the shape of the educated or cultured person. The word *Bildung* is especially associated with the shaping and formation of the mind. Its cognates *Nachbild* and *Vorbild* mean 'image or copy' and 'model' respectively. It is interesting to note also that Kant's word for imagination is *Einbildungskraft*. Together, these words are to do with the activity of 'shaping', 'imaging' and 'modelling', and are obviously linked with the more technical sense of 'imagination'. Clearly with this concept we are close to the heart of the epistemology which we have been seeking to arrive at here.

For Gadamer, *Bildung* has to do with the business of keeping oneself open in 'conversation' with one's own society and others. This 'shapes' the person in an educative sense. It is surely not without significance that Gadamer maintains that *Bildung* is an 'inner process of formation' and that 'it is not accidental that in this the word Bildung resembles the Greek physis' (Gadamer 1979 p.12) [10]. It is a dynamic inner formation within a conversation. Gadamer uses this notion in his philosophical hermeneutics in relation to texts. The interpreter of texts is the one who is in conversation with the text. Gadamer speaks of the 'fusion of horizons' which takes place when the horizon of the text is fused with the horizon of the interpreter. The logical structure of openness which is required in this process is what is meant by 'conversation'. This openness lies at the heart of the shaping within the conversation. Gadamer says that 'the fusion of the horizons that takes place in understanding is the proper achievement of language' (p.340). The unity of language and thought is 'intimate' (p.364) within the open structure of conversational knowing.

The conversation is the encounter in which we come to know the partner in dialogue. This involves entering into the horizon of the other and truly listening to the other. The point here is not to establish a foundational truth or to mirror a 'glassy essence' but rather to test concepts and be led into an exchange in which each is respected, but in which new insight might emerge. Gadamer contrasts this 'dialogic structure of understanding' with a straightforward 'statement'. The dialogic structure of understanding is based in the question-and-answer process. For Gadamer the Socratic *docta ignorantia* is an important part of the structure of knowing. The Socratic questioning, constantly leading the enquiry forward, lies at the heart of knowing. He says that 'the emergence of the question opens up, as it were, the being of the object. Hence the logos that sets out this opened-up being is already an answer. Its sense lies in the sense of the question' (p.326). The Socratic method of not knowing, the negative way, opens up the nature of what is to be known. There is a union between the question and the answer.

Gadamer's contribution to modern hermeneutics has placed interpretation upon a new map. His major concern was with texts, but it is already clear that his insights can be used in relation to the knowing mind and the world which it knows. The process is personal, active and passive in relation to what it knows. It retains its identity and integrity whilst also respecting these in its partner. The unity and distinction within the process of knowing are once again stressed. It is the dialectical process which establishes the unity of knowing. Gadamer says, 'Dialectic as the art of conducting a conversation is also the art of seeing things in the unity of an aspect (sunoran eis hen eidos) ie it is the art of the formation of concepts as the working out of the common meaning' (p.331). This dialectic does not only involve the 'fusion of horizons', but also a necessary 'tension' which should not be ignored but brought out from within the fusion (p.273). All this is in relation to texts, of course, but it is of equal value in coming to understand the human conversation with the world and with the God of whom we speak metaphorically.

One final and basic area of concern must be noted. Gadamer relates his philosophical hermeneutics and his notion of the intimate relation between language and thought to the λόγος and more specifically to the mystery of the Trinity. He says that 'there really is something in common between the process of the divine persons and the process of thought' (p.384). The mystery of the Trinity is 'reflected in the phenomenon of language' (p.379). This link with the Trinity and the divine persons is crucial to Gadamer's notion of language and thought. We can see that the Incarnation of the Word of God is the basis upon which human language is linked with christology. It is this rootedness in the λόγος that prevents Gadamer's non-foundational epistemology from slipping into subjectivism. Gadamer says that within the process of conversation 'what emerges in its truth is the logos, which is neither mine nor yours and hence so far transcends the subjective opinions of the partners to the dialogue...' (p.331).

Here, in addition to the value of the concepts provided by both Gadamer and Rorty, we find once again the problem in theology of keeping a balance between the human and the divine. We are seeking to uncover the epistemology which lies behind a Chalcedonian view of language. It is clear that we wish to establish the distinction in unity which we have found in both christology and language. According to Georgia Warnke, Rorty has misread Gadamer on the full significance of *Bildung*. She says that:

> For Rorty, edification or *Bildung* therefore 'replaces knowledge as the goal of thinking'. Yet, despite the opposition that Gadamer himself establishes between *Bildung* and an objective knowledge of facts, on his view, *Bildung* remains more than an education into the pluralism of 'ways of coping.' Indeed, the connection between *Bildung* and a certain kind of knowledge remains fundamental... (Warnke 1987 p.159).

If we are to use the concepts provided by Gadamer and Rorty, we must bear in mind our concern with the 'distinction in unity' which we are seeking to articulate. Certainly if there is any question concerning just what the 'objective' status of knowledge is in Rorty's thinking, then Gadamer's articulation of *Bildung* clears this up and is closer to the epistemological structure which lies behind a Chalcedonian approach to language. In relation to *Bildung*, for example, Gadamer claims that 'like nature, Bildung has no goals outside itself' (Gadamer 1979 p.12). This does not however, mean that Gadamer has a subjectivist view of *Bildung*. On the contrary, it is rooted in the λόγος. It is of course, more than significant that it is Gadamer who has made the links with the Incarnation and whose view of the operations of language and thought are, therefore, ultimately the more balanced.

Knowledge and Chalcedon

In conclusion, we must briefly retrace our steps concerning the epistemological structure which lies behind a Chalcedonian approach to language and then underline the specific links with the Chalcedonian Definition itself. Language, knowledge and christology are inherently linked. Human language, especially of God, but also in general, is inherently metaphorical. It revolves around a basic 'is and is not' structure. We have also seen that christology has this inherent 'is and is not' structure. Because of the 'inner logic' of these related areas, the 'inner logic of knowledge' will be continuous with these. We have traced some of the main elements in Enlightenment epistemology and have called these 'foundationalist' because the main aim has been to secure certain knowledge based upon rational or empirical evidence. The patterns which emerged in the epistemology of the Enlightenment thinkers paralleled those which we had found in christology and language, and rejected. For this reason alone, they are not the patterns we seek.

We have seen that because human language is essentially metaphorical, the processes of human knowing are rooted in the imagination rather than in 'clear and distinct ideas' of the kind sought by Descartes. Even though some views of the imagination reveal patterns which are still inadequate, the view found in Coleridge articulates the very 'distinction in unity' which we are seeking. Next, we stressed that the union thus found was personal, as Ephraim of Antioch said. The thought of Polanyi provided further articulation of some of the structures of personal knowing. Finally, the notion of 'conversation' and especially the understanding of this found in

Gadamer shed even more light on the sort of knowing processes which lie behind a Chalcedonian view of theological language. The notion of knowledge which lies behind this view of language is essentially one of personal union, of a fusion of the two partners in conversation and yet also a simultaneous distinction. This epistemology is thoroughly continuous with the dynamic which is disclosed in the revelation of God in Jesus Christ and it also makes sense of a Chalcedonian view of human language about God.

We have seen that the rejection of Chalcedonian christology always brings with it a disturbance at the level of language. Lindbeck produced a 'regulative' notion of Chalcedonian categories and ended up with an inadequate notion of language. McFague rejected 'incarnational' christology and ended up with a view of language which frequently slipped into subjectivism. The point is that if we approach human language about God by way of Chalcedonian christology, such problems as we have encountered will appear in a different light. The epistemology which then emerges will be in keeping with this. We can see now that the personal union which exists between the human and the divine at the level of ὑπόστασις and the distinction which exists at the level of φύσεις are fundamental to christology and also to language and knowledge. The 'unity in distinction' is the crucial feature and the three areas, bound together at the deepest level, all bear this characteristic. A Chalcedonian notion of human language about God leads us to a view of knowledge as 'heuristic conversation' rooted in 'imaginative rationality'.

A final observation confirms the link between the Chalcedonian Definition and human knowledge. In his classic study, *The Council of Chalcedon*, R.V. Sellers associates the unity of the human and the divine in Christ with the faith of believers. The distinction between the two elements, he associates with the believers' capacity for enquiry [11]. In noting this, Sellers draws attention to a crucial link between the christology of Chalcedon and the epistemology which inheres in it. The unity of the two elements in Christ is the root of an epistemological unity between the knower and the known. We can see that this has special links with the positive element in metaphorical language about God. Sellers sees the difference between the two elements in Christ as the root of an epistemological distinction between knower and known. Here we can see special links with the negative element in metaphorical language about God. Both the unity and the distinction are central to christology and to language. Both are central to knowledge.

In conclusion, it is clear that approaching notions of human language about God in relation to the Chalcedonian Definition requires a basic inversion of the epistemological features identified by Gunton. Individualism, spatial distance and foundationalism, linked with the 'active mind/passive perception' dichotomy do not provide us with an adequate account of how we know things and certainly not of how we know God. Within the context of a 'heuristic conversation' between mind and world in which 'imaginative rationality' predominates, we will find that knowers know in union with the object known and that the 'conversation' is personal, dynamic and non-foundational. Furthermore, although the object known is constitutive within the knowing process, in this case, the revelation of God himself, the knower is also active in the making and shaping of knowledge. The business of human knowing is a continually moving process in which we know, but do not come to manipulate and possess. Marjorie Grene says that 'the knower is the knowing person, in hazard, gambling on making contact with reality, and the reality he seeks contact with is the real world, though for ever eluding his ultimate, self-sufficient, systematic grasp' (Grene 1966 p.152). This feature is especially the case where knowledge of God is concerned. It also characterizes the form of epistemology which is continuous with a Chalcedonian approach to human language about God.

VII

CONCLUSION

Christology, Language and Knowledge

We began with the question of how we are able to speak of the God whom we know in revelation, but who also remains hidden from us. Lying as it does at the centre of communal experience in worship, in theological articulation and in philosophical reflection, human language is the powerful and immediate medium of communication, consciousness and knowledge. We have, therefore, been initially concerned with language rather than with knowledge *per se*. In examining the views of two recent writers on the nature of theological language we found that whilst they provided us with many of the elements which are important, there were some serious defects.

Neither Lindbeck nor McFague made the crucial connection between their view of language and their christology. We found that their comments on christology, made almost in passing, were very revealing of the inner workings of their theologies. We found, furthermore, that this was not a feature which was peculiar to these two writers. Schleiermacher had already made a significant alteration at the level of christology and his notion of language began to follow suit (while Aquinas worked with notions of analogy not overtly connected with christology at all). Tillich's view of symbols suffered for similar reasons. On the contrary, where the crucial relation between the divine and the human was kept in sight, a more balanced view of theological language emerged, as, for example, in Coleridge.

We argued, therefore, that human language about God should be understood in the light of christology and especially the Chalcedonian Definition of the Faith. In looking at the Chalcedonian Definition we traced the presence of two dominant traditions, the Antiochene stressing the 'model of distinction' and the Alexandrian stressing the 'model of unity' in relation to the person of Christ. We then saw that these two models came together in the Chalcedonian christology producing an essential tension of 'is and is not' at its heart. The 'inner logic of christology' lay in its simultaneous 'distinction in unity', the distinction in unity of the human and the divine. The interpretation of this christology through the notion of ἐνυπόστατος, especially that of Ephraim of Antioch, stressing the personal union or 'composite hupostasis', provided us with the essentially personal nature of this essentially tensive christology.

In looking more specifically at human language about God, we turned first to Aquinas' notions of analogy because we found there a perfect example, this time in the mediaeval period, of the regrettable separation of christology and language in Christian theology. Here we showed that the various notions of analogy offered us a great deal but were ultimately inadequate because Aquinas had not made the necessary links with christology. In turning to consider the way in which metaphors and models work, we discovered the richest area of language and the most important dimension of the theological naming process. Here we were able to show that certain views of metaphor were in fact inadequate and that christology, with its inherent 'is and is not' logic, enabled us to find the best notion of metaphor. The heart of language and the heart of christology had come together. Because symbols are so closely related to metaphor, we turned next to consider the contributions of Tillich and Coleridge and found essentially the same relation between christology and language that we had found in our opening chapter.

Finally, we turned to the question of knowledge in order to expose the epistemology which lies behind a Chalcedonian approach to human language about God. Rejecting Enlightenment patterns of knowledge, we found that the basic views needed inverting. Rather than individualism, spatial distance, foundationalism and a false 'subject-object' divide, we found an 'imaginative rationality' which operated within a 'heuristic conversation'. Again, as in christology, the union between knower and known, or human and divine, was essentially personal and dynamic. The relation between subject and object was one of union, distinction and personal interchange.

Having stressed the inner relation between christology and language and having seen the inherent parallels between the logic of Chalcedon and the logic of metaphor, which we take to typify the richest dimensions of human language, we have concluded that Chalcedonian christology is a wholly appropriate light in which to view notions of theological language and knowledge. Here, the two elements of humanity and divinity co-exist in a certain sort of relation. Let us now illustrate this one more time.

Chalcedon and Language

In conclusion, we shall reaffirm the basic argument using different material. We shall consider first a view of language in which a recent author *has* associated language and christology, but in which there are still problems. This enables the value of the Chalcedonian approach to emerge even more clearly. Secondly, we shall illustrate the basic Chalcedonian approach in relation to notions of metaphor, the heart of human language and knowledge of God.

The view of language in which the author *has* made the links between language and christology is that found in the writings of Ian Ramsey. We referred to his work earlier in the section on models. Ramsey makes an important contribution and comes closer to the point we are making here than many recent writers on theological language. It is all the more striking, therefore, that he does not achieve what he might have done. In his main work *Religious Language*, Ramsey is out to achieve an 'empirical placing of theological phrases'. His aim is to make sense of theological language in a predominantly empiricist climate. Ramsey begins by attempting to say something about situations which are essentially 'religious'. He is correct that human language about God is rooted in experience of the divine. Although his notion of revelation is not brought out fully, it is certainly stronger than it was in the writings of Lindbeck and McFague. Ramsey calls the situations which form the context of religious language 'disclosure situations'. These are situations in which we experience 'depth' or 'insight' and in which something more than the merely visible is 'seen'. These situations, according to Ramsey are 'logically odd' because they deal with more than the purely empirical.

The depth or insight found in certain things or events gives rise to a 'discernment' in association with which we use the word 'God'. Christians are then 'committed' to this and the combination of 'discernment' and 'commitment' form the 'logically odd' context in which religious language finds its meaning. Ramsey says that '...we must expect religious language to be appropriately odd, and to have a distinctive logical behaviour. Otherwise it would not be currency for the strange kind of situation about which it claims to speak' (Ramsey 1957 p.49). It is in this context that metaphors and models, for example, have their meaning for Ramsey. If we do not take into account their logical oddness, then we shall lose the entire meaning of religious utterances. Ramsey thus separates the empirical base of scientific language from the 'logically odd' base of theological language.

It is in this context that Ramsey contributes his notion of models and 'qualifiers'. When a model is used of God, it is accompanied by a 'qualifier' which enables it to function in relation to the 'logically odd'. When God is spoken of as 'first cause'; 'infinitely wise'; 'infinitely good'; 'creator *ex nihilo*'; or 'eternal purpose', he is spoken of on the basis of a human model which is qualified by a word which enables it to be used of God. Thus, 'infinitely wise' uses the model of human wisdom which is then qualified by the word 'infinite', thus showing the extent and limitations of the model. This enables Ramsey to place language about God within an empirical setting. The models can make sense whilst also being qualified by words which show them to be operating in a way other than the primary sense of their meaning. For Ramsey, all Christian language, including biblical language, operates in this way.

So far, so good. All this is very positive, but there are some fundamental difficulties in what follows. The difficulties come at the most positive point in Ramsey's discussion. This is when he associates his concept of language with christology. He refers regularly to the system of 'qualifiers' as a 'logic' of language and clearly has in mind a notion of language which will account for the workings of all religious language. He sees that concepts such as λόγος, ὑπόστασις and *communicatio idiomatum* are crucial for understanding the way human language about God works. However, his view seems to limit the language to a 'regulative' role and falls into all the pitfalls which one might expect of a 'Christian empiricism'. As with Lindbeck, the importance of the christology seems to be at the regulative level and certain crucial links are missing.

Throughout his discussions of models, Ramsey is concerned to underline the usefulness and richness of many models. He is attempting all the way through his work to avoid the common supposition that religious language operates on the same logic as any other language. In establishing his case, however, and in the attempt to secure the recognition of mystery in the use of models, he slips into the same trap as McFague. Ramsey asserts that 'all models are bound sooner or later to show their inadequacy' (p.168). In overemphasizing the importance of the limitation of models, Ramsey tends to leave us where McFague left us, that is with an 'experiential-expressivism' which loses sight of the positive element in the models we use. This is perhaps noticeable in his insistence on 'mystery'. He is of course correct that mystery is important in theology and in the theological use of metaphors and models. His claim, however, that 'the heart of theology is permanent mystery' (Ramsey 1964 p.60) suggests that the affirmative element in theological language has slipped from view.

This dualism at the level of epistemology, between the language and what is spoken of, is especially interesting because it is linked with christological elements which are stressing unity. That is, Ramsey refers to ὑπόστασις and *communicatio idiomatum* in his christological emphases, but fails to secure the union in his epistemology. This reminds us immediately of the rationalism and empiricism of Enlightenment foundationalism. It combines unity and distinction, but these are inside out. The christology is, in fact, not linked with the language at precisely the point it needs to be. This can be seen most clearly, perhaps, when Ramsey actually refers to Chalcedon and then immediately asserts a dualism in relation to how our models operate. In speaking of how theology must acknowledge the limitations of its models, he says:

> It must necessarily in this sense exhibit always a Chalcedonian bankruptcy: like many other people's banking accounts at the present time, it will only show an active healthy condition when its

store of empirical models is overdrawn. For it has invisible assets -
mystery - of which the models take no account (Ramsey 1957 p.170).

Here we are back where we began, with Temple's confusing use of the
'bankruptcy' metaphor. For Ramsey, this 'Chalcedonian bankruptcy' refers
to the inadequacy of models understood purely at the empirical level.
Ramsey sees that there must always be 'more' than the model itself, but
then fails to sustain the essential link between the models and the mystery.
The potential of Chalcedon itself for understanding theological language
has slipped through Ramsey's fingers at the crucial moment. In his later
work *Models and Mystery* in which he discusses the importance of
metaphors, the link with christology is not made at all (Ramsey 1964
passim).

In all this it is interesting to note that Ramsey has set out to provide
'an empirical placing' for human language about God. He makes an
important contribution to our understanding, but his scheme is still riddled
with dualisms which prevent him from achieving an adequate picture.
His concern with 'empiricism' inevitably pulls him in the direction of
empiricism itself and in this sense he loses touch with the very mystery
he is out to guard. He has been correct to root human language in the
divine life itself, in 'disclosure situations'. Here, at least, is the attempt to
provide an objective rooting for the language. However, as many of his
critics have observed, he has failed to maintain that rooting by not using a
model appropriate enough to carry the objectivity. Thus, his 'disclosure
situations' could be interpreted as entirely subjective. Ramsey's notion of
disclosure is weak and needs developing into a doctrine of revelation.
Soskice comments that 'Ramsey's purposes would have been better served
had he rid himself of "Christian empiricism" and turned to a theological
realism' (Soskice 1985 p.147). Indeed, she rightly sees empiricism as
'bankrupt' in this respect (p.144).

Such a 'theological realism', of a critical sort, is enabled by approaching
human language about God by way of Chalcedonian christology. There,
the two natures are fused into a personal union. The link between the
human and the divine is articulated as a 'distinction within unity'. The
christology and the language are linked. Language about God, and models
and metaphors operate in connection with what they are about. They are

not simply loose expressions unattached to the God of whom they speak. The language is of God, even though it is simultaneously human, limited and changeable. From this angle, we can see that Ramsey's scheme is inside out. He has dualism at the level of language (or models) and epistemology, and unity at the level of christology (using *communicatio idiomatum* and ὑπόστασις). His notion of language founders, however, because of an imbalance between the two. By way of Chalcedon, these elements of distinction and unity are safeguarded. We move now, finally, to the heart of just how this is the case with metaphor.

A Master of Metaphor

At the present time there is a serious need to rehabilitate an appropriate understanding of human language about God. It is only recently, after a long history of neglect, that the metaphorical element in language is being taken seriously as a medium of truth-telling. Theologians writing before the Enlightenment were aware of the need to illustrate their theology through metaphor, in spite of its more general lack of popularity. Origen, approaching his christology through reflections about perception, uses illustrations such as the 'iron in the fire' and the example of a painting to illustrate man made in the image of God, also used by Athanasius. Origen's aim is to bring his christology to speech as adequately as he can, although he notes frequently that such illustrations are always inadequate [12]. The Fathers of the Reformation also knew the need to use metaphor, especially in relation to the atoning death of Christ [13]. In the post-Enlightenment western world the respectability of such metaphors is in serious decline. A renewed sense of the importance of metaphor is arising, however, and it is essential that an understanding of the christological dimensions of metaphor arises with it. We have argued that such an understanding is enabled by way of the Chalcedonian Definition of the Faith.

We have seen that establishing an adequate notion of the way human language about God works is a difficult and often vexing matter. There have been many notions of theological language and we have seen that words about God have be made to mean many different things. Lewis

Carroll raises the question of whether words or users of words are more important:

> 'When I use a word', Humpty Dumpty said, in a rather scornful tone, 'it means just what I choose it to mean - neither more nor less.' 'The question is', said Alice, 'whether you can *make* words mean so many different things.' 'The question is,' said Humpty Dumpty, 'which is to be master - that's all' (Caird 1980 p.38).

The concern throughout this investigation has been with which *meaning* is to be master. The answer has been that because language and christology are so intimately related, christology is the 'master of metaphor'. Neither language itself, nor users of language are the master, but rather God in his revelation in Jesus Christ is the 'master of metaphor'.

The 'inner logic' of this view should now be clear. The christology of the Chalcedonian Definition set out to avoid two major pitfalls in articulating the relation between the human and the divine in Christ. Through its language of ὁμοούσιος, πρόσωπον, ὑπόστασις and φύσις and its 'four negative adverbs', the christology provided us with a 'distinction in unity' at the heart of the relation between the human and the divine in Christ. Indeed the very structure of the central section of the Chalcedonian document itself is concerned with these two elements, the first half occupying itself predominantly with the unity and the second half with the distinction. The distinction between the two natures was preserved within the 'hypostatic union'. Relton commented that the aim of the Chalcedonian Definition was 'to exclude two possible explanations of the mystery' (Relton 1917 p.37). The aim was to exclude possible drifts into confusion and into separation of the elements.

One of the main words used at Nicaea and Chalcedon is ὁμοούσιος. Prestige noted that this word 'conveyed a metaphor drawn from material objects' (Prestige 1952 p.209). The words ὑπόστασις and πρόσωπον also indicate metaphor. Their use, as we have seen, was to do with asserting unity. The fact that metaphors are used here is significant and reminds us that at the heart of christology we find the need for metaphor in order to speak of God. The level of distinction between the 'two natures', or φύσεις, it will be recalled, was a dynamic and fluid relation of two elements also in unity. Here at the heart of christology we come also to the heart of metaphor. It is here that the two things can be shown to exhibit exactly parallel features. Furthermore, because of the inherent relatedness of human language and christology, these parallel features are thoroughly continuous with each other.

The Chalcedonian approach has operated here especially in relation to metaphor, which lies at the heart of theological language. As in christology, so in metaphor, there are tendencies to divide the elements and tendencies to unite them. Thus, we may well find views of metaphor drifting into 'comparison' or into plain literalism, that is, taking the metaphor at face value. The real power of a metaphor in 'speaking of one thing in terms of another', however, is in preserving the distinction within the unity. The two elements which are brought together in a metaphor operate in such a way that there is an essential 'tension' at its heart. Aristotle says that '...the greatest thing by far is to be a master of metaphor. It is the one thing that cannot be learnt from others; and it is also a sign of genius, since a good metaphor implies an intuitive perception of similarity in dissimilars' (*Poetics* 1459a). The metaphor operates around the perception of these two elements together and perceiving this 'similarity in dissimilars' constitutes the essence of being metaphorical [14].

In metaphor, furthermore, we have two levels in unity. 'God is a rock' is clearly false at its primary level. This is the negative element or 'distinction'. This relates to the 'is not' of the metaphorical tension. The level at which the meaning is positive is the metaphorical level. This relates especially to the 'is' of the metaphorical tension. These two levels relate to the 'is and is not' of Chalcedonian christology. However, the two elements are not separate. There is a clash of meaning, here, and both the positive and the negative are simultaneously required in order to achieve the meaning. The 'is and is not' is a tension produced simultaneously by both elements together. Ricoeur, whose notion of 'split reference' has some weaknesses, still has some insights to offer here. He says:

> ...metaphor displays the work of resemblance because the literal contradiction preserves difference within the metaphorical statement; 'same' and 'different' are not just mixed together, they also remain opposed. Through this specific trait, enigma lives on in

the heart of metaphor. In metaphor, 'the same' operates *in spite of* 'the different' (Ricoeur 1978 p.196).

'The same' operates in spite of 'the different'. Here is the semantic tension or clash within metaphor. Here, also, is the heart of Chalcedonian christology. Indeed, it is in this 'sameness in difference' that we find the heart of both metaphor and christology. Chalcedon forms the required model precisely because it preserves in the language what should be acknowledged if the ontological groundedness and objectivity of that language is not to be compromised. With this approach, a full notion of the 'is and is not' of God's revelation and hiddenness is preserved.

In theological language we are dealing with the 'unity in distinction' of the two elements, one of which is God. The essential 'is and is not' is crucial. The language has both unity with what it is about and yet is also distinct from it. Here we are back with trying to avoid McFague's 'idolatry' and 'meaninglessness' and with Lindbeck's various views. The notion of metaphorical tension is certainly the way forward here. Berggren says that 'a more systematic application of the notion of metaphorical tension to the problem of religion would also be worthwhile, thus counteracting the annihilating dangers of both mythical fundamentalism and mystical silence' (Berggren 1962-63 p.258). If language is thought to operate straightforwardly in its primary or literal sense, then we slip into idolatry. If it is thought to be too unlike what it is talking about, then we slip into meaninglessness. The heart of the issue here is that human language both 'is and is not' meaningful in relation to God. It retains unity at the metaphorical level whilst being false in its primary or literal sense. Both 'falsity' and 'unity' are central to achieving that basic meaning. The heart of metaphor and the heart of christology come together in Chalcedon. The Chalcedonian christology, therefore, provides us with the most adequate way in which to preserve the central tension which lies at the heart of human language about God.

If we approach notions of human language about God in relation to Chalcedonian christology we shall find the most adequate view emerging, eliminating the pitfalls which we have observed. In particular, a Chalcedonian approach enables the most adequate notion of metaphor, the heart of the human speaking and knowing processes, because it pre-

writers' neglect of christology. McFague spoke of metaphor as the heart of theological language and of the 'is and is not' tension as the heart of metaphor. She did not, however, make the link between the tensive nature of metaphor and the tensive nature of christology. Taking up the christology which these two writers had neglected, we examined Chalcedon and saw that the essential tension which is required in an adequate notion of language is provided there. The inherent link between christology and language strengthened the case. The point at which these writers were at their weakest became the point at which the real nature of language could be exposed. That is, when it is seen in the light of Chalcedonian christology.

Finally, we can see here and from the observations made throughout the book, that although human language works in a wide variety of ways and may achieve its meaning in different ways in different contexts, human language about God is best understood in terms of metaphor. Ramsey made the point that language about God must be 'logically odd', but this is true only by empiricist standards. Indeed, the logic of human language about God can now be seen to be rooted in the revelation of God in Christ, in a form of metaphorical and imaginative rationality. Theological 'logic' then begins to look rather different. The revitalization of notions of language about God must reintroduce a sense of the riddle at the heart of our speaking of him. Metaphor in particular provides the most adequate way of speaking about the God who is revealed to us and yet remains unknown. Even with metaphor, however, there are many views and some of these undermine the real power of what happens when we speak metaphorically. We are especially keen here on preserving the 'essential tension' at the heart of metaphor. There are many ways of encapsulating this notion. Bedell Stanford calls it 'stereoscopic vision'. Ricoeur speaks of 'split reference'. Whatever we call it, it is the essential tension at its heart which must be preserved.

If we are to speak about God responsibly, we need metaphor and we need adequate notions of metaphor. The christology of the Chalcedonian Definition of the Faith has been seen to enable this. Indeed, it is here that we are concerned with the Incarnation of the Word. Far from being 'bankrupt' in Temple's earlier sense, the definition sustains a tension which turns out to enable an adequate understanding of human language about God and of the relation between humanity and divinity. The definition can only be said to be 'bankrupt' in the sense that it does not 'explain once and for all' and this is its strength. Human language does really speak about God, however, and Ramsey was wrong to think of bankruptcy as the protection of 'permanent mystery'. As in Exodus 3:14, the naming of God is in a riddle, but he is truly named. 'Bankruptcy', of course, is a difficult matter and in any case metaphors can be so easily misunderstood.

We conclude then, that notions of human language about God, and especially metaphors, can be guided by the christology of Chalcedon. Approaching human language about God in the light of the Chalcedonian Definition of the Faith will enable both the human and the divine and their relation, to be kept in view. As Relton said, the Chalcedonian Definition is a sign-post for future seekers, a safeguard but not a solution [15]. It is in this sense that christology can condition notions of human language about God and in this sense that God in Christ is the 'master of metaphor'. William Temple was confused about the Chalcedonian Definition of the Faith, but he knew a wise question: 'What is God like?' and a wise answer: 'Christ'.

ENDNOTES

Introduction

[1] See Martin Buber *Eclipse of God* (1952). 'Eclipse' is a particularly appropriate metaphor for articulating the conditions which have arisen in the western world in relation to theological language and knowledge.
[2] All references to Aristotle are to *The Works of Aristotle* ed. by W.D. Ross.
[3] These are Humpty Dumpty's words to Alice. See George Caird *The Language and Imagery of the Bible* (1980 p.38).

Part One

[1] In his *Tractatus* Wittgenstein says, 'A proposition is a picture of reality: for if I understand a proposition, I know the situation that it represents' and 'A proposition is a description of a state of affairs' (1974 p.21).
[2] See Alister E. McGrath *The Genesis of Doctrine* (1990 p.16).
[3] In 'An Empiricist's View of the Nature of Religious Belief' Braithwaite says that religious assertions are 'primarily declarations of adherence to a policy of action, declarations to a commitment to a way of life' and that 'the meaning of a religious assertion is given by its use in expressing the asserter's intention to follow a specified policy of behaviour' (1971 p.80). In *Radicals and the Future of the Church* Cupitt says, 'language now looks like an improvization, purely human, ever-changing, and bound into the human practices that it facilitates and furthers. Words do not share any qualities with the things out there in the world that they are used to refer to. Strictly speaking, words are related only to each other. There is no 'finalistic' or pre-established bond at all between language and reality. Reference is merely conventional. There is no Meaning out there and no

Truth out there. Meaning and truth belong only within language, and language is only human, an historically-evolving and changing thing' (1989 p.11).

[4] Rejecting Augustine's notion of language in the *Confessions*, Wittgenstein immediately takes his understanding into the market-place with an example of buying and selling apples. The view in the *Philosophical Investigations* is that 'the meaning of a word is its use in the language' (1967 p.20). Also, 'the term "language-*game*" is meant to bring into prominence the fact that the *speaking* of language is part of an activity, or of a form of life' (p.11). See also D.Z. Phillips 'Religious Beliefs and Language Games' (1971).

[5] In his article 'Lindbeck's Regulative Christology' Stephen Williams concludes that 'no good grounds have been offered' for Lindbeck's conclusions concerning Nicaea (1988 p.174). This obviously has implications against Lindbeck's entire notion of Christian doctrine.

[6] In speaking of doctrines in Christianity, Lindbeck says that 'faithfulness to such doctrines does not necessarily mean repeating them; rather, it requires, in the making of any new formulations, adherence to the same directives that were involved in their first formulation' (1984 p.81). Also, 'there may, on this reading, be complete faithfulness to classical Trinitarianism and Christology even when the imagery and language of Nicaea and Chalcedon have disappeared from the theology and ordinary worship, preaching, and devotion' (p.95). However, in his own work this faithfulness remains 'regulative' only at the level of language.

[7] The notion of christology as 'regulative' for theological language can be understood in a more or less reductionist sense. Some see it as merely grammatical whilst others regard it as rooted in ontology. Although he does acknowledge a metaphysical dimension here, R.A. Norris says of Chalcedon that 'the definition's terminology can best be treated as *second-order language*. Functionally considered, the nature-substance terminology reflects not a metaphysic but something more elementary: a view of the logical structure of the normal sentence. Hence it becomes intelligible in its Christological use when it is understood not as a direct account of the constitution of the Person of Christ, but as a definition of the normative form of any statement about Christ, without consideration of the metaphysical framework...'. See R.A. Norris 'Toward a Contemporary

Interpretation of the Chalcedonian Definition' (1966 p.76). Furthermore, D.M. Mackinnon in his article '"Substance" in christology - a cross-bench view' treats the 'homoousion' as a 'second order proposition': 'we have to say that it is not about Christ, but about statements about Christ' (1972 p.291). The concern in the present work is to keep the link between language and ontology more firmly in view.

[8] The works are: Sallie McFague TeSelle *Speaking in Parables* (1975); Sallie McFague *Metaphorical Theology* (1982); *Models of God* (1987) and *The Body of God* (1994).

[9] McFague says 'I have not found it possible as a contemporary Christian to support an incarnational christology...nevertheless, I have found it possible to support a "parabolic" christology' (1982 p.x).

[10] Colin Gunton, in a study of McFague's work entitled 'Proteus and Procrustes. A study in the Dialectic of Language in Disagreement with Sallie McFague', says that 'Professor McFague's theory of metaphor has much of projectionism about it...' and later that 'the systematic weakness of *Metaphorical Theology* and its successor is the inadequacy - indeed, almost absence - of the author's concept of revelation' (1992 pp.66 and 70). We shall stress the importance of revelation in relation to language in the next section.

[11] McFague contrasts Atonement theology which she sees as 'a good illustration of metaphorical theology' with 'the neatness of the Nicene and Chalcedonian formulas' (1982 p.117). Again, she fails to see the 'tensive' character of these formulas.

[12] Both Schleiermacher and Ritschl wrote in the wake of Kant. In his work *The Christian Doctrine of Justification and Reconciliation* Ritschl emphasized ethics and soteriology over christology, separating 'value-judgement' from 'scientific knowledge' : 'But if Christ by what He has done and suffered for my salvation is my Lord, and if, by trusting for my salvation to the power of what He has done for me, I honour Him as my God, then that is a value-judgment of a direct kind. It is not a judgment which belongs to the sphere of disinterested scientific knowledge, like the formula of Chalcedon' (1900 p.398).

[13] In *The Christian Faith* Schleiermacher objects to using the word 'nature' for God because God and nature are different. This begs the question, but Schleiermacher's definition of nature shows us why he thinks this:

'...always we use it solely of a limited existence, standing in opposition to something else...' (1928 p.393).

[14] Schleiermacher also says that 'all attributes which we ascribe to God are to be taken as denoting not something special in God, but only something special in the manner in which the feeling of absolute dependence is to be related to him' (1928 p.194). This does not of itself indicate that Schleiermacher sees language about God as reducible to the feeling of absolute dependence. It is, however, rooted in that consciousness and the question remains as to what extent language about God relates to God himself. Claude Welch attempts to defend Schleiermacher on this point but still speaks of Schleiermacher's 'difficulties' and 'failure' in maintaining a genuinely dialectical perspective on the divine-human relation. He also likens Schleiermacher to Kant when he says that they both hold that God 'cannot appear in a concept'. See Claude Welch *Protestant Thought in the Nineteenth Century* (1972 pp.81 and 77).

[15] Tillich is unhappy with the 'conceptual tools' of Chalcedon and especially with the term 'nature'. See Part Two p.133f here, and also Paul Tillich *Systematic Theology* (1978b p.142).

[16] There is a possible exception in Theodore when he refers to 'one hupostasis'. The authenticity is disputed. If it is authentic, it would be a forerunner of the Chalcedonian 'one hupostasis'. See A. Grillmeier *Christ in Christian Tradition* (1975 p.438).

[17] I am dependent here upon H.A. Wolfson *The Philosophy of the Church Fathers* (1970 p.372f) and R.A. Norris *Manhood and Christ* (1963 p.67f) for the material from Aristotle on 'mixing'.

[18] See Wolfson (1970 p.383).

[19] This problem forms the major concern in Plato's *Cratylus*. The basic issue lies with whether human language relates to reality through nature or through convention, that is, whether it arises out of 'phusis' or out of 'thesis'. The view taken in the present work is not that words are in some sense 'glued' onto things, but that language arises from our being in nature. Human language about God relates to God in that it arises out of his creation and revelation. Rorty says that the physical universe 'grows knowers'. See Richard Rorty *Philosophy and the Mirror of Nature* (1980 p.297). We can see that it also 'grows speakers'.

[20] Lonergan draws attention to the divisive element in this materialist

understanding and to the way in which the Fathers wished to avoid it. He then adds: 'One may ask, however, whether, when we exclude every materialistic interpretation of the definition "of the same stuff", we are left with even a metaphor. For the naïve realist this is a genuine difficulty; for he thinks of the real in terms of what is presented to the senses. It is not a difficulty for the critical realist, or for one who is at least a dogmatic realist; for the dogmatic and the critical realist think of the real, not as what is sensible, but as what is known through true judgment'. See Bernard Lonergan *The Way to Nicea* (1976 p.90). In the present work we are developing a 'critical realism' in which metaphor is a natural form of language.

[21] See Christopher Stead *Divine Substance* (1977 p.191).

[22] The occurrences in Clement are in his *Stromateis* and *Excerpta*. For the references to these see Stead (1977 p.206f).

[23] On Origen's metaphors see e.g. *De Principiis* (1979): the sun and its rays (p.247); the image (p.247); the statue (p.249); the stainless mirror (p.251); the iron in the fire (p.283) and the ointment (p.283).

[24] Kelly says that the Council of Nicaea was 'content to affirm the Son's full divinity and equality with the Father, out of Whose being He was derived and Whose nature He consequently shared. It did not attempt to tackle the closely related problem of the divine unity, although the discussion of it was inevitably brought nearer'. See J.N.D. Kelly *Early Christian Doctrines* (1977 p.236). Furthermore, the notion of identity is complex here. In terms of the Godhead it could indicate Modalism. On the other hand, two things can be 'identical' without being the same thing. Clearly the concern here is to emphasize the unity and continuity between the Father and the Son. This, at least, was established both at Nicaea and Chalcedon.

[25] See A. Grillmeier (1975 p.473f) on Cyril.

[26] In *The Shape of Christology* John McIntyre considers Ephraim's notion of ἐνυπόστατος to solve a number of problems raised by other notions of this. It 'secures the wholeness of the humanity'; it 'secures the totality of the atonement of man'; God is still in control of the union and any suggestion that human autonomy is formative is ruled out; 'it answers to the way in which we speak about the events of the incarnation', that is, it begins to shed some light on how to interpret events in the gospel

narratives (1966 p.100f).

[27] Cyril, for example, speaks of 'one out of two' and 'one out of both' and of 'the one and sole Christ out of two different natures'. Sellers emphasizes that Cyril himself does not slip into Eutychianism here, but it is clear how easy this might be. See R.V. Sellers *Two Ancient Christologies* (1940 p.90f).

[28] Of the two natures formula, John Hick says that it 'remains a form of words without assignable meaning' and 'is as devoid of meaning as to say that this circle drawn with a pencil on paper is also a square'. See Hick in *The Myth of God Incarnate* (1977 p.178). Interestingly, Hick also has a low view of metaphor: '...the incarnational motif should in fact be understood as a basic metaphor. If this is right, the centuries-long attempt of Christian orthodoxy to turn the metaphor into metaphysics was a cul-de-sac. For the metaphor has always evaded attempts to convert it into a coherent theory or hypothesis'. See Hick in *Incarnation and Myth: The Debate Continued* (1979 p.48). Hick's comments raise important questions concerning both metaphor and epistemology which will be addressed later in this work. See also Hick's more recent discussion of Chalcedon and metaphor in his work *The Metaphor of God Incarnate* (1993) and for a more positive view of Chalcedon see Adrian Thatcher, *Truly a Person, Truly God* (1990).

[29] Arguing in relation to the christology of John Owen, Alan Spence has recently stressed the dynamic content of Chalcedon in terms of the coming together of inspiration and incarnation. He says that 'to recognise this inspirational dimension underlying Chalcedonian christology is to discern its dynamic and functional possibilities, rather than merely the static and ontological categories that have usually dominated its interpretation'. See Alan Spence *Incarnation and Inspiration* (1989 p.25).

[30] The expression occurs frequently in Irenaeus' *Against Heresies* (1981): e.g. 1.9.2; 3.16.2f; 3.16.8; 3.17.4; 4.6.7.

[31] It is worth noting that not only are these terms not wholly negative in intention, they are also actually adverbs, not adjectives, in the Greek text. Hence, the usual 'without confusion, without change, without division, without separation...' is not so appropriate.

Part Two

[1] In the modern period this problem has emerged in some interesting places. Demea in Hume's *Dialogues Concerning Natural Religion* says 'The question is not concerning the *being* but the *nature* of God. This I affirm, from the infirmities of human understanding, to be altogether incomprehensible and unknown to us' (1980 p.13). Wittgenstein, at the end of his *Tractatus* says 'What we cannot speak about, we must pass over in silence' (1974 p.74). Karl Rahner has stressed the mystery, incomprehensibility and hiddenness of God in a number of articles in the *Theological Investigations*. See Vol 4 (1966 pp.36-73); Vol 16 (1979 pp.227-243 and pp.244-254); Vol 18 (1984 pp.89-104).

[2] According to Aristotle, Heraclitus maintained that 'you cannot step into the same river twice'. Cratylus, taking the scepticism further, claimed that 'you cannot step into the same river once'. See *Metaphysics* 1010a.

[3] See B. Mondin *The Principle of Analogy* (1963) on analogy in a number of major thinkers. On analogy in Aquinas, see also Brian Davies *The Thought of Thomas Aquinas* (1992 Chapter 4). For a discussion of analogy and metaphor within the wider context of revelation, see Richard Swinburne *Revelation. From Metaphor to Analogy* (1992).

[4] In *Analogy and Philosophical Language* David Burrell maintains that Cajetan obscures Aquinas' real contribution (1973 p.11f).

[5] Burrell interprets Aquinas' understanding of analogy in the light of Wittgenstein's later work. The emphasis is off a 'doctrine of analogy' in favour of seeing analogy in relation to how human language about God is used. Once again we need to keep both the language and its content in view if we are to be faithful to Aquinas and to human language about God.

[6] Michael J. Buckley says that 'in the *Summa Theologiae*, Christ makes a central appearance only in the third part - after the doctrines of god, providence, the nature of the human person, creation, and human finality have already been defined'. Michael J. Buckley *At the Origins of Modern Atheism* (1987 p.55).

[7] See, for example, Aquinas *Summa Theologiae* (1964c p.65).

[8] Cited in Colin Gunton *The Actuality of Atonement* (1988a p.27). For a discussion of literal and metaphorical language in relation to talk about

God, see William P. Alston *Divine Nature and Human Language. Essays in Philosophical Theology* (1989 Part 1).

[9] Aristotle's discussion of metaphor in the *Poetics* comes under a section on 'nouns' and 'verbs'. His tendency seems to be to limit his notion of metaphor to the single word and to the noun, although his is not so narrow a view in this respect as is often made out. See *Poetics* 1457b and *Rhetoric* 1404b.

[10] See C.M. Turbayne *The Myth of Metaphor* (1962 Chapter 1) .

[11] Barr says that 'the linguistic bearer of the theological statement is usually the sentence and the still larger literary complex and not the word or the morphological and syntactical mechanisms'. James Barr *Semantics of Biblical Language* (1961 p.269).

[12] Isocrates' *Evagoras* (190 D). Cited in W.B. Stanford *Greek Metaphor* (1936 p.3).

[13] See M. Black 'How Metaphors Work: A Reply to Donald Davidson' (1979a p.188).

[14] Henri Bergson emphasized creativity and dynamic interrelatedness over against determinism and atomism.

[15] See Janet Martin Soskice *Metaphor and Religious Language* (1985 p.46).

[16] Soskice says that 'the tenor and the vehicle are not necessarily two terms of the utterance at all' (p.46).

[17] William Empson *Seven Types of Ambiguity* (1991) and Israel Scheffler *Beyond the Letter* (1979).

[18] Speaking of 'linguistic transfiguration', Frank Burch Brown says that 'the epiphoric element within metaphor discloses that which we recognize as like, or analogous to, what we already know: God's love as like a parent's love, for example. On the other hand, the diaphoric element within religious truth and language is that which confronts us as paradoxical...'. See his 'Transfiguration: Poetic Metaphor and Theological Reflection' (1982 p.49). In fact, these elements within metaphor do not separate quite so neatly. The 'is and is not' structure operates in more of a 'criss-cross' manner: for example, God's love is also *not* like a parent's love.

[19] See Soskice (1985 p.86f).

[20] e.g. Romans 5:21-31 and 1 Corinthians 7:23.

[21] See Ian Ramsey *Models and Mystery* (1964 pp.60 and 61).

[22] Richard Boyd has spoken of 'epistemic access' in relation to the use of

metaphor in the sciences and this is obviously also important in relation to models. See Richard Boyd 'Metaphor and Theory Change: What is "Metaphor" a Metaphor for ?' (1979 p.377).

[23] See Soskice (1985 p.102).

[24] Speaking of 'symbolical revelation' and 'symbolical divinity' in *The Divine Names*, Dionysius says that 'at present we employ (so far as in us lies), appropriate symbols for things Divine' (Rolt 1940 p.58). See also Lubheid *Pseudo-Dionysius. The Complete Works* (1987).

[25] Tillich uses this notion frequently in his discussions of revelation in his *Systematic Theology* (1978a).

[26] Tillich maintained at first that there are no non-symbolic statements about God and that 'all knowledge of God has a symbolic character'. See William L. Rowe *Religious Symbols and God* (1968 p.26). However, by the time of the first volume of the *Systematic Theology* he says that 'the statement that God is being-itself is a non-symbolic statement. It does not point beyond itself. It means what it says directly and properly...' (1978a p.238). By the time of the second volume of that work, he claims that 'the question arises...as to whether there is a point at which a non-symbolic assertion about God must be made. There is such a point, namely, the statement that everything we say about God is symbolic. Such a statement is an assertion about God which itself is not symbolic' (1978b p.9).

[27] Aristotle says that 'spoken words are the symbols of mental experience and written words are the symbols of spoken words' (*De Interpretatione* 16a). Aquinas sees the sacraments as 'signs' of the Incarnate Word of God. He says that '...when we speak of the sacraments we have in mind one specific connection with the sacred, namely that of a sign' (Aquinas *Summa Theologiae* 1975 p.5).

Part Three

[1] See Colin Gunton 'No Other Foundation. One Englishman's Reading of *Church Dogmatics*, Chapter v' (1988b). Gunton discusses both Barth and Polanyi in relation to restoring a comprehensive epistemology.

[2] Gunton emphasises this feature in Part One of his *Enlightenment and*

Alienation (1985a p.11f).

[3] The element of alienation which has arisen from Enlightenment epistemology is emphasized by Gunton in his *Enlightenment and Alienation* (1985a passim). In drawing out the dangers of absolutizing Enlightenment epistemology, he comments that 'excess of light can blind' (1985a p.2).

[4] In addition to Gunton (1985a), Nicholas Maxwell has drawn attention, from the scientific side, to this aspect of contemporary western culture. He advocates a turn away from 'knowledge' and 'information' to 'wisdom'. See his *From Knowledge to Wisdom* (1984 passim).

[5] For William Wordsworth the human 'imagination' is 'but another name for absolute strength | And clearest insight, amplitude of mind, | And reason in her most exalted mood'. See *The Prelude* Book XIII (1984 p.582).

[6] In the *Biographia Literaria* Coleridge says 'The very words *obiective* and *subjective*, of such constant occurrence in the schools of yore, I have ventured to reintroduce, because I could not so briefly or conveniently, by any more familiar terms, distinguish the percipere from the percipi' (1907 I, X, p.109).

[7] See Colin Gunton's article 'Creation and Recreation: An Exploration of Some Themes in Aesthetics and Theology'. He says 'the divine activity in creation is that which enables us to repeat the divine truth which precedes us' (1985b p.12).

[8] The notion of making and finding *together* is crucial here and is well articulated by Wordsworth. In *The Prelude* Book XII, he speaks of 'A balance, an ennobling interchange | Of action from within and from without...' (1984 p.578). Similarly, in 'Lines Written a Few Miles Above Tintern Abbey', he speaks of '...eye and ear, both what they half-create, | And what perceive' (p.134).

[9] Helmut Kuhn draws attention to the way in which Polanyi's work is a move forward out of the present crisis in philosophy. He says that Polanyi 'reconciles what tends to fall apart, at any time and especially in the present crisis of philosophy: the proud firmness of conviction on the one hand and the humble awareness of the fallibility of all our reasoning on the other.' See H. Kuhn 'Personal Knowledge and the Crisis of the Philosophical Tradition' (1968 p.134). An epistemology which is continuous with Chalcedon keeps both these features in view.

[10] *Bildung* and *Physis* are clearly related to metaphor in that all are

concerned with the 'shaping' and 'forming' of human life. For Derrida, the quest for truth concerns 'the unveiling of nature (physis)'. Also, 'nature gives itself in metaphor' and 'the metaphoric capacity is what is proper to man'. See Jacques Derrida 'White Mythology' (1982 pp.237,244,249).

[11] Sellers emphasizes the role of 'faith' and 'enquiry' throughout his study of the Chalcedonian Definition and associates these with the positive and negative elements in the christology. He draws out the epistemological dimension further when he says that the Greek word γνωριζόμενον (gnorizomenon) used in relation to the two natures, means both 'made known' and 'recognized'. See R.V. Sellers *The Council of Chalcedon* (1953 p.216). He says that 'much of the criticism of Chalcedon has arisen through a failure to appreciate the significance of the word gnorizomenos in the formula' (p.345) and that 'this statement...expresses what lies at the heart of Chalcedonian faith' (p.349).

[12] We have cited some of Origen's metaphors from the *De Principiis* (See Part One Endnote 23). Origen says that 'although no one is able to speak with certainty of God the Father, it is nevertheless possible for some knowledge of Him to be gained by means of the visible creation and the natural feelings of the human mind' (1979 p.252). On other occasions, however, he is less confident: God's nature 'cannot be grasped or seen by the power of any human understanding' (p.243). See also Athanasius' *De Incarnatione* (1971): the king (p.155); the portrait (p.167); the wrestler (p.193); the straw (p.247).

[13] On the metaphors used by the Early, Mediaeval and Reformation Fathers, see Gustaf Aulén *Christus Victor* (1931) and Colin Gunton *The Actuality of Atonement* (1988a).

[14] The dynamic element in metaphor is underlined by the observation that Aristotle's word in his phrase 'the greatest thing by far is to be a master of metaphor' is a verb. That is, it would be better translated 'the greatest thing by far is to be metaphorical'. See Paul Ricoeur *The Rule of Metaphor* (1978 p.23).

[15] See Maurice Relton *A Study in Christology* (1917 p.37). Karl Rahner's words concerning Chalcedon and doctrinal formulae generally are also pertinent here: '...they are not end but beginning, not goal but means, truths which open the way to the - ever greater - Truth'. See Karl Rahner *Theological Investigations* (Vol.1 p.149).

BIBLIOGRAPHY

A list of the main works discussed or cited
in the text.

If more than one article is cited from a single work,
that work appears as a separate entry.

Alston, William P., (1989) *Divine Nature and Human Language. Essays in Philosophical Theology*. Ithaca and London: Cornell University Press.

Aquinas, Thomas, (1952) *De Veritate* in *Truth*. Vol.1. Questions 1-1X. trans. Robert W. Mulligan. Chicago: Henry Regnery Company.

_____ *Summa Theologiae*. (1964a) Vol.1 trans. Thomas Gilby; (1964b) Vol.2 trans. Timothy McDermott; (1964c) Vol.3 trans. Herbert McCabe; (1975) Vol. 56 trans. David Bourke. Oxford: Blackfriars.

Aristotle, *The Works of Aristotle*. ed. W.D. Ross. London: O.U.P.

Athanasius, (1971) *De Incarnatione* in ed. Robert W. Thomson *Athanasius. Contra Gentes and De Incarnatione*. Oxford: Clarendon Press.

Aulén, Gustaf, (1931) *Christus Victor. An Historical Study of the Three Main Types of the Idea of the Atonement*. London: S.P.C.K.

Bacon, Francis, (1905) *Novum Organum* in ed. John M. Robertson *The Philosophical Works of Francis Bacon*. London: George Routledge and Sons.

Barbour, Ian, (1966) *Issues in Science and Religion*. London: S.C.M. Press.

_____ (1974) *Myths, Models and Paradigms. The Nature of Scientific and Religious Language*. London: S.C.M. Press.

Barfield, Owen, (1960) 'The Meaning of the Word "Literal"' in eds. L.C. Knights and Basil Cottle *Metaphor and Symbol*. London: Butterworth

Scientific Publications pp.48-63.

_____ (1984) *Poetic Diction. A Study in Meaning.* Middletown, Ct.: Wesleyan University Press. First published in 1973.

Barr, James, (1961) *The Semantics of Biblical Language.* Oxford: O.U.P.

Barth, J. Robert, (1977) *The Symbolic Imagination. Coleridge and the Romantic Tradition.* Princeton: Princeton University Press.

Barth, Karl, *Church Dogmatics.* (1936) I/I trans. G.T. Thomson; (1957) II/I and (1956) IV/I. ed. G.W. Bromiley and T.F. Torrance. Edinburgh: T. and T. Clark.

_____ (1949) *Dogmatics in Outline.* trans. G.T. Thomson. London: S.C.M. Press.

_____ (1960) *Anselm: Fides Quaerens Intellectum.* trans. by Ian W. Robertson from the second German edition of 1958. London: S.C.M. Press.

Beardsley, Monroe C., (1958) *Aesthetics: Problems in the Philosophy of Criticism.* New York: Harcourt, Brace and Company.

_____ (1962) 'The Metaphorical Twist' in *Philosophy and Phenomenological Research* 22 pp.293-307.

Berggren, Douglas, (1962-63) 'The Use and Abuse of Metaphor' in *Review of Metaphysics* 1962: 16.2 pp.237-258; 1963: 16.3 pp. 450-472.

Bernstein, Richard J., (1983) *Beyond Objectivism and Relativism: Science, Hermeneutics and Praxis.* Oxford: Basil Blackwell.

Bindley, T. Herbert and Green, F.W., (1950) *The Oecumenical Documents of the Faith.* London: Methuen and Co. First published in 1899.

Black, Max, (1962) 'Metaphor' in Max Black *Models and Metaphors: Studies in Language and Philosophy.* Ithaca, New York: Cornell University Press pp.25-47.

_____ (1979a) 'How Metaphors Work: A Reply to Donald Davidson' in ed. Sheldon Sacks (1979) pp.181-192.

_____ (1979b) 'More About Metaphor' in ed. Andrew Ortony (1979) pp.19-43.

Boyd, Richard, (1979) 'Metaphor and Theory Change: What is "Metaphor" a Metaphor for?' in ed. Andrew Ortony (1979) pp.356-408.

Braithwaite, R.B., (1971) 'An Empiricist's View of the Nature of Religious Belief' in ed. Basil Mitchell (1971) pp.72-91.

Brown, Frank Burch, (1982) 'Transfiguration: Poetic Metaphor and Theological Reflection' in *The Journal of Religion* Vol.62 no.1 pp.39-56.

Buber, Martin, (1952) *Eclipse of God. Studies in the Relation between Religion and Philosophy*. Hassocks, Sussex: The Harvester Press.

Buckley, Michael J., (1987) *At the Origins of Modern Atheism*. New Haven and London: Yale University Press.

Burrell, David C., (1973) *Analogy and Philosophical Language*. New Haven and London: Yale University Press.

Caird, George, (1980) *The Language and Imagery of the Bible*. London: Gerald Duckworth and Co.

Cassirer, Ernst, (1953) *Language and Myth*. New York: Dover Publications. First published in 1946.

Coleridge, S.T., (1912) *Coleridge's Poetical Works*. ed. E.H. Coleridge. London: O.U.P.

_____ (1907) *Biographia Literaria*. ed. J. Shawcross. Oxford: Clarendon Press. First published in 1817.

_____ (1853) *Aids to Reflection* and *The Statesman's Manual* in ed. Shedd *The Complete Works of Samuel Taylor Coleridge* Vol 1. Also *Table Talk* in Vol.6. New York: Harper and Brothers.

Collingwood, R.G., (1945) *The Idea of Nature*. Oxford: Clarendon Press.

Copleston, F.C., (1955) *Aquinas*. Harmondsworth: Penguin.

_____ (1958) *A History of Philosophy*. Vol IV. London: Burns Oates and Washbourne Ltd.

Cupitt, Don, (1989) *Radicals and the Future of the Church*. London: S.C.M. Press.

Dalferth, Ingolf U., (1988) *Theology and Philosophy*. Oxford: Basil Blackwell.

_____ (1989) 'Karl Barth's Eschatological Realism' in ed. S.W. Sykes *Karl Barth: Centenary Essays*. Cambridge: C.U.P. pp. 14-45.

Davidson, Donald, (1979) 'What Metaphors Mean' in ed. Sheldon Sacks (1979) pp.29-45.

Davies, Brian, (1982) *Introduction to the Philosophy of Religion*. Oxford: O.U.P.

_____ (1992) *The Thought of Thomas Aquinas*. Oxford: Clarendon Press.

Derrida, Jacques, (1982) 'White Mythology: Metaphor in the Text of Philosophy' in Jacques Derrida *Margins of Philosophy*. Hassocks, Sussex: The Harvester Press pp.207-271. First published in English in *New Literary History* 6 (1974) pp.5-74.

Descartes, René, (1967) *The Philosophical Works of Descartes*. Vol. 1. trans. Elizabeth S. Haldane and G.R.T. Ross. Cambridge: C.U.P.

Dulles, Avery, (1988) *Models of the Church*. Dublin: Gill and MacMillan. First published in 1975.

Eco, Umberto, (1984) *Semiotics and The Philosophy of Language*. London: Macmillan.

Eliot, T.S., (1921), 'The Metaphysical Poets' in ed. John Hayward (1953) *T.S. Eliot. Selected Prose*. Harmondsworth: Penguin pp.105-114.

_____ (1969) *The Complete Poems and Plays*. London: Faber and Faber.

Empson, William, (1991) *Seven Types of Ambiguity*. London: The Hogarth Press. First published in 1930.

Fawcett, Thomas, (1970) *The Symbolic Language of Religion*. London: S.C.M. Press.

Fergusson, David, (1990) 'Meaning, Truth and Realism in Bultmann and Lindbeck' in *Religious Studies* 26 pp.183-198.

Foss, Martin, (1949) *Symbol and Metaphor in Human Experience*. Princeton: Princeton University Press.

Gadamer, Hans-Georg, (1979) *Truth and Method*. London: Sheed and Ward, Stagbooks. First published in 1975.

Gardner, Helen, (1972) *The New Oxford Book of English Verse*. Oxford: Clarendon Press.

Greer, Rowan, (1961) *Theodore of Mopsuestia. Exegete and Theologian*. London: The Faith Press.

Grene, Marjorie, (1966) *The Knower and the Known*. London: Faber and Faber.

Griggs, E.L., (ed.) (1956) *Collected Letters of Samuel Tavlor Coleridge*. Vol 1 1785-1800. Oxford: Clarendon Press.

Grillmeier, A., (1975) *Christ in Christian Tradition. Volume One. From the Apostolic age to Chalcedon (451)*. London: A.R. Mowbray. First published in 1965.

Gunton, Colin E., (1983) *Yesterday and Today: A Study of Continuities in Christology*. London: Darton, Longman and Todd.

_____ (1985a) *Enlightenment and Alienation. An Essay Towards a Trinitarian Theology*. Basingstoke: Marshall, Morgan and Scott.

_____ (1985b) 'Creation and Recreation: An Exploration of Some Themes in Aesthetics and Theology' in *Modern Theology* Vol.2 no.1 pp.1-19.

_____ (1988a) *The Actuality of Atonement. A Study of Metaphor, Rationality and The Christian Tradition*. Edinburgh: T. and T. Clark.

_____ (1988b) 'No Other Foundation. One Englishman's Reading of *Church*

Dogmatics Chapter v' in ed. Nigel Biggar *Reckoning With Barth. Essays in Commemoration of the Centenary of Karl Barth's Birth.* London: S.P.C.K. pp.61-79.

———— (1992) 'Proteus and Procrustes. A Study in the Dialectic of Language in Disagreement with Sallie McFague' in Alvin F. Kimel, Jr. *Speaking the Christian God. The Holy Trinity and the Challenge of Feminism.* Leominster: Gracewing; Grand Rapids, Michigan: Eerdmans pp.65-80.

Harnack, Adolf von, (1958) *History of Dogma.* Vol. 4. trans. by Neil Buchanan from the third German edition. New York: Russell and Russell. First published in 1896.

Hartwell, Herbert, (1964) *The Theology of Karl Barth: An Introduction.* London: Gerald Duckworth and Co.

Hick, John, (1977) 'Jesus and the World Religions' in ed. Hick *The Myth of God Incarnate.* London: S.C.M. Press pp.167-185.

———— (1979) 'Is there a Doctrine of the Incarnation?' in ed. Michael Goulder *Incarnation and Myth.* London: S.C.M. Press pp.47-50.

———— (1993) *The Metaphor of God Incarnate.* London: S.C.M. Press.

Hill, William J., (1987) 'On "Knowing the Unknowable God": A Review Discussion' in *The Thomist* Vol. 51 no. 4 pp.699-709.

Hobbes, Thomas, (1985) *Leviathan.* ed. C.B. Macpherson. Harmondsworth: Penguin. First published in 1651.

Hume, David, (1896) *A Treatise of Human Nature.* ed. L.A. Selby-Bigge. Oxford: Clarendon Press. First published in 1739.

———— (1980) *Dialogues Concerning Natural Religion.* ed. Richard Popkin. Indianapolis: Hackett Publishing Company. First published in 1779.

Irenaeus of Lyons, (1981) *Against Heresies* in ed. Alexander Roberts and James Donaldson *The Ante-Nicene Fathers.* Vol.1. Grand Rapids, Michigan: Eerdmans Publishing Company pp.315-567.

Jüngel, Eberhard, (1989) 'Metaphorical Truth. Reflections on the theological relevance of metaphor as a contribution to the hermeneutics of narrative theology' in ed. J.B. Webster *Eberhard Jüngel. Theological Essays.* Edinburgh: T. and T. Clark pp. 16-71. First published in German in 1974.

———— (1983) *God as the Mystery of the World. On the Foundation of the Theology of the Crucified One in the Dispute between Theism and Atheism.* trans.

Darrell L. Guder. Edinburgh: T. and T. Clark. First published in German in 1977.

Kant, Immanuel, (1933) *Critique of Pure Reason*. trans. Norman Kemp Smith. London: Macmillan. First published in 1781/1787.

_____ (1977) *Prolegomena to Any Future Metaphysics*. trans. Paul Carus, revised by James W. Elrington. Indianapolis: Hackett Publishing Company. First published in 1783.

Kelly, J.N.D., (1972) *Early Christian Creeds*. London: Longman. First published in 1950.

_____ (1977) *Early Christian Doctrines*. London: A. and C. Black. First published in 1958.

Kittay, Eva Feder, (1987) *Metaphor. Its Cognitive Force and Linguistic Structure*. Oxford: Clarendon Press.

Kuhn, Helmut, (1968) 'Personal Knowledge and the Crisis of the Philosophical Tradition' in ed. Thomas A. Langford and William H. Poteat *Intellect and Hope. Essays in the Thought of Michael Polanyi*. Durham, North Carolina: Duke University Press pp. 111-135.

Kuhn, T.S., (1970) *The Structure of Scientific Revolutions*. Chicago: University of Chicago Press. First published in 1962.

_____ (1974) 'Second Thoughts on Paradigms' in ed. Frederick Suppe *The Structure of Scientific Theories*. Urbana, Illinois: Illinois University Press pp.459-482.

Küng, Hans, (1971) *Infallible? An Enquiry*. London: Collins. First published in German in 1970.

Lakoff, George and Johnson, Mark, (1980) *Metaphors We Live By*. Chicago: University of Chicago Press.

Lampe, Geoffrey, (1961) *A Patristic Greek Lexicon*. Oxford: O.U.P.

Lindbeck, George, (1984) *The Nature of Doctrine. Religion and Theology in a Postliberal Age*. London: S.P.C.K .

Locke, John, (1823) *An Essay Concerning Human Understanding* in *The Works of John Locke*. A New Edition, Corrected. Vols 1 and 11. Aalen: Scientia Verlag. First published in 1690.

Lonergan, Bernard, (1976) *The Way to Nicea. The Dialectical Development of Trinitarian Theology*. London: Darton, Longman an Todd.

Lubheid, Colm, (trans.) (1987) *Pseudo-Dionysius. The Complete Works*. London: S.P.C.K.

McCloskey, Mary A., (1964) 'Metaphors' in *Mind* 73 pp.215-233.

McFague Teselle, Sallie, (1975) *Speaking in Parables. A Study in Metaphor and Theology.* London: S.C.M. Press.

McFague, Sallie, (1982) *Metaphorical Theology: Models of God in Religious Language.* London: S.C.M. Press.

_____ (1987) *Models of God. Theology for an Ecological Nuclear Age.* London: S.C.M. Press.

_____ (1994) *The Body of God. An Ecological Theology.* London: S.C.M. Press.

McFarland, Thomas, (1969) *Coleridge and the Pantheist Tradition.* Oxford: Clarendon Press.

McGrath, Alister E., (1990) *The Genesis of Doctrine. A Study in the Foundations of Doctrinal Criticism.* Oxford: Basil Blackwell.

McIntyre, John, (1966) *The Shape of Christology.* London: S.C.M. Press.

Mackinnon, D.M., (1972) '"Substance" in Christology - a cross-bench view' in ed. S.W. Sykes and J.P. Clayton *Christ Faith and History.* Cambridge: C.U.P. pp.279-300.

Macquarrie, John, (1979) 'Foundation Documents of the Faith 111 The Chalcedonian Definition' in *Expository Times* 1979 Vol. 91 no.3 pp.68-72.

Maxwell, Nicholas, (1984) *From Knowledge to Wisdom. A Revolution in the Aims and Methods of Science.* Oxford: Basil Blackwell.

Middleton Murry, John, (1931) 'Metaphor' in Middleton Murry *Countries of the Mind. Essays in Literary Criticism.* Second Series. London: O.U.P. pp.1-16.

Mitchell, Basil, (ed.) (1971) *The Philosophy of Religion.* Oxford: O.U.P.

Mondin, Battista, (1963) *The Principle of Analogy in Protestant and Catholic Theology.* The Hague: Martinus Nijhoff.

Norris, R.A., (1963) *Manhood and Christ. A Study in the Christology of Theodore of Mopsuestia.* Oxford: O.U.P.

_____ (1966), 'Toward a Contemporary Interpretation of the Chalcedonian Definition' in ed. R.A. Norris *Lux in Lumine. Essays to Honour W. Norman Pittenger.* New York: Seabury Press pp. 62-79.

Origen, (1979) *De Principiis* in ed. Alexander Roberts and James Donaldson *The Ante-Nicene Fathers.* Vol. 1V. Grand Rapids, Michigan: Eerdmans Publishing Company pp. 239-382.

Ortony, Andrew, (ed.) (1979) *Metaphor and Thought.* Cambridge: C.U.P.

Pannenberg, Wolfhart, (1968) *Jesus - God and Man*. London: S.C.M. Press.

Patterson, Robert Leet, (1933) *The Conception of God in the Philosophy of Aquinas*. London: Allen and Unwin.

Phillips, D.Z., (1971) 'Religious Beliefs and Language Games' in ed. Basil Mitchell (1971) pp.121-142.

_____ (1988) *Faith After Foundationalism*. London: Routledge.

Plato, (1875) *The Dialogues of Plato*. ed. B. Jowett. Second edition. Oxford: Clarendon Press.

Polanyi, Michael, (1958) *Personal Knowledge. Towards a Post-Critical Philosophy*. London: Routledge and Kegan Paul.

_____ (1959) *The Study of Man*. Chicago: University of Chicago Press.

_____ (1967) *The Tacit Dimension*. London: Routledge and Kegan Paul.

Polanyi, Michael and Prosch, Harry, (1975) *Meaning*. Chicago: University of Chicago Press.

Popper, Karl, (1959) *The Logic of Scientific Discovery*. London: Hutchinson. First published in German in 1934.

Prestige, G.L., (1952) *God in Patristic Thought*. London: S.P.C.K. First published in 1936.

Rahner, Karl, *Theological Investigations*. Vol.1 (1965) trans. Cornelius Ernst; vol. 4 . (1966) trans. Kevin Smyth; Vol. 16 (1979) trans. David Morland; Vol. 18 (1984) trans. Edward Quinn. London: Darton, Longman and Todd.

Ramsey, Ian T., (1957) *Religious Language. An Empirical Placing of Theological Phrases*. London: S.C.M. Press.

_____ (1964) *Models and Mystery*. Oxford: O.U.P.

Raven, Charles E., (1978) *Apollinarianism. An Essay on the Christology of the Early Church*. New York: AMS Press. First published in 1923.

Relton, H. Maurice, (1917) *A Study in Christology. The Problem of the Relation of the Two Natures in the Person of Christ*. London: S.P.C.K.

Richards, I.A., (1950) *Coleridge On Imagination*. London: Routledge and Kegan Paul. First published in 1934.

_____ (1936) *The Philosophy of Rhetoric*. Oxford: O.U.P.

Ricoeur, Paul, (1978) *The Rule of Metaphor. Multidisciplinary Studies of the Creation of Meaning in Language*. trans. by R. Czerny and others. Toronto and Buffalo: University of Toronto Press.

_____ (1979) 'The Metaphorical Process as Cognition, Imagination, and

Feeling' in ed. Sheldon Sacks (1979) pp.141-157.

Ritschl, Albrecht, (1900) *The Christian Doctrine of Justification and Reconciliation. The Positive Development of the Doctrine.* trans. H.R. Mackintosh and A.B. Macaulay. Edinburgh: T. and T. Clark. First published in 1872.

Rolt, C.E., (trans) (1940) *Dionysius the Areopagite. The Divine Names and The Mystical Theology.* London: S.P.C.K. First published in 1920.

Rorty, Richard, (1980) *Philosophy and The Mirror of Nature.* Oxford: Basil Blackwell.

Rowe, William L., (1968) *Religious Symbols and God.* Chicago: University of Chicago Press.

Ryle, Gilbert, (1986) *The Concept of Mind.* Harmondsworth: Penguin. First published in 1949.

Sacks, Sheldon, (ed.) (1979) *On Metaphor.* Chicago: The University of Chicago Press.

Scheffler, Israel, (1979) *Beyond the Letter. A Philosophical Inquiry into Ambiguity, Vagueness and Metaphor in Language.* London: Routleage and Kegan Paul.

Schleiermacher, F., (1928) *The Christian Faith.* Edinburgh: T. and T. Clark. First published in 1821-2.

Schoen, Edward, (1985) *Religious Explanations. A Model From the Sciences.* Durham: Duke University Press.

Sellers, R.V., (1940) *Two Ancient Christologies. A Study in the Christological Thought of the Schools of Alexandria and Antioch in the Early History of Christian Doctrine.* London: S.P.C.K.

_____ (1953) *The Council of Chalcedon. A Historical and Doctrinal Survey.* London: S.P.C.K.

Sherry, Patrick, (1976) 'Analogy Today' in *Philosophy* 51 pp.431-446.

Soskice, Janet Martin, (1985) *Metaphor and Religious Language.* Oxford: O.U.P.

Spence, Alan John, (1989) *Incarnation and Inspiration. John Owen and the Coherence of Christology.* Unpublished Ph.D. Thesis, King's College, University of London.

Stanford, W. Bedell, (1936) *Greek Metaphor. Studies in Theory and Practice.* Oxford: Basil Blackwell.

Stead, Christopher, (1977) *Divine Substance.* Oxford: O.U.P.

Swinburne, Richard (1992) *Revelation. From Metaphor to Analogy*. Oxford: Clarendon Press.

Temple, William, (1912) 'The Divinity of Christ' in ed. B.H. Streeter *Foundations. A Statement of Christian Belief in Terms of Modern Thought*. London: Macmillan pp.211-263.

_____ (1924) *Christus Veritas. An Essay*. London: Macmillan.

Thatcher, Adrian (1990) *Truly a Person, Truly God*. London: S.P.C.K.

Thiemann, Ronald F., (1985) *Revelation and Theology. The Gospel as Narrated Promise*. Notre Dame, Indiana: University of Notre Dame Press.

Tillich, Paul, *Systematic Theology*. (1978a) Vol.1; (1978b) Vol.11. London: S.C.M. Press. First published in 1951 and 1957 respectively.

_____ (1957) *Dynamics of Faith*. New York: Harper and Brothers.

_____ (1959) *Theology of Culture*. ed. Robert C. Kimball. New York: O.U.P.

_____ (1962) 'The Religious Symbol' in ed. Sydney Hook *Religious Experience and Truth*. London: Oliver and Boyd pp.30-321.

Turbayne, Colin Murray, (1962) *The Myth of Metaphor*. New Haven and London: Yale University Press.

Waldrop, Charles, (1984) *Karl Barth's Christology. Its Basic Alexandrian Character*. Amsterdam: Mouton Publishers.

Warnke, Georgia, (1980) *Gadamer. Hermeneutics, Tradition and Reason*. Oxford: Polity Press.

Warnock, Mary, (1976) *Imagination*. London: Faber and Faber.

Welch, Claude, (1972) *Protestant Thought in the Nineteenth Century*. Volume 1, 1799-1870. New Haven and London: Yale University Press.

Wheelwright, Philip, (1954) *The Burning Fountain. A Study in The Language of Symbolism*. Bloomington, Indiana: Indiana University Press.

_____ (1962) *Metaphor and Reality*. Bloomington, Indiana: Indiana University Press.

White, Roger, (1982) 'Notes on Analogical Predication and Speaking about God' in ed. Brian Hebblethwaite and Stewart Sutherland *The Philosophical Frontiers of Christian Theology. Essays Presented to D.M. Mackinnon*. Cambridge: C..U.P. pp.197-226.

Williams, Stephen, 'Lindbeck's Regulative Christology' in *Modern Theology* Vol.4 no.2 pp.173-186.

Wittgenstein, Ludwig, (1974) *Tractatus Logico-Philosophicus*. trans. by D.F. Pears and B.F. McGuiness. London: Routledge. First published in 1921.

_____ (1967) *Philosophical Investigations*. trans. by G.E.M. Anscombe. Oxford: Basil Blackwell. First published in 1953.

Wolfson, H.A., (1970) *The Philosophy of the Church Fathers* Vol.1 'Faith, Trinity, Incarnation'. Cambridge, Mass.: Harvard University Press. First published in 1956.

Wordsworth, William, (1984) *William Wordsworth*. ed. Stephen Gill. Oxford: O.U.P.

Young, Frances, (1983) *From Nicaea to Chalcedon. A Guide to the Literature and its Background*. London: S.C.M. Press.

INDEX